The Future We Deserve

100 essays about the future

Editors: Vinay Gupta, Cat Lupton, Noah Raford

Title: The Future We Deserve

Subtitle: 100 essays about the future

Editors: Vinay Gupta, Cat Lupton, Noah Raford

Created on: 2012-11-16 12:43 (CET)

Produced by: PediaPress GmbH, Taunusstrasse 61, Mainz, Germany, http://pediapress.com/

The content within this book was generated collaboratively by volunteers. Please be advised that nothing found here has necessarily been reviewed by people with the expertise required to provide you with complete, accurate or reliable information. Some information in this book may be misleading or simply wrong. PediaPress does not guarantee the validity of the information found here. If you need specific advice (for example, medical, legal, financial, or risk management) please seek a professional who is licensed or knowledgeable in that area.

Sources, licenses and contributors of the articles and images are listed in the section entitled "References". Parts of the books may be licensed under the GNU Free Documentation License. A copy of this license is included in the section entitled "GNU Free Documentation License"

All third-party trademarks used belong to their respective owners.

Create your own custom Wikipedia-Book at http://pediapress.com

collection id:
pdf writer version: 0.10.1 mwlib version: 0.14.1

Contents

Articles 1

Dedication 1

Introduction 3

Foreword - Shaun Chamberlain 5

Without Divine Justice, Human Rights - Gaia Marcus 6

Gods or Goats - David Jennings 9

A 'Playbour' of Love for the Next Twenty Years - Pat Kane . . . 10

Untitled, 2010 - Maria Elvorith 12

We Deserve A Future Of Good Governance - Patri Friedman and Brad Taylor 13

The World Needs Wives - Zoe Lee 15

The Food We Deserve - Christopher Brewster 16

Rediscovering the Stuff We Forgot to Remember - Joe Turner . . . 17

Reclaiming Awesome - Emma Bryn-Jones 19

Panarchy - Paul B Hartzog 19

On the Future We Deserve... - Antonio Dias 20

There is No Future - Eleanor Saitta 22

This is Mental. - Rohan Gunatillake 23

Monastech - Nathan Rosquist 25

The Futures We Deserve or, Even Bankers Might Have Uses - Edmund Harriss 26

Memes that Kill - Thomas Bjelkeman 28

The Tiny Army - Vinay Gupta 29

A Four-Bladed Scissors - Arthur Doohan 31
One in Six, a Strategy for Reduction - Glenn Hall 33
Of Arms and the Man - James Hester 34
A Knowing World - Chris Watkins 36
A Picture, a Person, a Time and a Location - Thomas Bjelkeman . . 37
Decline and Fall - Tom Stafford 38
We Deserve to Evolve - Sam Rose 40
The Knowledge and Action Platform - Mark Roest 41
The Joy of Open - Erik Moeller 44
6 Ways to Live - Chris Malins 45
Solar Photovoltaic Energy Replication - Joshua Pearce 47
The Future We Deserve or The Future We Desire - John Byfield . . 48
Zombies and Vampires, Oh My! - Antonio Dias 50
The Future of Information Freedom - Smári McCarthy 51
My Vision of the Future - Otis Funkmeyer 53
The Matter of Place - Catherine Lupton 54
The Locavores' War: A History of America's Future - Frank J. Popper 55
A World in Common - The Socialist Party of Great Britain 59
The Story Our Children Will Tell - Curtis Faith 60
The Abolition of Scarcity - Kevin Carson 62
Cities of Freedom Chariots or Four-wheeled Demons? - Cindy
    Frewen Wuellner PhD, FAIA 64
A Healthy and Smiling Planet - Anil Prasad 66
The Future We Deserve and the Earth Charter - Jeffrey Newman . . 67
The Feet We Deserve - Steve Wheeler 69
Sex & Singularity: Sex in the 21st Century - Julian Powell 70
...middle... - Nick Taylor 71
If You Want to Go Fast, Go Alone. If You Want to Go Far, Go
    Together. And If You Want to Transform..? - Shaun Chamberlin 75
Just 4: A Macroscale Social Model - Woody Evans 77
Open Source Appropriate Technology - Joshua Pearce 79

Who Will Save Our Souls? - Thembisa Cochrane 80

Art Monasticism - Nathan Rosquist 82

Personal Futures and Futures Therapy - Jessica Charlesworth 84

Deep Lessons - Alan Chapman 86

Semantic Organization and Connectivity - Anne McCrossan 87

The Education We Deserve - Pamela Mclean 88

Moving Towards a Post Penal Society - Anton Shelupanov 91

A Future Without Childhood - Julia Macintosh 94

Online Open Distance Learning - Anil Prasad 95

The Future of Television - Glenn Hall 98

Citizen Centred Participation - Phil Green 99

The Future We Got–Earth Date Zero Plus Twenty - Pamela Mclean 101

The Onion and the Satellite - Lucas Gonzalez 103

Ode to the Tech Fix - Chris Malins 105

Deserving The Future We Want - Eldan Goldenberg 106

Re-envisioning Our Relationship With Micro-Organisms - Brian Degger 107

The Spaces We Deserve - Dougald Hine 108

The Age of Warlords Cookbook - Michael Swifte 110

Using Science Locally - Ian Simmons 112

Seed Saving for Local Food Security - Lisa Erwin 113

Challenging Education and the "Harry Potter Letter" - Edmund Harriss 115

Credibility & Calories: A Perspective on Information - Woody Evans 117

The Future of Programming - Andy Broomfield 119

Higher Education for the Future We Deserve - Lisa Erwin 121

A Systemic Revolution, or, the Need for a Post-Scientific Approach - Andy Novocin 122

An Ideal World - Paola Di Maio 124

My Ideal Panflu - Lucas Gonzalez 125

Report on the Planet Earth from the Intergalactic Study Group on Worlds in Transition - Gary Alexander 126

A Hypothetical Vision of What the Property Sector in the Future Might Look Like - Bonnie O. Wong 128

The Future is Here - Kenneth Lo 130

Hacking Society and a Proposal for Beta Towns - Andy Broomfield 133

The Age of Phlight - Lionel Wolberger 135

Designing the Future - David Braden 137

Collaboration for Introverts or, How to Make Friends and Tolerate People - Steve Wheeler and Alex Fradera 138

Hundreds of Sovereign Singapores - Jon Southurst 140

Working Together: Unleashing Collective Intelligence - Fabio Barone 142

Clash for Civilization - Arthur Doohan 143

Seawater into Food - Thomas Bjelkeman 145

Collapsarithmetic - Chris Malins 147

Our Future and the Sun - Vinay Gupta 148

Bootleg Oil - Al Razi Masri 149

Time For Resilient Tribes to Step Up and Show the Way - Kuldeep Brar 151

The Music We Deserve - Allen Wentz 152

All the World's a Stage - Alex Fradera 154

Success in the Twenty First Century - Mark Charmer 156

On Lying to Children - Peep 158

We Deserve the Time and Space to Be Human - Alex Bowyer ... 160

Opening the Floodgates - Ben Werdmuller von Elgg 161

The Future of Art - Nick Stewart 163

The Human Rite of Living - Bembo Davies 164

No Island is an Island - Lucas Gonzalez 165

Getting The Future We Deserve - Paul Graham Raven 167

Berlin, Berlin - Liam Breslin 168

We Deserve a Future - Jason Louv 169

Aftermath - Thinking the Unthinkable. Asking What is Not Asked - Thomas Bjelkeman 172

Appendix 175

References 175
Article Sources and Contributors 180
Image Sources, Licenses and Contributors 183

Article Licenses 185

Index 187

Dedication

The Future We Deserve is dedicated to Maria Elvorith (1982-2010), cover artist, contributor and pure soul.

May our future be as beautiful as you.

Introduction

If you don't know the story of how the book was written, it's very simple: I asked on twitter.

"@leashless I'm putting together a book called The Future We Deserve, open brief, 500 words, sign up at http://www.appropedia.org/The_future_we_deserve."

Actually it started a day before that, when Noah Raford and I stood in a playground in Forest Hill watching his two year old interacting with a large metal duck on a spring, discussing the future.

Three days after the tweet, by the magic power of twitter and networks, 70 people had decided to write for the book, and the long, slow process of putting it together had begun. It took about three months to get 90+ pieces in. We did a Kickstarter, because I began to realize how big a job I'd gotten myself into. Many people donated, some of them hundreds of dollars, and this is part of what kept the project alive when I thought "there's no way I can get this right." I'd committed, I'd taken people's money, and I had to see it through. So I'd like to thank everybody who helped make this book a reality, authors, donors and especially those who gave both their work and money, and Kickstarter for existing.

When I sat down and did the first reading, what I discovered stopped my mind for most of a year. I went from being confident that I understood the broad narrative outline of the future to being **absolutely certain** that I did not. Every page or two there was a deep insight, something that once-seen could not be unseen, and gradually my implicit, unacknowledged confidence and boldness about my understanding of the future faded away into a *conscious unknowing*.

There is too much going on for us to hope to control.

Cat Lupton got me out of this rut - she provided the editorial input, the time editing and managing, and the enthusiasm that I needed to finally admit that I could not do this alone, and dealing with the implications was not a precondition to publishing it. Solo work at the heart of a community project is not sensible, and I want to thank Cat for caring enough to get this moving and done.

This book is an interactive process. I'm hoping for reading groups, for annotated versions of the articles, for interviews and interaction with our authors, and for a second book, nominally titled *The Present We Have*. The hub for these activities is http://thefuturewedeserve.com/1/

Our hash tag for twitter (and other media) is #TheFWD / @TheFWD.

Part of the fluidity of this project is the power of the new infrastructure. Ward Cunningham's seed of genius, the Wiki, and the fine chaps at Appropedia who in addition to hosting and managing the world's largest online appropriate technology library, also have a very liberal, inclusionist attitude to side projects like this book. The New Public Thinking book which my collaborator Dougald Hine just released is also on this platform.

Finally, there's our printing process. PediaPress is a phenomenal service which exists to turn wikis into books. I'm not sure that they ever realized just how potent the MediaWiki/PediaPress combination is for producing new work, but the streamlining of workflow and the simple "just leave this to our software" mechanism by which the books are produced is truly revolutionary and liberating. It's not just print-on-demand, but the total fluidization of the concept and execution of the book as a mass-collaborative object.

And beyond finally, to our authors: this is, literally, your book. When I started this, I had an elitist notion of the future as, in some way, the domain of specialists who thought about the future a lot. What you've taught me is that the future is where every one of us will live our lives, and people know their own business best - you wrote about what you knew, and you wrote about what you cared about, and in the process, you created a work that has broadened my horizons, and deepened my appreciation for just how brilliant and talented people are.

You taught me that we know nothing about where we're going, and that the future is a dialogue between nine billion people, striving to find a common voice.

To the future!

Vinay Gupta London, 29 Feburary 2012

Supporters

With heartfelt thanks to for their kind support, without which this book would certainly never have been produced. Thank you.

Futuryst, Pedro, Darren Beale, Al Billings, Thomas Bjelkeman-Pettersson, Daren Forsyth, Lucas Gonzalez, Neal Gorenflo, Rohan Gunatillake, Carol Gunby, Glenn Hall, Justin Hayward, David Jennings, Wendy L Schultz, Russell Smithers

About the cover

Dragonfly, by Maria Elvorith.

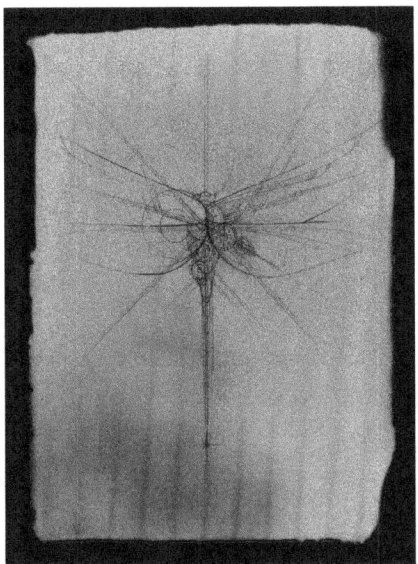

Foreword - Shaun Chamberlain

"Five hundred words on the theme of the title". A simple brief, but having just read the first proof of *The Future We Deserve*, that simple brief has conjured forth a wonderful mélange of foresight, insight, powerful fiction and playful speculation.

From cyber-monasteries to socialism, from taking 'phlight' to the importance of introspection, the contributors have taken those four titular words and run with them in myriad directions. Indeed, some even appear to have run *at* them. I expected an abundance of different takes on "future", but "deserve" is challenged, "we" is questioned, and even "the" doesn't get off scot-free!

In the face of the dauntingly poor track record of futurism, this book adopts a radically different approach, and not just in terms of the diversity of authors. Remembering the Chinese proverb that **"when men speak of the future, the Gods laugh"**, it perhaps seeks to humbly laugh along with them, embracing a healthy diversity of disparate and even opposed visions, ideas and plans – the useful attitude that the postmodern theorist Ewa Ziarek termed 'dissensus'.[1]

In grappling with an uncertain future, this exploration of many paths may be only appropriate, reflecting nature's own evolution, which never seeks to reach consensus on the ideal life-form, but simply creates, creates, creates. Such dissensus also underlies the Transition movement, with communities exploring diverse paths towards preparedness for likely future scenarios, even where the detail of any threats may remain unclear.

Trying to agree on one grand unified story of the future is a waste of energy because whatever we may decide upon, reality surely has other plans. It may be possible (and useful) to discern trends, but the specifics will always elude us. Accordingly, resilient approaches are those which make sense across a wide range of possible futures. They are humility in action, and they keep our eyes open. So let us explore dissensus – explore our various curious projects, inspirations and stories – secure in the understanding that while some of them will thrive and others die, our task is not to foresee the future, but rather to enable it.

I wrote in **The Transition Timeline** that we will certainly get the future we deserve. As one contributor puts it herein, let's work for a future worth deserving. And who can know which obscure passion, vocation or tale might turn out in retrospect to have provided a defining contribution to our collective future? **The Future We Deserve** is a ground-breaking collection of candidates, and while reading it I find myself always wondering whether some of them may be fated to shape our world, and whether the future collaborators may find each other through these pages.

I hope to see many more books like it, for it feels like fertile ground.

Shaun Chamberlin has been involved with the Transition Network since its inception, co-founding Transition Town Kingston and authoring the movement's second book, The Transition Timeline (Green Books, 2009). He writes at www.darkoptimism.org

Without Divine Justice, Human Rights - Gaia Marcus

*"It would, of course, be a little odd that there should be such rights attaching to human beings simply qua human beings... **There are no such things as rights, and belief in them is one with belief in witches and in unicorns...**"* (Alaisdair MacIntyre, 1981)

I believe that we deserve human rights with or without God, or Gods, or any divine purpose. Not because human beings are good, but because we can be very, very bad. Humans need rights for the very reason that these rights do not, in of as themselves, exist.

I believe that human rights pertain to and are necessary for our current conception of human beings, just as laws pertain to and are necessary for our current conception of society. Laws are not a priori transcendental truths, and neither are human rights. They are societal constructions rendered necessary by our current mode of existence. Without rule of law and monopoly of force, this structure breaks down.

I am a secular human rightist who subscribes to an essentially pessimistic view of human nature. I believe that any idea of inherent human dignity is socially constructed, that we are equal in being essentially meaningless, and that science has stripped us of all but our flesh and blood. By the same token, I believe in kindness, empathy and human beings' amazing capacity to create and thrive through ingenuity and tenacity.

Human rights cannot be seen to be an externally verifiable truth; they do not exist in the same way that a person exists. However, they are a representation of something inherently human: an idea of fair and ingrained empathy, however opportunistic. Alasdair Macintyre's critique of human rights – the "failure of the enlightenment project" – charts the two broad arguments used to uphold man as 'moral sovereign' when morality loses links to theology or divine law. On the one hand, we have rights as justified by societal utility; on the other, "the appeal to moral rules as grounded in the nature of practical reason".[2]

MacIntyre argues that this appeal to reason leads us to a paradoxical contemporary moral standing where we are told that man has an autonomous morality that must not be interfered with, yet we spend our lives trying to manipulate lest we be manipulated: "The incoherence of our attitudes and our experience arises from the incoherent conceptual scheme we have inherited".[3]

This does strike a nerve, for without religion or other cosmological or metaphysical schemas of the world, human rights believers are stuck in Habermas's 'striking cognitive dissonances'. They may be "suffuse[d] ... with a glow of certainty,"[4] but still human hacks human to pieces. Human is mere means to economic speculation, human is an anonymous face on which to exert power, human is an anonymous cavity from which to extract pleasure.

The critique of reason as overarching rationality is one that attacks not only human rights, but also the whole of our enlightenment inheritance. The appeal to reason is indeed circular:[5] man reasons that he has reason/rationality; man reasons that rationality is man's defining characteristic; man reasons that man's rationality is so noble or moral a thing as to warrant a transcendental dignity; man reasons that man's inherent dignity, due to his rationality, means that man has inalienable rights.

So without divine mission, and still reeling from the 20th century bankrupting of human reason, where do we turn? "We hold that these truths are self-evident," yet we know there are no self-evident truths. The twentieth century has perpetually called into question what it means to be human: the progressive codification of a human rights regime concurrent with the failure to act in Rwanda.

With fallen Gods and fractured reason, I would turn to fair. The idea of fair can be traced as a recurrent thread throughout human history – lost, sullied and broken at times, often selfishly motivated, but to be found even in babies. Beyond humans it is to be found in dogs and monkeys, just as empathy's mirror neurons were first discovered in chimpanzees.

Our understanding of fair is mediated by our understanding of society: if one man has the God-given right to rule, it is fair that he should. Fair is that distribution of benefits and duties that reflects our conception of human beings. If we understand all human beings to be equal, then that distribution should reflect this. If a woman is worth half of a man, then so too is her testimony.

This understanding of fair provides a unifying thread: Major religious texts such as the Jewish Bible, Buddhist texts, the New Testament and the Koran "incorporate moral and humanist principles, often phrased in terms of duties".[6] These tend to be phrased in terms of duties, not rights, although a commonly accepted argument is that these can be interpreted as implying each other – thou shalt not kill becomes the right to life, and so on.[7] Although a direct correlation between rights and duties is difficult,[8] it helps establish the idea of a common good and consequent idea of fairness in ancient texts.

The oldest surviving code of law, the Babylonian Hammurabi codes, is a good example of the utility of this concept of fairness. It contains the principle of eye for eye, tooth for tooth. However, the reciprocal nature of crime and punishment only apply if the offender and victim are of the same status. If a freeman injured a commoner, he would pay money, not in kind.[9] On the other hand, doctors were paid according to whom they treated: a freeman would pay more than commoners or slaves.[10] Here we find that the codified rights (to health) and duties (to give redress for a crime) were mediated by social relations.

By stripping all levels of status, meaning and mission from human beings, we essentially make them pounds of flesh: in a secular society, these pounds should be equally of value or not value, lest we be accused of being unfair. Given existing power relations and the perpetuation of status, we find that some pounds of flesh become more equal than others. To maintain our understanding of human beings as ends and as equals, normative human rights become necessary.

If we strip human beings of divine rights, moral purpose and higher reason, we need this concept of human rights, hinged around a concept of fairness, lest we all become mere bones, blood and sinew.

Gods or Goats - David Jennings

"We are as gods and *have* to get good at it," says Stewart Brand, the self-styled eco-pragmatist.[11] Planet Craft, as he calls it, involves choosing among potential geo-engineering levers and pulleys, which could buy us some time to rethink our way of life before billions of homeless climate refugees change it for us. Actually, it's not a question of levers and pulleys; it's more aerosols in the upper atmosphere and making the clouds over the ocean shinier so that they reflect light and absorb less heat. Still, this is a classic Newtonian clockwork view of a universe that we can keep running smoothly with some judicious hacking of our planet's physics and governance.

Do you feel like a god? No, me neither. Do presidents and prime ministers feel like gods? No? Then what about Branson or Gates, the oligarchs and the world's many secret billionaires? Some of them may have the means - like Bond villains - to undertake unilateral geo-engineering projects with global consequences.

Such gods as these are fallible and potentially vengeful, closer to those of Greek and Norse myth than to the kind to whom all hearts are open and all desires known. As individuals, they are prone to well-documented psychological biases - biases that no amount of study or reprogramming can reliably unlearn.[12]

With that in mind, you can see why scientist, Gaia theorist and planet hacker James Lovelock suggested, "We are as incapable of saving the planet as a goat is of being a gardener."[13]

One problem is that it's hard for us to imagine our collective behaviour getting less dysfunctional without us becoming individually smarter and more god-like. The one does not necessarily follow from the other.

Kurt Vonnegut understood that in his post-collapse parable *Galápagos*, "Human brains back [before the collapse] had become such copious and irresponsible generators of suggestions as to what might be done with life, that they made acting for the benefit of future generations seem like one of many arbitrary games which might be played by narrow enthusiasts - like poker or polo or the bond market, or the writing of science fiction novels..."[14] Fortunately, natural selection, after the collapse, favours those who can swim best, with streamlined heads and thus smaller brains.

Our science and engineering do not have to go back to the Dark Ages (though that would be one way of reducing their carbon footprint). Massive data sensing and number crunching may be cornerstones of astute Planet Craft, yet mastery of this craft may not be the preserve either of an elite of technocratic magi or of a new super-smart citizenry.

In terms of simple capacity, and maybe raw processing power, we actually passed "peak brain" tens of thousands of years ago. But we've been able to evolve smaller, more efficient brains by externalising intelligence in our tools, words and the design of our habitats - and in each other.

Being as gods doesn't mean evolving into Master Craftsmen of planets, but evolution in a different direction. A direction where, like brain cells, we are individually not all that smart, but our patterns of "activation" describe a grander intelligence - one which neutralises our individual biases. Could it be that being collectively as gods, we are individually as goats?

The secret to realising how we may be as gods is to understand that this is not the same "we" that we are used to. The frame of our collective cognition and action has to change. Long Now thinking encourages us to think in longer time frames.[15] We need a Connected We that encourages us to think in wider relationships.

As with the contributions to this book, the wisdom and mastery that gives us power is to be found in the links between us, not in the individual nodes.

A 'Playbour' of Love for the Next Twenty Years - Pat Kane

To measure the impact of the new mainstream culture of play on the rest of society, we have to be specific about what kinds of play we're talking about. There are two essential dimensions to play: it takes reality lightly, and it is something voluntarily entered into. So there are many opportunities for organisations of all kinds to read play cultures wrongly. For example, it may look as if the guild loyalty, commitment to routine and skill-acquisition, and lust for success and awards that are on display in the average synthetic world (e.g. World of Warcraft) is the return of a new work ethic online - a 'playbour' that can be redirected to enterprise efficiency. In my view, that would be a bad judgement. Players in these games are freely choosing their worlds and are embracing the labours within these worlds as an attraction of the overall immersive experience. Make a game out of the day screen-job of selling insurance, and there's a great risk of extreme alienation. Play is a step towards a semi-utopian alignment of passions and opportunities, or it's nothing.

And a generation of players is much more of a challenge to the very divisions of labour and occupations we currently toil under than it is an opportunity to adapt them (via a few avatars and power-up competitions) to the exigencies of Business As Usual.

"Playbour" - incidentally, first coined by the video-game theorist Julian Kucklich, and as a pejorative, not an aspiration - is a critical term that can be applied to any interaction, simulatory or networked experience that uses the techniques of play (absorption, immersion, repetition, recombination) to extract some kind of labour from a user that might contribute to a corporate bottom-line. A paradigm example is our interactions on Facebook through chat and games, enriching their database so that 'sentiment analysis' can take place to better serve their advertisers. Apple's various touch interfaces are potential playbour moments.

I'm not sure how it'll specifically develop in the '10s, other than to become a commercial aesthetic that will smear across most screens and interfaces, but I am vaguely interested in the possibility of 'civic playbour' - that users can be appealed to as good citizens and asked to use their devices to help process information that clearly has social or collective use, the grind of the labour in playbour being mitigated by its ethical outcome. SETI@home or Wikipedia meets the game platform. There are early versions of this (see The Extraordinaries[16]). And I think public services might get smarter at gameifying their services, under the general constriction of funds over the next few years, which are compelling the discourse of 'co-production' of services. Games can be 'co-productions' in that sense. But the danger is, as ever, that too much coercion and duty presses into the game experience. The voluntarism of play is always key.

There might be an opportunity for new models of citizenship for the Millennials, based on play-game offers coming from social enterprises and the state. But there is a crucial consequence involved in bringing play cultures into the heart of your infrastructure - they are sprawling, messy, generative, and always pushing at bureaucratic or commercial time-money constraints. The New Economic Foundation's recent report on the 21-hour week can be read as a plea for more 'play-time' in our lives - meaning more time beyond strict economic considerations to proliferate lifestyle experimentation, self-determination, and processes of conviviality and creativity in our lives. 'Playbour' as a ludic dressing-up of the same old produce-to-consume paradigm of Western capitalism will easily be rumbled by the Multitude (see Antonio Negri and Michael Hardt).

'Playbour' as the ideal reconciliation of social duty and semiotic flexibility, in a steady-state, sustainably-aware post-carbon economy, might be an entirely new social ethic. A true 'play ethic', as I would say.

Untitled, 2010 - Maria Elvorith

"The war that matters is the war against the imagination all other wars are subsumed in it."

– Diane Di Prima

With each day we move towards a necessary revolution. Resource depletion, mass species extinction and the risk of runaway climate change highlight the great flaws in our current worldview and the society it has built. It is in this nebulous inner realm of intuition and story that a revolution quietly gathers strength.

And it is in this realm that art has a unique power. Its intrinsic nature allows it not only to powerfully mirror 'the now', but to inspire and demonstrate a vision of where we can go from here.

However, if society is not engaged with these pressing issues or actively debating the absurdity of the current system, then most artists won't be either. It has taken a painfully long time for the predominant Western civilisation to begin to acknowledge the devastating consequences of its current systems. Perhaps then it is no wonder that a lot of the artwork produced in the 21st century comments on excess, commoditisation, self-immortalisation and isolation.

Artists are a part of society, and once they are aware of or involved in a debate, they will inevitably create works that communicate this understanding, whether through content, creation or presentation. But to ask an artist to respond to something that they have little or no understanding of – or interest in – invariably produces work which is contrived and short-lived.

The greatest and most striking artworks tend to emerge instead from the expression of a tension within the artist, usually without a planned agenda. Take, for example, Picasso's *Guernica*,[17] painted almost immediately after the devastating casual bombing of the town of Guernica during the Spanish Civil War and famous for its depiction of the horrors of war. When asked to explain the symbolical references in the painting, Picasso would often refuse.

"...this bull is a bull and this horse is a horse... If you give a meaning to certain things in my paintings it may be very true, but it is not my idea to give this meaning. What ideas and conclusions you have got I obtained too, but instinctively, unconsciously. I make the painting for the painting. I paint the objects for what they are."[18]

And herein lies our Catch-22. The urgency with which we need to respond to these issues calls for the inspiration that artists carry with them, which could help to move the debate forward into actualisation. Dr. Gerald Bast describes this well:

'The true beauty of art lies in its ability to move us intellectually, motivate us to follow new paths, shape awareness and character, demonstrate interconnectedness and teach us to employ all the things that surround us in a conscious manner. The achievement of social effectiveness can neither be the aim or the purpose of art. Nonetheless, art has a social influence, either in the sense of change, or in the spirit of affirmation and conservation."[19]

Yet, unless artists themselves are genuinely intimately involved in the exploration and can escape from the commoditisation of the arts sufficiently to find their true voice, the need for their distinctive contribution may go unmet.

In a sense, the future we deserve is inevitable – we will reap what we sow. But if artists can be released from their bind, then their ability to unite our hearts, minds and imagination could catalyse the creation of a future we all hope for.

We Deserve A Future Of Good Governance - Patri Friedman and Brad Taylor

We deserve a future of good governance in which people live under high-quality rule sets suited to their preferences. Rules are enormously important to human welfare – just look at the differences between those on opposite sides of an arbitrary border, such as that separating North and South Korea[20].[21] Rules are a meta-technology that determines how well people can cooperate to achieve their goals, and the potential benefits of improvement in this area dwarf those of any other effort to improve the world.

Proposals to improve government are common, but few are ever tried. Those that are tried generally end badly. The clearest example is communism, which claimed more than a hundred million lives[22][23] and left billions poor and miserable. It's no wonder that conservatives see radical reform as dangerous[24].[25]

The central difficulty of improving governance is like any product: we don't know what will work ahead of time. Products improve not by some grand plan that maps progress from start to finish, but by a series of decentralized experiments that allow ideas to be retained or discarded based on performance in reality. This is why we have such amazing phones today: entrepreneurs tested ideas against technological constraints and consumer preferences. Good ideas were retained and bad ideas abandoned – without anyone needing to die. Over time, we progressed from clunky machines to modern smartphones.

In governance, though, such low-stakes experimentation is currently impossible. Those wishing to improve politics have the impossible task of creating proposals without incremental feedback from reality. If they get things wrong, millions of people may suffer or die. Rather than groping in the dark for the right solution, as utopian philosophers do, we need to bring progress to politics by lowering the barriers to experimentation and making failure less costly. If new countries could be created by those with good ideas, and citizens could move to whatever country best suited their preferences – and leave if it got unpleasant – we would see the decentralized experimentation that drives progress in other areas.

Historically, this has happened on the frontier, but since every square inch of land is currently claimed by some existing government, we need to look elsewhere. In the long run, space will provide a vast blank space for experimentation, but there is another frontier here on Earth which is ready now: the ocean.

By developing the knowledge we need to permanently live on the ocean comfortably at a reasonable cost, my colleagues and I at The Seasteading Institute[26][27] hope to transform the market for governance. The political vacuum of the ocean would itself make seasteading worthwhile (we don't have to fight anyone for it). As it turns out, the ocean has another important property: shifting large objects is much easier in water than on land (that's why the ocean is our global highway for goods). With modular ocean cities, people could move countries without leaving their house. Seasteading makes it easier to create and compete in the nation-state industry.

While settling the ocean may sound utopian and unrealistic, it is far more humble and realistic than the alternatives. We admit our ignorance about the ideal society, so we want to let a thousand nations bloom[28][29] to see what works. And by transforming a political problem to a technological one, we avoid the problems endemic to large-scale politics[30].[31] While the technological challenges[32][33] are large, they are far easier than convincing a majority of the population that your utopia is worth the whole country trying. The cruise ship industry[34][35] shows that people can live comfortably at sea for around $200 per day. Our mission is to drive comfort and safety up and cost down while finding better ways to make a living at sea[36].[37]

Settling the oceans is a realistic way of increasing quality, diversity, and innovation in governance. It avoids the hubris of top-down reform, and there is a clear path from here to there. While there is much work to be done, the potential benefits are huge. We hope you'll join us in supporting seasteading as a powerful way to move towards the Future We Deserve.

The World Needs Wives - Zoe Lee

Men have made a mess of the world. They don't care for the world in the same way they don't care for their families. They just assume someone else will take care of the messy chores.

While women of the minority world can now participate in the men's world, the majority of men continue to avoid the women's world of being available to soothe hurts, feed endless appetites, make the bed, clean the floor and otherwise work to provide a safe, secure, healthy environment for those who can't provide for themselves. "Women's work" is hugely unpopular, unrecognised and largely unpaid. When we do pay someone to do it, they don't do as good a job, they don't care for your home, your children or your dear demented mother the way a good wife/mother/daughter would.

Institutions fail because money can't buy the care traditionally given by a wife or mother. The dependent – the disabled, the chronically ill, the young, the elderly, the environment – all need personal relationships with people who ensure they are able to live to their fullest potential, provided with support when needed. These relationships take time, commitment, appreciation and empathy – the kind of love that accepts and honours intrinsic values; the antithesis of the abuse and neglect that institutions and "individual independence" produces.

Traditional societies work because they prevent women from participating in society in any function other than wife or mother. This ensures an adequate supply of devoted carers while depriving society of the talents of half its population. In the minority world, we have population decrease because, given the opportunity of participating in a man's role, many women avoid fulltime caring for the family. It is ironic that we pay people to nurse, teach, organise our lives but those who do the same job unpaid don't feel valued.

We should pay "professional wives" (regardless of gender) to care and educate; they are given the task of keeping track of their family, ensuring they are living healthy, safe, productive lives engaged in education, their communities, and democracy. These wives will also be advocates, responsible for the legal and financial blunders their charges get into. Wives would be paid per head, with additional provision for food, board and live-in care if needed. They have a maximum number they can care for with minimum contact hours per week for each member of their family up to 40 hours employment per week. They will have qualifications, professional codes of ethics, compulsory health and safety standards, best practice syntheses, minimum holidays, sick leave, employment contracts, complaint procedures, bonuses, (perks ?), monthly reports, quarterly reviews, annual plans, professional development and a supervisor.

Forget obesity campaigns – give the wives clear guidelines of the expected individual weight targets as part of their performance criteria.

Everyone who wants to be looked after by the government will be told to get a wife who will manage the beneficiary's affairs professionally and apply for monetary support on their behalf. Getting a wife would be like finding a midwife or doctor – finding someone whose manner suits but whose professionalism is to be assumed. Currently, at least sixty percent of the tax dollar pays for health, education or social security (including pensions). It's ineffective and inefficient – people are not staying healthy or making educated choices and they are expecting the government to rescue them when things go wrong. If you don't want a wife, you can become one. But with responsibility comes accountability.

Wives integrate lives, co-ordinate community and build resilience by maintaining webs of relationships enabling everyone to pursue their passions and fulfill their responsibilities.

The future will be what we deserve when men become wives because that's when we'll know wives are valued.

The Food We Deserve - Christopher Brewster

The tomato did not deserve this.

It was clearly culpable but hardly responsible. People wanted nice red round tomatoes. Or they just wanted ketchup. Or they were told they just wanted ketchup. So all colours (orange, gold, yellow, purple), all variety of shape (misshapen, oval), were bred out or merely forgotten. People wanted tomatoes all year round, so they were grown in glasshouses, even heated hothouses, all through the winter. This was possibly one of the most environmentally damaging fruit and vegetable production processes then undertaken[38]. Most people did not care how the tomatoes were grown, or who grew them, and so other people, out of sight and mind, suffered birth defects, cancer and other illnesses from pesticides and chemicals in order to provide us with these tomatoes[39]. Standardised hard balls which needed gas to turn the standardised red and become apparently acceptable for most consumers, transported across great distances, packaged in plastic wrappers, labelled as good for you, one of your "five a day". This belonged to a time when it made sense for some to grow tomatoes on the nutrient poor soil of Florida or use North Sea gas to heat greenhouses based on hydroponics. The tomato did not deserve this maltreatment, it did not deserve to be complicit in a long abusive supply chain, abuse of our environment, abuse of people, and for an aesthete, the supreme crime, abuse of our taste buds. Most people in fact never ate real tomatoes, rather they ate some form of processed tomatoes in pizzas and ketchup, as part of the infinitely varied, completely non-nutritious modern industrial diet[40].

In the future we deserve, our tomato will not be available in northern climes, in mid winter, out of season. But when it does come to our local farmers' market, we will celebrate its arrival, we will thank the seasons for its return once more, in all its variety, its different colours, and variegated shapes. We will taste that tomato and it will bring back memories of childhoods, of delicious lunches and dinners with friends, of picnics by a river with past or present loves, of juices spilt and sauces poured. In the future we deserve, fresh food will come a short distance to us from farmers whom we either know or can easily get in touch with. Food will carry a story from the past and the present, it will be a central part of human communication and community, it will be a tool for conviviality.

In this future food will be recognised as central to human existence and humanity's cohabitation with the flora and fauna upon the earth. Our agricultural practices will be in harmony with the environment because these practices produce more, reduce poverty, improve nutrition and reduce the possibility of climate change[41].

Rediscovering the Stuff We Forgot to Remember - Joe Turner

The 'future we deserve' is a phrase that can be taken at least two ways:
- In a positive sense, we might use it to affirm that we have rights as citizens of the world and that we collectively should be working towards a future that we all – collectively – deserve.
- The phrase has resonance with the idea of getting the 'politicians we deserve' – meaning that if we are as apathetic about our future as our body politic, we'll get what we deserve, i.e., a lot less than we would have had we thought and planned for a better future.

We live in wildly enlightened times, or, perhaps more accurately, wild and enlightened *space*. We expect *our* futures to be better than our past, even if we are not really able to articulate what we want from the future that is better than we have today – nor how we will be able to show that things are better when we get there. A large proportion of those of us who live in wealth have, by many measures, lives which have never been better – and it is difficult to imagine a world where it could get any better for us. We are slow to realise that our future will be shared with billions of people whose urges for improvement are more urgent, more demanding, more ethical than ours. Mostly, we want them to develop, but relatively slowly and **not at our expense**.

But that is **not an option** in the future we all deserve. On a planetary scale, not all will survive, and the rich are the least able to cope with change, so most of us (include me writing this and you reading) are going to need to swallow a lot of humble pie and remind the rump of humanity why we are worth keeping.

If we (the 'old' rich) have something to offer, we have a chance of surviving with our poor brethren. And, actually, I think we do. For example, in the field of agricultural improvement.

The history of British Agriculture contains many lessons – for example, the humble *Chenopodium album*, commonly known as Fat Hen, is one of British Agriculture's top 10 weeds (attracting huge amounts of pesticide usage for its removal), yet it used to be a staple food in Southern England. At one point in history, there was a choice between fat hen and cabbage, and ultimately we chose the cabbage.

The British developed skills in agricultural improvement, which meant that new species and cultivars and varieties developed very rapidly compared to other parts of the world. The trade-off was that the old knowledge of species and varieties was lost.

So part of our legacy to humanity is this: We made a lot of agricultural mistakes and learned our way out of them. We did it before, we can do it again. And we can do more than we think we can do, particularly with regard to agriculture and soil management.

If we are to be more self sufficient – and my guess is that we're either going to have to choose to depend more on our own resources or be forced to – we need to learn to survive on the things we throw away or ignore. Remarkably, we can; we've merely forgotten to remember how to do that.

Reclaiming Awesome - Emma Bryn-Jones

Awesome! The ubiquity of its enthusiasm, soiled with cynicism already – how long before it makes its sorry path to the heap of ne'er-do-wells and its predecessor awful? The tautology of "awesome wonder" in the not-so-ancient hymn "How great thou art" (published as we know it in 1954) holds the clue, for awesome is not a word without spin.

By origin, awe is an Old English word for dread, which the Church first appropriated in the Middle Ages to make the "Fear of God" reverential. The Creator remained awful for some four hundred years, until the Reformation saw fit to bestow an echo of this greatness around kings with divine rights, when the word awesome came into being. For a further three hundred years, awe had two strands: brimming to the full of it or characterised by some of it. In any case, awe was good for those captive of its benevolence.

Awful took a turn for the worse during the Industrial Revolution, so it is uncanny that awesome prevails in the current Virtual Revolution. With the demise of awful, only two hundred years after the birth of its relative, awesome, the latter rose as a beacon of hope in the aftermath of mass production and two world wars. Losing its value rapidly as it is shunted around the globe, what will become of awesome a hundred years from now?

In the correlation between dread and wonder is the recognition that no creation exists without measures of good and bad. Twenty years since the Internet's creation, users are emerging as content creators or consumers and thus the power of communication thrives, with a mere chink of opportunity before it is once again under control. Awesome – isn't it time you defined how we use it?

Panarchy - Paul B Hartzog

"What makes political systems cross over the threshold into parameter transformations? Some breakpoints occur when a technological development enables individuals to engage in previously unimagined activities and collectivities to pursue previously inconceivable policy goals... a turning point that occurs when the resources or practices of a system can no longer cope with one more increment of change and its parameters give way under the cumulative load."[42]

In times of great transformation, civilization finds itself in T.S. Eliot's Wasteland.[43] Old rules become increasingly useless and do not result in the same successful outcomes as they did in the past, but a new Kuhnian paradigm has yet to emerge from the chaos of turbulent times.[44] The discovery of a new path lies in the process of recognizing and illuminating patterns in the vectors that are operating in the transforming civilization.[45]

The primary hypothesis that I will endeavor to support is that leveraging the benefits of network organization constitutes a new source of power and a new way of accomplishing global governance. As individuals and groups engage each other globally, the locus of global governance shifts from state-centered activities to distributed networks. The cumulative effect of the shift from hierarchies to networks is a system of overlapping spheres of authority and regimes of collective action called "panarchy."[46]

Complexity + Networks + Connectivity => Panarchy

On the Future We Deserve... - Antonio Dias

The Future: Our "now" is continually replenished. We notice trends and run vectors to imagine "the future." Modernism – long-scale, 15th Century to Present – fetishized the future, a dream-scape we inhabit vicariously. Other cultures did this with the past, or an after-life. Our tendency is to imagine Heaven or Hell, and foresee Utopia or Apocalypse.

We: Our reflex is to identify parochially or globally, "people just like me," or we try to be all-inclusive. In either case we project a stereotype ahead in time.

Deserve: Cause and effect exists. We tend to conflate causality with expectations based on morality or fairness resulting in language like "deserving." Depending on how we feel about our "we," we deserve Heaven or Hell, and posit a Utopian or Apocalyptic "future."

We can never break out of our subjectivity, but that doesn't nullify the exercise. Realizing the impossibility of entering a realm in which our assumptions line up with reality is a first step towards changing how we interact with our world, leading us to look at the future in a fundamentally different way, stepping beyond our modernist habits. Instead of building fanciful scenarios upon wishful foundations, it requires us to be disciplined and humble. We can define elements that may impact our future, we can generate thought-experiments to gain experience beyond the actual, we can habituate ourselves to change – but we do so with a greater awareness of our limited abilities, not only to predict, but to drive change that does not simply make things worse.

We live in an emotional landscape defined by optimism, pessimism, willfulness and hope. These cardinal points mean more to us than any reality. We measure the world from our favorite quadrant. Unless we challenge this compass, we wander our landscape with no way to see beyond our desires. This is a fact we cannot ignore, but we can acclimate ourselves to subjectivity and improve our chances of finding an effective engagement.

If this project is to be useful, it needs to step beyond "What if?" – where we take our wishes, optimistic or pessimistic, as starting points and apply our brand of willfulness or hope as we imagine how they might play out. To fail in this way is to admit we are only hammers looking for nails and ensures we have little or no agency as we remain trapped within our illusions.

Here is where our future will play out. Can we maintain our desire for effective agency? Can we deal with intractable decline? Can we develop acceptance? Can we keep from spinning out imagined futures, either worldly or heavenly, and simply inhabit our present as each 'now' comes upon us?

You hit what you're aiming at as all those skid-marks ending at solitary poles and trees testify. If we limit our aim to what we currently envision, we are bound to run into whatever we fear lies behind it. The only way out of this trap is to remain present. This can potentially cycle us into realms beyond our current view. To accept this choice is to wager: pitting certain failure, if we stay on our customary path of attempting to plan and control our reality, against the chance that we can broaden our range of possibility by letting go of the wheel.

We inhabit – or would, if we stopped looking past it – a wondrous unfolding present. We are, or can train ourselves to be, witnesses to that unfolding. The discipline and humility required to inhabit our present, to live within a gift, is in itself a corrective that might lead us to a future we cannot predict. If we fail to inhabit our present we lose the only thing we know we have. Unless we turn our meditation on the future into motivation to focus on our present, we give up a "sure-thing" to remain within a chimera, a fantasy of heaven or hell, imagined brightly or darkly, arrived at actively or passively but assuredly nowhere.

There is No Future - Eleanor Saitta

Futures are funny things. We plan for them, think about them, and obsess over them, as individuals and as families, groups, cities, even cultures. We expect our futures to create a coherent narrative with our past. Our media is saturated with experts, telling us how the future will unfold. Even when they're telling us they don't understand what's happening, they do so from a position of expertise, a position that says, "Not to worry, chaps, our top minds are working on the problem. We'll have this whole 'future' thing wrapped up in no time."

We do the same thing with the past. There, we call it history — the cherry-picked and miniscule subset of past events, strung together as the supporting evidence for the image of ourselves that we desire. Narratives are no more present in actual history than in any other random sequence of events. The future, or what we think of as the future, is this process in reverse.

We understand a lot of small-scale natural processes, but we're only just beginning to grasp how interlinked they are. The way those large systems change and fail is a cause of ongoing surprise, worry, and increasingly tragedy. Our reach has outstripped our vision.

The natural world is only a small part of our future, however, and we're even worse at understanding people. People are a big part of why we construct narratives. We need to understand what they're going to do to choose our current actions, and when we're working with other people, we need to share our understanding of the world and our intent. Narratives are a great tool for this, but they're plagued by mistaking the map for the territory and the story for the world.

Our production of narratives runs very deep. We create the "self" as a distinct entity, different and separate from the world, and create a narrative about how that self has interacted with the world through its history. This, even, is where the problems start. We try to live in that narrative, instead of in the real world. The self we create doesn't really exist, and the narrative we create is more fiction than real.

The future, the real future, doesn't come from the stories we tell, it comes from the actual lives of people. To effect real change, we need to look to those lives and the contexts in which they're lived. Understand lives and contexts, and you understand the now and the future. Change lives, change contexts, and you change the future. Of course, humanity is big and incredibly interconnected. Just like no person is going to understand all seven billion lives, let alone the implications of their interconnections, no one gets more than a glimpse of the future. Those glimpses come from seeing through the narratives to the real people and understanding their lives with real compassion. Foresight starts with our first narrative — it starts by getting rid of the fictions that you've built up around who you are, stopping the pretence that you are separate from the world, or indeed that your "self" is meaningful at all.

If we want to act, we can only act in the now, and interact with the actual existing conditions in the world. For the purpose of action, there is no future. This isn't to disregard the power of narrative to shape people's actions — the shared understanding still functions, and it can trigger other people's actions in the now. It's a dangerous tool, though, because it carries with it and reinforces the seeds of illusion.

When I say that the future doesn't exist, I'm not saying that it won't happen, obviously. When it happens, though, it will just be more now, with all the messiness, ugliness, and, sadly, suffering that that implies, but also with the beauty and the joy that can only be experienced in the moment.

Each new instant arises from the decisions and tensions of its predecessor. When the new now appears to have shifted very quickly from past ones, it's because of millions of small decisions, not a few big ones. The narratives we tell, what we hear on the evening news, only tell us about the big and often meaningless decisions. As such, those narratives are increasingly useless, especially as they become more and more time-sliced and schizophrenic, with less space for the analysis of real lives.

There is no plan. There is no actual grand narrative. Think about what may happen later, but live, learn, and act in the now. Look into the dark corners that narratives want to forget and that make you uncomfortable. Don't ignore the truth just because it doesn't agree with the world you want, because it's the world you're going to get.

This is Mental. - Rohan Gunatillake

In this book you will find dozens of people more knowledgeable, more informed and more equipped than I am. I encourage you to listen to them carefully, as I certainly will do, for they are talking to us about the challenges we face as a species and as a planet, and they are pointing us to strategies by which we might use this critical window in human history for not only survival but for genuine transformation. And while I bow to my fellow writers here and acknowledge that the future of the world is important, what I believe is even more important is the future of how we relate to the world.

Human conscious experience — colloquially known as life — has two components. First there is the stuff — rocks, cars, trees, the planet, animals, people we know and people we don't. (This is not an exhaustive taxonomy but you get the idea). The second component is our relationship to that stuff, the elements of our inner or mental experience that results in our either liking, disliking or being indifferent to whatever is happening. And when we look closely, more often than not we see that wherever we find difficulty in our lives, it's ultimately bound up in the relationship — our mental attitude — rather than the stuff itself. Ok. So what?

The so-what is in the unavoidable fact that most of our challenges will be most effectively solved, not by tinkering around with the stuff (e.g., better, cleaner fuels) but by radically changing our relationship to it (e.g., not wanting to travel in the first place). So what we are talking about is our changing our relationships, changing our behaviours and ultimately changing our minds. Therefore to give our advances in stuff the absolute best chance of delivering the change we need, we need to develop our minds in lockstep.

Again, taking climate change as an example challenge, the mental qualities we could most benefit from building up together are awareness of what is actually going on and a greater sense of how we are all systematically connected. Or in other, more Buddhist-y words, wisdom and compassion.

All the great contemplative traditions have wisdom and compassion at the heart of their teachings and practice, but Buddhism is fairly unique in its highly systematic approach, its appealing atheistic/agnostic position, and its rich history for evolution across cultures. And while I am certainly not advocating that we all become Buddhist meditators — as someone who has spent much of the last decade in Buddhist circles, I honesty cannot think of anything worse — I am, however, advocating that we as a society up our mental game.

And from my limited viewpoint, it is already happening. Mindfulness meditation-based approaches are now widely recognised as effective therapeutic tools against a wide range of mental health issues both in the UK and globally. And as traditionally alien practices such as yoga and caring about whether our food is drowned in pesticides become increasingly accepted as mainstream, I believe (or is it hope?) that transformative mental development is the next step for the "conscious" shopper and exerciser. And it's not only the uptake of clinical meditation therapies that energise me, but also the bloom of the positive psychology movement and the well-being and happiness agenda more generally.

But to get there — to get to a culture where sensitivity, awareness and high levels of inner literacy are the rule — there has to be a presentation of why we should and how we can practically develop these qualities in a language that speaks to where the majority of us are — and that is a language that avoids the religious, avoids the clinical, and avoids an association with the limp spirituality of pop Orientalism or the anti-modern brigade. It has to be relevant, urban and now, because the challenges we face are relevant, urban and now.

Monastech - Nathan Rosquist

Monastech is how monasticism interfaces with technology to help us build the future we deserve. Monastech helps you grow your own Otherhood — create your very own monastic order — or monasticize your existing community's future. It is an open-source monastic university, an online cyber-monastic community, as well as a model of community living that confronts the increasingly secular, technological, and complex future we're facing.

Monastech futurism

"What wisdom does transhuman power demand?" —Joel Garreau in *Radical Evolution*

Secular monasticism + technology;give us the equanimity, compassion and capacity to create the future we deserve.

For example, in fields of genetics and cognitive, neuro-, computer, and information science — folks who are working on artificial intelligence and human enhancement — it will be the scientists and engineers who have dealt significantly with their own consciousness who will have the first, best answers to questions like:

- What is life?
- What is awareness?
- Is artificial intelligence the same thing as artificial consciousness?
- Does artificial consciousness require a body?
- Does compassion require a mortal body?
- How do we concoct a "Friendly AI"?

Corporate Monastech

High tech companies will pay employees who go on month- or year-long sabbaticals in a monastery. The halls of Google and Microsoft are already crowded with monkish personalities. Giving these employees incentives to spend time in a monastery (perhaps one designed specifically with high tech in mind, or in an art monastery that would expand their creative capacities to new levels) would make good business sense, as they would operate at a significantly higher level — with greater focus, clarity, equanimity, compassion and insight — than other employees upon returning to the work force.

Cybermonasticism

There will be monasteries that exist only online and in the bedrooms and minds of millions of householder monks. The monks will all get up at the same time, chant together, meditate together, eat together. Some cybermonks will work normal jobs, some will work to support the cybermonastic infrastructure. Some will live together in real monasteries. All will be joined in a Universal Otherhood of Otherhoods.

Online tools for collaborative mindfulness will turn their collective conscious power into real, compassionate action. The mindfulness grids and awareness engines they power will guide artificial intelligence, robotics, and nanotechnology.

e.g., 'The International Otherhood of Artmonks.'

Monasticism in a minute

With technological upgrades to the power of human consciousness, future monks will have what subjectively feels like a 12-year silent retreat in the Himalayas in a matter of seconds.

Monastech for weathering a dystopian age

In a negative future, monasteries will serve the same role they did in the last dark age: preserving knowledge, culture and compassion.

The Futures We Deserve or, Even Bankers Might Have Uses - Edmund Harriss

My son often asks me "Which do you like best?" before going on to list two things that are (to my mind) simply not comparable. As a mathematician, I would describe this sort of thing as a partial ordering. I can easily say which I prefer out of, say, Rachmaninov and Britney Spears; however, ask me to compare Rachmaninov to Leonard Cohen, or Britney Spears to Christina Aguilera, and I would be stumped. Essentially, a partial ordering lets you order some things but not everything. This is in contrast to a total ordering — numbers, for example. If you give me two different numbers, one will always be greater than the other (for maths geeks, I am talking about real numbers here).

What has this got to do with the future? It comes down to the stories that we tell each other; in particular, that we deserve the best. At first glance this seems obvious, maybe even moral if you take into account the effects on other people.

We also want to know that we are doing well, not just by our own standards but by the standards of the community. As communities and individuals, therefore, we seek to impose a total ordering on everything in society, even though many things cannot be compared. As everyone wants the best car, house, and job, we are pulled into a trap where most people have the same things.

For other reasons, the banks in the early 21st century were doing the same. They had one model of risk. They justified this, saying that everyone would be safe as they used the same model. This did not end well, and we all saw the consequences when the model broke.

Finally, we are always encouraged to seek efficiency and best practice. This trend is shown clearly in the spread of Walmart, who makes just three-and-a-half cents profit on every dollar spent, or, alternatively, Dilbert's boss insisting we should "work smarter not harder".

What can we do instead? The potato farmers in the Andes have a solution. They do not grow a single type of potato; they grow hundreds. The wild plants in their hedges add even more to the genetic mix. Each year, their crop gets a variety of weather conditions, and some varieties do well. Other varieties do badly. These can switch from year to year. There are even some varieties that do poorly in all conditions but always give something. Only considering those plants would ensure poverty, yet when the conditions are really bad they can be essential, helping survival to the next year.

To flourish in all the possible futures we need the diversity of humanity. This is easy to see. To actually embrace it as individuals is harder. The idea of best, the idea of safety by not standing out, and a worship of efficiency are harder than you would think to break. This is because when something is truly diverse there are many things that you might consider bad, as well as those that are just good for other people.

The first step is to cultivate different friendships. When you meet people who you can get on with but fundamentally disagree with, do not write them off. Argue with them, perhaps, but cultivate the friendship. Understand that any one of us is wrong about many things. This helps you to become more diverse as an individual. Also recognise that something that seems useless, or even evil, can have a purpose in some situations. Not understanding how that might be is not a justification to reject it. Of course, there are some fundamental rules that you might consider sacred, but question even those. On the other hand, this is not passive acceptance of everything. When certain things start to dominate, you should work against them. Easy when you disagree, but sometimes you have to move against things you actually love.

In conclusion, do not pin your hopes on one future. We do not know what might be 'round the corner — good, bad or simply transformative. Whatever happens, different people will experience the same future differently. By keeping our options as wide as possible we can maximise humanity's greatest asset: to adapt.

References

- Recipe for Disaster: The Formula That Killed Wall Street[47] Wired Magazine 23 February 2009
  - Article on the Gaussian Cupola, the risk model that the banks went for. A little harsh on the mathematics, rather than the greed of those who used it.
- Walmart's Operating and Profit margins[48]
- Original (I think) Dilbert comic with "Work smarter not harder"[49]
- The Botany of Desire[50], Michael Pollan, 2002
  - In a chapter on agricultural monoculture, especially for the potato, Michael Pollan discusses the different approach of Andean farmers.

Memes that Kill - Thomas Bjelkeman

Virus pandemics are scary things. "The 1918 pandemic, by most estimates, killed 50 million from a 2000 million global population."[51] The 2009 pandemic could have been this bad, or even worse. Many were scared that it would be really virulent and maybe reach the type of levels of death in the population which the Black Death caused. "The Black Death is estimated to have killed 30% to 60% of Europe's population, reducing the world's population from an estimated 450 million to between 350 and 375 million in 1400."[52]

But there are even more virulent things than viruses or bacteria that kill. Some things that we have no large scale healthcare systems to deal with. We have no quarantine system that will function on them — and the fact that these things can be deadly is not even widely recognised, even though it is easy to prove that they are. So what are they? They are memes. Memes that kill.

What is a meme?

"A meme is a unit of cultural ideas, symbols or practices, which can be transmitted from one mind to another through writing, speech, gestures, rituals or other imitable phenomena."[63]

Memes are more virulent than viruses or bacterial plagues, as two people can transmit the meme between them without even being in the same country. The telephone system, TV, radio and lately the internet are the transmission vector for the meme. One person can in fact "infect" millions of people with a particularly successful meme and nearly at no cost.

What are some deadly memes, then?

Government regulated, or "social" health care is worse than market regulated health care US style. This meme seems to have infected a rather large part of the US population, and it makes it much more expensive to run the US health care system, which as a result kills people. How many it kills I don't have the numbers for, but when you compare the cost for healthcare in the EU compared to the US, the latter gets worse healthcare (life expectancy: US 78.2; EU 78.7)[54], costing significantly more (US: 14.5% of GDP, EU: 9.5% of GDP).[55] (5% of US GDP is about US$ 730 Bn.) These billions could instead be used to save lives every year. Many lives. Certainly more than what the 2009 virus pandemic killed in the US.

Climate change is a hoax. This meme has taken root among a fairly substantial part of the population in the Western world. The result will be that many people will die due to effects of climate change in places like Bangladesh, with increased flooding, or East Africa due to droughts.[56]

MMR vaccination is dangerous. The MMR vaccine is an immunisation shot against measles, mumps and rubella. This was a meme that made people think that vaccinating their children was more dangerous than not, as those who got this meme thought that their children would develop autism if they took the vaccine.[57]

So the question is: What is the next big meme that is going to kill on a massive scale? Something as big as Nazism, which killed several tens of millions of people in only six years.[58]

The Tiny Army - Vinay Gupta

In the end, there were only seven of us in the army. Harald built the lab, Frieda and Alok manufactured or bought the reagents, Ali designed the distribution systems and Micky selected the targets. Sweet, brilliant Chen built the humanitarian pandemic organism. I did logistics and communications, so that the others never had to meet. I don't run the errands myself, of course. There's a rather good underground syndicate that trades routine favors on deliveries and such, like using smurfs, and generally if you generate a bit of noise on the network, they're reliable. Of course, it would be easier in a corporate lab if we were engineering sterile mosquitos or enslaving cotton farmers, but we're not. We're working on a final solution to the ills of humanity.

We're going to kill all the alpha males.

The rising destructive power of small groups is one of the biggest worries of national security types. The "force multiplier" effect of weapons has increased to the point where ten men can paralyze a city, and fifty can execute terrorist attacks that cost a trillion dollars to repair. As technology delivers longer and longer levers, the ability of a small group to render immense harm has increased. A single person, if they were a skilled virus author, could paralyze large parts of the internet.

When you add biotechnology to this equation, things darken dramatically. Rumors have circulated for years about nations, such as Israel, researching gene-specific bioweapons — because to defend against a genetic final solution, one would have to know if one was possible.

What to do? What to do? Are we to have Science Police who intrude into every aspect of life looking for the technical capability to kill? Perhaps compulsory mental screening, but then what to do with the numerous people who might, but never do? At fifteen, how do you tell Lex Luthor from Luther Burbank?

Like all wicked problems, it is going to take many approaches combined to get a lid on small group power. Some loss of civil liberties for those working in dangerous areas is inevitable - those with advanced knowledge of how to do dangerous things are going to have to become socialized to heightened personal surveillance and occasional mental health screening. A licensing approach to these technologies is not the whole answer, but an acceptance that working with them makes you a risk to the world and gives the world the right to scrutinize seems necessary. It is one of the few areas where enhanced transparency solves many problems.

The most dangerous actors will still be profit-seeking corporations. The people who are crazy enough to want kill the world are usually too ineffective to do it. But the corporate psychopath, seeking profit above all other goals, is sleek and well-organized, and willing to run this year's risks for next year's profits. We must open the labs to inspections, as we do for weapons testing, but to free us from the risk of regulatory capture those inspections must have tight public oversight.

The final guard is that the violent reformers, generally speaking, are trying to kill their way to a better world. In a twisted way, they value life and quality of life. Few of the most dangerous people operate out of hatred. Rather, it is the vision of the better future that guides them.

As a result, there may be a certain self-correcting aspect to small group destructive power. People who are resorting to violence to change the world do not want it destroyed. Perhaps we will find that even the most violent of extremists shy away from deploying self-replicating weaponry, be it bio or nano in nature, because of the risk it will destroy what they only wished to control.

This is scant hope, but it is all I have for you.

A Four-Bladed Scissors - Arthur Doohan

Mankind is better at creating problems than solving them.

We created plenty of pointless, bloody wars. We now know that, inadvertently, we created the conditions that spread plagues amongst our own and other tribes and nations. In the previous century, we did solve a few problems. A stalemate that kept a nuclear war at bay was devised. Some very old plagues were eradicated, an achievement never dreamed of before, let alone accomplished.

But in the main, mankind is very poor at problem solving on a societal or cultural scale. We either endure or we throw enough resources to either overwhelm the 'enemy' or exhaust ourselves. In the main, our experience has been of tackling one problem at a time. The literature from Tainter, Diamond and others suggests that a civilisation often fails to cope when beset by more than one factor type problem.

We now have a vast array of tools for generating complex analysis about our dilemmas. We also have a very poor apparatus for deciding what to do about our problems. So we know more about what we are facing into but we are hamstrung from doing anything about it.

Some of the problem stems from the fact that we have a largely reductive science and our toolset currently reflects this state of affairs. We have only recently begun to tangle with the issues raised by dynamically interacting problem-spaces, such as DNA-protein interactions, weather systems and networked autonomous computers.

Frankly, we are not good at seeing the wood for the trees. I would like to throw a 'framework' onto the bonfire of our vanities to see if it helps at all.

First of all, our problems can be divided into categories of physical/real and cultural/artificial. Secondly, they can be divided in categories of what we want and what is available. These form Cartesian axes of Availability and Actuality.

Peak resources of all kinds (but principally, crude oil) fall into the category of negative or declining Availability but positive Actuality. Peak Population is positive for both Availability and Actuality.

Peak Debt is negative for both Availability and Actuality. A better way of thinking of Peak Debt might be in terms of an optimal ratio for debt/equity rations for a given technological/EROI situation; clearly, we are in negative territory with regard to global debt/equity ratios.

Peak information is clearly positive and increasing. Information and its hoped-for corollary, knowledge, are intangible and therefore on the 'Artificial' side of the graph but on the positive side of the Availability axis.

	Y-Axis – Rate of Change
Information	**Population**
X-Axis - Tangibility	
Debt/Equity Ratios	**Resources** (Environmental Dividend, Mineral Stock)

From my point of view, masses of population and information are good things, but it must not be forgotten that they both imply constraints. Information is not knowledge and it is most certainly not wisdom. It has to be managed and used creatively. Equally, a population has to be fed, watered and housed before it can start to produce anything, whether that be food, art or knowledge.

There are very real negatives in this picture that we are very well aware of.

You might well be asking where climate change is in all of this 'graphology'. It is in amongst Peak Resources because I view the renewable output of the planet (food, air, water) as a 'dividend' of the physical wealth of the planet and, in the same way as we have damaged the debt/equity ratios of our imaginary/intangible assets, we have done the same to the 'real assets' and will face declining 'real dividends' until we repair the damage done.

Although I have classed Information and Population as 'Positives,' they are not costless and they can be problems unless they are handled correctly.

Which leads me to my final and unhappy conclusion.

I started this article by saying that 'Mankind' had not shown much aptitude to date for handling problems, even if they came one at a time. Each of these four issues constitutes a serious problem for humanity. Worse, each of these represents a constraint on the other.

A blade can be a tool or a weapon. Two blades in opposition to each other is commonly called a scissors and is much more likely to be used as a tool than a weapon arising from its configuration. Humanity faces a 'four bladed' scissors, each blade of which cuts on the other.

Our information and our population mean that we are poised on the cusp of enormous potential, but our history tells us that we are likely to end up with bloody fingers before we get the hang of the 'tool'.

One in Six, a Strategy for Reduction - Glenn Hall

There are too many of us on this planet. We use too much. We create too much back end to our activities in the form of waste. We are greedy. We have too many children. We are intolerant. We consume. We eat too much. We aspire. We live. We drive. We want.

I am a member of we, I do many of these things, and I *am part* of the problem.

Radio plays get me thinking; this piece is inspired by H.G. Wells' *The War of the Worlds*[59] meets *Blade Runner*[60] meets *The Day of the Triffids*[61]. It should scare the hell out of you.

> *Imagine you are driving along, and you round a bend and find a checkpoint. You can see about 30 cars in front of you. There is activity, but you can't understand what it is. You are deeply uncomfortable. A uniformed person appears and signs a car near the front to move to a side lane. A crusher appears; the car and its occupants are gone. The sixth car. The uniform moves up the line, to no 12. Crush. Gone. You start to count your on position in the line. Thirteen, Fourteen, Fifteen, Sixteen, Seventeen. The uniform approaches you. You sweat. The car behind you. Crush. Gone.*
>
> *At the supermarket, you are in a line at the checkouts, a long line. The sixth person is pulled aside by uniformed people and taken away. You count. Seven.*
>
> *You are at work later. An email arrives; you are called to a room. Immediate. A quarter of your room empties, there are twenty-four desks. You do not return.*
>
> *You go to collect your children from school. You wait, and some you know arrive at the gate. They are wearing bright tabards. You have seen this before, they carry the school logo. Your child is late. You turn and look at the earlier children walking up the road. They have large numbers on their backs. One. Two. Three. Four. Five. You sweat.*

You drive onto your own road to your house, which is number 30, halfway round the second bend. As you go past number eleven, you notice a whole house has gone. You sweat.

Too much, too much. If the Future We Deserve is to be brought into being, then we must prepare for reduction. One-in-six of everything. People, cars, lives, babies, buildings...

In our world, we have granted ourselves a great luxury: the right to decide what is and what is not, what lives and what does not. We declare that human life is sacrosanct. One-in-six lives are not.

The idea behind this is to begin, and to pursue, some really hard dialogues in the whole of this world. For over fifty years, Europe has been (mostly) peaceful, whereas earlier the (mainly male) population of young men were slaughtered in war, regularly, and with visible statistical evidence of population rate change. So, we could get our heads around the concept of reduction, yet we hid behind 'doing it for the nation' or conscription.

We need to look at being choice conscious. Can we choose the one-in-six? Who is on your list? Can you look that person in the face?

I'm sweating, I'm scared. We need to survive and build our future of less. Less does mean that one-in-six of what we have now will go. We deserve that future, therefore we must face up to making the space for the Future We Deserve to happen.

What's your number?

Of Arms and the Man - James Hester

I'm going to talk to you about weapons.

There. Feel that?

That vague discomfort in the back of your mind? That reaction to this topic is, historically speaking, a new phenomenon, a couple of centuries old at most. Further back, whether it was the knife or sword worn every day or the musket propped behind the door, weapons were part of everyday life — a useful tool and an effective mode of defence if things should unexpectedly get ugly.

Weapons are today either reviled or glorified, with very little going on in between. We are content to delegate the use of force to others (the police and the military) and not concern ourselves with it. Owning one, you run the risk in some places of being labelled a violent weirdo, a criminal, or some combination thereof. Even those who legally own weapons for legitimate reasons make some people uncomfortable.

A yob with a steak knife stabs someone in a pub. A gangster puts two rounds in someone's chest for 'disrespecting' him. This is what happens when people get hold of dangerous objects with no understanding of or regard for what they have. Nor is this aggression representative of common human behaviour. Just as animals do not fight unless they determine that there are no other options (to do otherwise would be needlessly risky), it takes a lot to drive the average person to violence. Most would rather flee or attempt to diffuse the situation through other means. Tendencies towards conflict avoidance are only overcome through psychosis or training.

I propose that a person can be armed and capable of using arms with deadly effect and not be a violent person. That a society can be peaceful, take up arms and use them decisively when it is necessary, and then put them away and go back to once more being peaceful. The key to this is education.

According to UN crime statistics from 2008[62],[63] the United States had a homicide rate of 5.221 per 100,000. Here, many weapons (firearms and others) are for the most part legal. Public opinion towards the ownership of weapons is generally positive, although this depends on where you are. What awareness training there is comes either from home or through government programs that differ state to state (both with varying degrees of comprehensiveness and quality).

The United Kingdom clocked in at 1.19 per 100,000. Here, handguns are illegal, and many other weapons (knives, rifles, shotguns, etc.) are either also banned or heavily regulated. Weapons awareness is heavily angled toward inspiring aversion so that, with the exception of hunters, target shooters, or collectors, the popular opinion towards owning weapons is largely negative.

Switzerland is defended by a citizen militia. Every male between 19 and 34 completes compulsory military training (voluntary for women) and remains effectively on-call. Members are issued with assault rifles and ammunition which they are to keep in their homes and maintain themselves. Let me repeat that: **practically every Swiss household with a male between the age of 19 and 34 contains an assault rifle, a box of ammo, and someone with military-grade training in using them.** Weapons are generally looked-upon positively; bearing them competently is seen as a duty and a source of national pride. The 2008 homicide rate for Switzerland? 0.716 per 100,000; one of the lowest in the world.

A community, taught from an early age what weapons are, what they can do, and how to use them carefully and responsibly, will not descend into violence. Imagine being brought up viewing weapons as neither bad and forbidden, nor glorious and cool, but as just another part of life. A tool. Most would in all likelihood never have to use this knowledge. They would reserve it for the rare instances when stupidity occurs, requiring them to defend themselves, and perhaps their communities, from inescapable danger.

This piece takes its name from the opening line of Virgil's Aeneid: *'Of arms and the man I sing...'*

A Knowing World - Chris Watkins

Knowledge and action — we need both. Wise action depends on knowledge and a breadth of knowledge. Knowledge of what has gone before us, of what strategies and designs that have worked and not worked. As Isaac Newton stood on the shoulders of giants, we stand on the shoulders of many pioneers and support others on our own shoulders.

Newton was not merely a genius; he was a genius at the right place and time. The secrecy of alchemy was giving way to the sharing of knowledge in a modern era of science. In that tradition, we can benefit from an openness of sharing. We may no longer have a genius like Newton who stands out from society in his vast understanding because now understanding is shared so widely, and we stand on the shoulders of *so many* that it is collective wisdom that is awesome in its depth and breadth.

Our success as a species comes primarily from our ability to understand, to share that understanding, and to build on the understanding gained by others. The quality of our future depends in part on the work we do now to take this to a new level.

Our success as a species is now undermining itself. Our evolved character, which takes and extracts whatever is useful, and which wants to build bigger and more impressively, is threatening our security and our quality of life. Our need to survive will stop us eventually — but changing the fundamental model of human society is a mammoth task. We see this by the lip service paid to change and in the minimal action to date. On our current trajectory, we will destroy much before we begin to protect and rebuild the planet that sustains us.

So, what do we need to create the Future We Deserve (or, perhaps more accurately, the future that the next generations deserve)? Something that might help us pull one out of the fire is wisdom and knowledge — answers and feedback at our fingertips.

What does it look like in practice?

- Metadata, notes on the information: Who is it from? What are their biases? How well are they trusted and *who* trusts them?
- Openness and filters: allow all wisdom out but ensure that the *best* of it is shared and that *all* of it is accessible.
- Tools to wring out the data and make it tell us what we need.

A Picture, a Person, a Time and a Location - Thomas Bjelkeman

I have been going around for a number of months now telling the following story and then asking a question.

Imagine that you had an application on your camera phone which would only take a photograph when it had a good GPS fix, i.e. the application knows where in the world the phone is by getting data from the satellites in the Global Positioning System. Imagine that you took a sequence of photographs, the first picture is of yourself. Each photograph gets the current time as told by the satellites, the GPS coordinates, the phone number, the phone identity and potentially a text message added to it. The whole bundle is digitally signed and uploaded to a server on the internet. The signed bundle is verified by the server to ensure that the bundle has not been manipulated. We now have a set of pictures of something, taken by a person we can identify, at a particular time and a particular location.

The question I ask is:

How would you use this type of system?

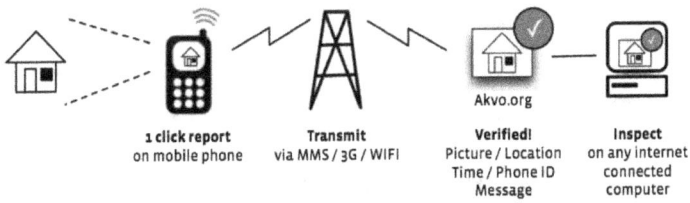

| 1 click report on mobile phone | Transmit via MMS / 3G / WIFI | Verified! Picture / Location Time / Phone ID Message | Inspect on any internet connected computer |

I get many interesting answers. The first answer was from myself. I want to improve the way field reporting is done on development aid projects. The pictures could be of a new well being drilled, the foundations of a school being laid or a meeting being held. This is all part of the work we are doing at Akvo.org[64], giving every development aid project a voice. A voice which tells the story of what is going on with the project. There are many benefits from using a system like this, as opposed to the traditional 6-12 monthly reporting via thick Word documents.

Other really interesting answers have been:

An NGO that works with war crimes investigations would like to show a picture of something in a particular location, for example signs of a mass grave, at a particular time. It is good that they would only need a mobile phone to do the work as it is fairly sensitive work. If would be beneficial if the proof would be valid as evidence in court.

Someone working with elections in an African country told me he wanted to take pictures of the tally sheets that are sent with the ballot boxes to be centrally counted. So that one could provide independent verification of the counting.

A professor working with e-learning in developing countries would like an examination assistant to be able to take a picture of the students taking an exam, so that it could be verified that the right person is actually doing the exam.

A woman working with human rights issues wanted to be able to use the pictures to document an ongoing riot or crackdown by the government. Think the Iran election demonstrations in 2010, but with verified photographs.

A young man working with legal aid support and training, in countries where the legal system is pretty sketchy, wanted to be able to take a picture of anyone interned or arrested. The pictures would be able to prove that the person was actually held by the police at a particular time and location. People disappear.

I have had several proposed commercial uses of such as system as well, by both big and small companies.

We have a prototype of this system called Akvo Phone, running on a GPS equipped camera phone, integrated with the Akvo Really Simple Reporting[65] (Akvo RSR) system.

Tell me:[66] **How would you use this type of system?**

Decline and Fall - Tom Stafford

'Decline and Fall' is the latest computer game from DO Arts. It's a sim/civilisation game, but with a twist.

The game is half massively multiplayer on-line role playing game, half resource management, sim-city/Civilisation empire-building. Teams of players manage their way through the running of virtual civilisations, choosing to cooperate or compete as they so desire. They found colonies, invent new technologies, build monuments and foster communities as they balance the demands of their population's desires with the threats and opportunities of contact with their neighbours.

The twist comes after approximately 10 hours of game play-time, when the resources of the virtual world begin to run out, and all the player's civilisations face extinction.

Warnings of the radical shift in the game's parameters are built into the game, but many players choose not to heed them, preferring to continue to expand and compete according to the boundless growth model that the start of the game seems to accord to. Typical game-world scenarios move through a depressing sequence of ignorance -> denial -> resource-wars -> massive population decline. Players recriminate each other, report dissatisfaction with the design of the game-world and the inherent unfairness of the game's parameters.

But 'Decline and Fall' was never designed to be fair. It was produced in Italy, a collaboration between award-winning game designers DO Arts and Edwardo Gibbone, a social-psychologist at the University of Bologna. Gibbone's team are now studying the game outcomes as teams of players sign up from around the world.

"We wanted to investigate how the players managed the collective impact of enforced energy-use restriction. To do this we had to get them hooked on one way of managing their societies, and then see how they reacted to a change in this environment." says Gibbone.

"We designed the game-play to be open enough to afford multiple different strategies in response to shortages in fossil fuels, clean air and water, and food simultaneously with catastrophic climate change and a population explosion large enough to tax environmental carrying capacity even without the other pressures. In doing so we hope to study the psychology of groups in crisis."

Existing research on the psychology of trust has been restricted to relatively unrealistic experimental situations on the one hand, and non-repeatable real-life observation on the other. The 'Decline and Fall' project aims to establish exactly what conditions or behaviours are required to allow groups of people facing individual threats to cooperate.

Specific theories to be tested by Gibbone's research include the importance of trade links, democratic political organisation, free media, cultural exchange and technological development.

"The dynamics of the game are designed so that painless transition to low-energy use societies is possible at all points of the game, even the final hours. Winning strategies aren't hard to identify, in theory there are multiple routes to success — but the level of coordination required stops most groups of players from achieving it."

The project is due to complete in 2012, when an estimated 400,000 players from around the world will have played 'Decline and Fall'. Gibbone is due to make a presentation of the results and the implications for real world civilisation at the World Climate Change Conference in Geneva that year.

Early reports from teams playing the game have been unpromising. When asked how successful teams of players have faced down their global crisis Gibbone just says "We'll let you know when it happens".

We Deserve to Evolve - Sam Rose

Carrying Capacity

The human species now projects a World Footprint[67] that is the equivalent of 1.4 of our total planet system. This means that we have *already now exceeded the carrying capacity of the planet*.

Just keep adding more sand, until...

Current human activities, often based on industrial-era ways of human interaction with global biological and geological systems, are revealing themselves to be fashioned in a way that exceeds the Earth's ability to absorb and dissipate. The changes that result from our activities are *not* always equal to the activities that caused them. Stuart Kauffman, and other complex systems thinkers have discussed that in their observations of dynamics in many systems, transformation tends to display a Power Law[68] distribution in the quantity of the size, and frequency of changes. The work of Bak-Tang-Weisenfeld and their "Sandpile model"[69] offers an illustrative example. In the "Sandpile model", sand is continuously added to a pile a few grains at a time. As the sand pile builds up, it reaches a critical state and dissipates sand by way of both emergent large- and small-scale avalanches. When the critical state is reached, any new grain of sand may unpredictably have no effect, a small effect, or may cause the whole system to cascade into total avalanche.

The important lesson here is that on every scale of the Universe we are a part of, things are changing and evolving in a way where output is not directly proportional to input. Therefore, we cannot plan and engineer human society around assumptions where we believe that outcomes can be measured by current and past actions alone.

The "Sandpile model" is an appropriate model for observing the emergence of critical behavior in a variety of systems, where the nature of the system is "self-organized", or "emergent". As we co-evolve with planetary systems, our activities and interactions will result in a "transition" of phases, from old ways of adapting, to new ways of adapting. We have a chance, and a choice, now, as to how this transition will play out.

The emerging possibilities for adapting to the coming change

Sharing is the key missing dynamic in human activities worldwide. Sharing economies give people *alternatives* to market economies[70]. World-wide, humans desperately need to dramatically increase the volume of voluntary sharing taking place among people, *especially in relation to basic needs* like food, water, energy, physical production, access to information. Sharing resources formally and perpetually is plausibly the *fastest route* to bringing human activity back to within the carrying capacity of the planet. **Don't wait for permission to share.** Sharing is a human right, and arguably a *human responsibility*. The most important question we can ask now, to create the conditions for real change in human activity is: "what I am doing now that I can currently share with others?" The next most important question we can ask now is: "how can I work with others to co-create conditions for the co-governance of what is being shared?"

If your goal is to control a resource, you are likely really working towards a path to totally destroy the resource. This applies to physical resources such as water, raw materials, etc, as well as the freely shared time, energy, and goodwill of other people. The secret to giving up control is also working together with others to ensure that resources are shared equitably, and remain available in perpetuity.

The Knowledge and Action Platform - Mark Roest

How can Knowledge Management influence public policy? What if...

We create a global system that acts to give voice to the people of the world and to the scientists, prophets and healers who can see nodes, links and dynamics of the larger and smaller wholes, and want to teach about and respond to the world's needs. As Doug Engelbart calls for (Bootstrap Institute), we organize this knowledge into a working top-level tool for improving human effectiveness in every area of life – a dynamic, well-planned knowledgebase.

We facilitate and find support for translating the relevant parts of it into the languages used by the cultures who evolved in and live in partnership with the 667 ecosystems mapped with the sponsorship of National Geographic and the World Wildlife Fund, and the assistance of about 1200 ecologists and other scientists, so that the urban masses and the rural herders, farmers, fishers and others working in nature can access it and make their voices heard, regarding both events on the ground and the policies that are needed to deal with them sustainably and equitably.

We embed access to the knowledgebase in the phone systems as well as on computers in the earlier sense of the word. We support rural cultures in deploying sensors that report back via mesh networks, as well as comprehensive yet inexpensive information and communication technologies to support their stewardship of their lands, and their collaboration with their neighbors who will be doing the same.

We include visualization technology (digital earth imaging), and we systematically empower all people working on all issues of social and environmental justice and policy, as well as design and planning, at all scales of operation, to use it to comprehend the systems they are engaged in, with their senses as well as their intellects, and to engage their higher selves to grow community, and create guidance and direction that is of and by all, in partnership on the deepest levels.

We use the tools of whole system geographic and technological analysis in extended, multi-site charrettes (design conferences that empower participants) which unite inventors and those reviving ancient practices with ecologists and community activists, with the support and facilitation of urban planners, rural development experts and economists like Peter Burgess and his friends. These conferences do the actual design work for sustainable economies on a community and regional scale, and they include or create councils to represent them, as well as documentation embedded in the knowledgebase to detail the policies they adopt and communicate what policies and resources are needed at larger planning scales.

We make the system work for the inhabitants of rural and wild lands to use it to conduct their business, to rebuild the deep ethos of community that used to motivate people everywhere, and to create equitable prosperity, health, and a restored natural world around them.

We make the system work for the urban poor, to create efficient services and resources for all who live in the cities, and to help conceive, design, plan, fund and execute the rebuilding of the rural economies they came from, so those who wish to can gradually return and, collectively, build lives of meaning, abundance, and spiritual fulfillment in their cultures' homelands.

Teilhard de Chardin envisioned or perceived a sphere of consciousness permeating all life on earth, uniting it as one; he called this the Noosphere. Most indigenous cultures experience something like this in their daily lives, and shamans work with it. We can begin to recover our higher or deeper faculties if we can begin to understand the natural world around us more completely. We can do that if we have access to the almost infinite collective knowledge and intelligence held by people of good will. We can have that access if we structure information ecosystems that inherently reflect natural and cultural ecosystems, as well as the merging of awareness that happens when people who have been dislodged from their origins bump up with different others in the same situation (that is one function of cities and towns and factory dormitories).

One more major opportunity that impacts policy profoundly: by merging a copy of the input-output analysis database created by The Perryman Group (an econometric consulting firm in Texas that supports the New Apollo Alliance plan for revitalizing the USA) with the knowledgebase, so that both physical and process specifics and non-economic dynamics ('externalities') are represented in the transactions that the input-output database models, we could wind up with not just an operating manual for lifeship earth, but an operations system that we all can use to conduct our personal, family and community businesses, and to steer and grow and stabilize sustainable economies.

This could also support multiple, complementary currencies, such as Fernanda Ibarra is talking about (Coalition of the Willing camp 10-10-10).

Such a system would constitute the synthesis that completes a Hegelian dialectic comprised of:

1. thesis: capitalism (local economic decisions that aggregate through 'the invisible hand of the market' – but lead to increasing concentration of wealth and power),
2. antithesis: Marxist socialism (or the Soviet-style top-down planned economy)
3. synthesis: collective planning by everyone, interacting in a working model of the economies of the planet, with local focus and global reach, with transparency and accountability supported by all who choose partnership over domination.

Inspirations See Riane Eisler's work with the Partnership Paradigm.

The Joy of Open - Erik Moeller

When we talk about free culture, open source software, participatory society, sustainability, and a better tomorrow, it's not uncommon that what people hear is: *You're complaining. You're trying to make me do something that is inconvenient and unnecessary. You don't like me.*

The future we deserve is a joyful future. The truth is that free and open culture is deeply pleasurable, addictive even. It's not the smug satisfaction of being better than someone else. No, quite the opposite: it's the pleasure of learning and discovery through connections with other human beings.

If you share your knowledge on a project like Wikipedia, or you contribute to open source software, or you're part of the open maker community, or you share artistic works freely, or you work in a participatory organization, or you help develop sustainable solutions, or ... **then you know this.** You know how wonderful it is to make friends all over the world. You know how revelatory it can be to see others share and change something you started, or to directly build upon the knowledge of those who have come before you. You know the joy and the pride of discovering how much our communities have already accomplished.

We're in this together, because we know that we *belong* here.

When we're inviting people to be part of this future, it's not because we want to harangue or lecture them. It's not because we're afraid that bad things will happen if we don't. It's because unfettered sharing is *natural*, it's *rewarding*, it's *fun*. The universe is not about business models, it's not about monetization, it's not about legislation. It's a playground, and we're always looking for new friends to explore it with us. Wanna play?

6 Ways to Live - Chris Malins

Why isn't wealth enough? Why does the American dream deliver so many individual nightmares? Why does material 'success' not uniformly generate happiness?

Sociologists have demonstrated that beyond a certain level, increased wealth does not correlate with increased happiness. The 'leading causes of life'[71] provides a framework within which we can understand better the things which enhance our lives, but that economic metrics fail to encapsulate. A future worth deserving must contain more than apocalypse dodging; our future should nurture the life experiences that enrich.

The first 'cause of life' is coherence. A rich life is understood through a narrative that is meaningful to us. In traditional communities, coherence often links to religion. Coherence is expressed by our internal storytelling, fitting our experiences to a common framework. In the capitalist paradigm where meaning = wealth accumulation, coherence is reduced for those either systematically (e.g. the 'working class') or capriciously (victims of illness, misfortune and circumstance) denied this wealth.

Second is connection, the experience of life in community. A good experience is emptier without others to share it. Tools like the internet can connect some but drive isolation for others. A focus on wealth can undervalue connection, reduce family to inheritance[72], encourage uprootedness.

The third cause is agency, the ability to act effectively. Agency is self-determination, being a subject, not object, of your internal story. It is denied when Government, corporations, bullies, arcane rules and inflexible frameworks are a barrier to your goals –it is lacking to both the 'jobsworth' and his victim, denied when democracy is absent or failing.

The fourth is hope, living life in positive anticipation. Applying our agency to realise our hopes is crucial to sustaining our self-narrative. In capitalism hope can be reduced to the constant desire for more, something that can never be properly realised. A richer narrative of hope, empowered by and empowering to our connections, can take a wider view.

The fifth cause is intergenerativity, the experience of life as adaptive. Life is a series of transitions from one stage to another – biologically defined childhood and adolescence, socially defined marriage and retirement, individually defined shifts in outlook and aspiration. Intergenerativity links to connectivity: grandparents participating in the lives of their grandchildren; mentoring, teaching, nurturing; the growth of community; are all expressions of adaptive life.

The sixth cause I characterise as awe. It is the understanding of one's place in an ecology and the realisation that the human individual neither is nor needs to be the definitive element within that system. Today's casual pollution is a symptom of an exceptionalist human hubris. Without living in awe of nature we risk teetering from one existential crisis to another, cowering behind the brute force protection of technology.

The existing world order of GDP, careerism and consumption has put itself in conflict with the causes of life. The materialism common to capitalism and communism, the two political systems born in economics, fails to understand or affirm the value of these less measurable things.

A future can be built around systems that not only beat back death, but which foster life. We can envision a society that cherishes connectedness and inter-generativity – through reinforcing local institutions, normalising engagement with rather than alienation from our fellow citizens, through transport solutions that emphasise mobility and through a growing, changing world wide web.

A distrust of bureaucracy and big Government arises from the desire to protect our agency. Just as we currently assess the financial and environmental impacts of new rules, new systems should be tested against their ability to foster freedom, and to support rather than hinder the individual's ability to realise her hopes.

And in the insistent awe of nature, this future can foster the personal narratives that recognise the diversity available in life, and that there is infinitely more to be achieved than a growing hoard of treasure. The future we deserve should allow individuals to define their world and to succeed within it, understanding that their success is incompatible with rather than dependent on the failure of the people and environment with whom their world is shared.

Solar Photovoltaic Energy Replication - Joshua Pearce

Wouldn't it be cool if there was a magical device that sat on your roof and quietly provided your home with all the free renewable electricity you and your family needed for your entire life. Ideally the device would actually be your roof (to cut down on the cost of roofing). It would be even better if the device could be made out of something common and inexpensive (like beach sand) and draw on an energy source available everywhere people live – so everyone could enjoy it. Finally, it would need to be such a prolific electricity producer that it could produce enough electricity to make itself - to self replicate so your grandchildren and their grandchildren and so on, could enjoy it too.

Amazingly, such a device already exists and is becoming a reality for an exponentially growing number of people. The devices are solar photovoltaics (PV), which turns sunlight directly into electricity. Solar PV have been around for a while – you probably have an old calculator that was powered with them. The only reason that you may not have a solar powered house now is because in our somewhat arbitrary and highly subsidized economy, fossil fuels have been allowed to externalize the majority of their costs and thus solar electricity appeared more expensive. Fortunately, this is no longer the case for an ever increasing percent of the world's population. Solar PV has been expanding by double digits every year for decades and in some years even over 100%[73]. This expansion, which was first on a tiny scale is now is over 10 GigaWatts/year of new PV and challenging traditional (and environmentally disastrous) technologies for market share.

Even for those of us who study the physics that allow solar PV to work, they are still a little bit magical. First, because they are solid state devices, PV have no moving parts and last a very, very long time. Manufacturers will give you a guaranteed 25 or 30 year warranty, but you can expect them to last at least twice that long losing less than 1% of their power per year. Traditionally PV was made from crystalline silicon, which you can get from beach sand, but through a relatively complicated and costly process. Just as the cost of computers dropped quickly as more computers were built and economies of scale set in – the cost of traditional PV has been dropping quickly. At the same time, scientists and engineers have been experimenting with different PV materials and improving existing devices. For example, amorphous silicon cells decreased the active PV material in a solar cell by more than a factor of 400 to only weigh a gram per square meter! Such "thin film" solar cells are cheaper than what you deposit it on and are now sold commercially on glass, metal or plastic for a dizzying array of applications including roofing materials.

Solar PV also represents an exceptionally egalitarian energy source as almost everyone globally has access to sunlight, which is inherently non-concentrated. Where the vast majority of the population resides there is plenty of sunlight to provide for energy needs with existing solar panels. For example, a house in Ontario, Canada with half of its roof covered with PV can provide its annual electricity needs (Canada is one of the highest per capita users of electricity in the world). Even traditional solar cells could produce as much energy as was invested in their manufacture in less than five years – even in not-so-sunny spots like Canada. Now thin film PV has decreased this energy payback time even more – and thus solar PV technologies can replicate themselves in energy terms by more than dozen times.[74] These self replicating energy devices will eventually drive down the cost of clean renewable energy for all of the world's people – and keep it that way into the foreseeable future.

Solar PV has already reached so called 'grid parity' in a number of locations – meaning that the life cycle cost of the electricity generated from the sun is the same or less than the cost of traditional sources of electricity.[75] This is leading to a virtuous cycle, where the lower costs help more people to afford PV, which improves support for companies, which funds more research, which improves PV performance, which lowers costs of solar electricity, which sparks more demand, which increases the economies of scale, which continues to drive down costs, which opens up even more markets, which makes solar affordable for even more people, and so on. At this point the expansion of PV is essentially inevitable and people of good will can help to accelerate the process.

A sustainable solar powered society for all is our future.[76]

The Future We Deserve or The Future We Desire - John Byfield

In my mind, The Future We Deserve conjures up not a vision of a beautiful future where our water, air, and energy are all clean or a place where our food, bodies, and minds are all pure, and most certainly not a place where we have ended war and conquered poverty and disease. In my mind the future we deserve is a result of the present we have created as in "he got what he deserved" or "she deserved to be fired". On the other hand the future our descendants deserve is one of beauty and light and living on our planet in a way that does not destroy it. That is a future that without a monumental sea change in the way that we conduct almost every human activity is unlikely to happen.

I believe that the fundamental mistake that is being made is to believe that our planet is in peril. Our planet will be fine, albeit different, no matter what we do to it just like it was fine 65 million years ago when a large rock from the cosmos plowed into it. It wasn't fine for the dinosaurs any more, but in time the planet absorbed the change and reinvented itself and thrived anew. The ice ages, global warming caused by volcanism and all other types of global events that created dramatic climate change all produced similar results and again, the earth and its ability to support life remained constant. What changed was the planet's ability to support certain forms of life. If we continue on our current path something like the fate that befell the dinosaurs may happen to us. The Earth will no longer be a place that can support human life, and we will perish. It is not a race to save the planet but a race to save the human race and the thousands of other species that we endanger. The fundamental change that must take place is that to get the future we desire or perhaps any kind of future for the human race at all, we must entirely change the way we live.

Unfortunately the Green Movement is being bought and sold by the same people that brought us to this place. The big companies have all discovered green is good for business, and hope that by producing green products they can convince us that we can consume our way out of the looming environmental disaster. Yet you can no more consume your way out of the mess we have created than you can spend your way out of debt.

What we really lack is a vision for the future we desire and our children deserve. Richard Branson, a man who tells the world he is an environmentalist at heart, has a vision of a world where space planes criss-cross the planet punching hundreds of holes in the ozone layer and consuming mass quantities of rocket fuel as they carry the well-to-do around the planet. T. Boone Pickens envisions a world where nuclear power provides the "clean" sources of energy to continue our unsustainable lifestyle. While the technology of the future may be able to do some wondrous things and we can all hope that the solutions we need will be discovered, the real bottom line for giving our children the future they deserve is to absolutely and fundamentally reevaluate our entire way of life.

No matter how we live our current population levels are simply not sustainable, and at the current growth rate will smother the planet in the very near future. Add the desire of all these new people to have the lifestyle that the average American now enjoys, and there is no hope whatsoever for achieving sustainability no matter how many boxes of "eco-friendly" soaps we consume, or how many "clean" cars we drive. Our insatiable appetite for things like bigger homes, more cars, asparagus and oranges year round no matter where you live, Chilean Sea Bass that take 50 years to mature and above all for the incredible range of petroleum based products that account for a staggering array of almost all the products we consume including our entire food chain, must come to an end. In my vision of the future we will use our brains to achieve this, but we are off to a very poor start.

Worldwide famine, global epidemics, catastrophic climate change, ravaged oceans and diminishing natural resources, perhaps this is the future we deserve. I hope it is not the future we desire or the future we will give our children.

Zombies and Vampires, Oh My! - Antonio Dias

In **Ellul**'s *Propaganda* he declares that individualist and mass societies are in effect the same thing, that the existence of unintegrated individuals is what makes mass society possible. Between a living culture and mass society we find the difference between soil and concrete. Soil consists of integrated particles of varying sizes and types existing in "communities" varying by depth and location, all part of a larger living system. To make concrete you must strip particles of their organic connections and create an aggregate of "individualized," and therefore, interchangeable particles forced into a blend controlled by an outside deciding body. To this aggregate, the commodification of what had been soil, commodified water and lime are added to produce the commodity concrete. The result is unmoving, resisting and brittle; the makings of a tomb.

Today, those of us looking for a way forward recognize and chafe at forced commodification. We yearn to forge, create, develop, and nurture connections that will integrate us into a living body. We are aware this requires us to make contact with others; but we feel isolated, surrounded by zombies and vampires.

Zombies are the commodified masses fantasizing about their individual freedoms. They maintain their fantasies by strictly forbidding any contact with reality from touching their "lives." They are dangerous because they will react violently to anyone who appears not to be a zombie too.

Vampires are life-suckers, the *un-Dead*, who maintain their existence by actively removing the lifeblood of anything living they can overpower. They are dangerous because they are smart, powerful, and ruthless. They make up that outside deciding body in the process of commodification. They will eagerly destroy anything that shows signs of life, and they control the zombies.

We find ourselves isolated from living culture, afraid to be engulfed by zombies or annihilated to feed vampires.

This is our double-bind.

To integrate ourselves, to establish a living soil, requires a place, and it requires people – people and person apply to human and non-human beings alike. Zombies take up much of the space – what's left after the vampires have killed what they could exploit for their own use. The remaining, vibrantly living places are few and are constantly threatened by vampire depredations. They are so threatened and fragmented that taking them for our purposes, however laudable they might be, is an unacceptable impingement on what remains of their fabric. No "colonizing" national parks, no "joining" wild indigenous tribes.

This question of place is very difficult. It's also a fluid and moving target as places degrade or fall out of use by the zombies with more or less of their potential restore-able fabric intact.

The question of people is equally difficult.

The key seems to have something to do with the nexus of individuality and integration. We're individualistic, that trait has kept us from becoming zombies; and we desire integration, this is what kept us from becoming vampires.

We are all damaged goods living in damaged places. We're aware of that too.

Zombies want nothing more than to be made into concrete and vampires are desperate to maintain their un-Dead powers. We want to be well, we want to heal, ourselves and our world. We want to experience life in all its particularity.

Zombies threaten us by engulfment.

Vampires threaten us if we engage. They are so powerful and so seductive. Their power and their "beauty" exhorts us to engage with them. If we do, they win. This has always been so.

How do we avoid engulfment by zombies and maintain disengagement from the vampire's powers?

These questions will dominate our future.

The Future of Information Freedom - Smári McCarthy

Freedom of expression as known today is the philosophical descendant of hundreds of years of thought about the rights of man. The vindication of free expression came in its present form from the French and American revolutions, and were ingrained in the constitutions which followed.

But that was two hundred years ago. Since then we've had an industrial revolution, two world wars, and we've seen the dawn of an entirely new mode of communications which completely alters our perception of expression. Through these massive changes to our world, almost all countries have put in place an elaborate set of exceptions that limit or punish truly free expression, and in many countries around the world the right to free expression has never been granted.

Persecution or prosecution for exposing the truth, going against the grain of the reigning ideology or embarrassing the regime that implements it is not uncommon - it's common enough that naming examples from countries such as China, Iran or Sri Lanka would be superfluous. Less commonly known examples are the western countries which have implemented state or corporate censorship in a plethora of forms, many based on such obscure legislation that the chilling effect goes unnoticed, many based on such complex networks of ownership and influence that the depth of the problem is unseen through the opaque surface. Government transparency is to an alarming extent mythical, and where it exists it is obscured by poor information management and rampant jargon.

We deserve better.

We're two hundred years down the line, and we have developed our capacity for the aggregation and dissemination of information to a point where it is high time we reconsider freedom of expression. It needs to be redefined in terms of our knowledge of information theory, with clear rights for individuals to transmit, receive and store information in any form, and to apply transformations as they see fit.

We deserve a return to the guiding principle that no restraint on the publication of information is acceptable, and that punishment for infringement on social values must happen after the fact, not before.

We must grow out of our tendency to pay lip service to the notion of privacy without defining privacy in terms of its utility. If an argument is made for privacy that does not specifically protect the physical security or personal wellbeing of an individual, it it moot, and should be disregarded.

Corporate opacity is therefore unacceptable. There is no reason to hide the behavior of corporations behind veils of privacy, banking secrecy or trade secrets. No good has ever come of such secrecy, and no evils have ever come from exposing it. Those industries that are built around manipulating information and exploiting unequal access to information can be replaced with new industries. Prosperity needn't come at the cost of other peoples' freedom.

Further, we need to realize that the argument of "national security" is only valid insofar as we accept the concept of "nation" - this artificial construct and the governance models it is designed to support and protect may not be allowed to interfere with the right to know and the right to share what you know - exposure of government secrets has never harmed societies, only governments, and there is very little reason to believe that this will not be the case for all information.

The future we deserve is one where information freedom is absolute insofar as it does not harm *people*. Individuals, as the fundamental unit of society, and the rights of individuals, as is necessary to protect their existence, must be the one and only assumption upon which we base the freedom of information.

My Vision of the Future - Otis Funkmeyer

I see a future of unlimited possibility. Wait, that sounds lame. I see fruit-tree-lined boulevards–where all is free for the picking, making the abundant nature of the Gaian Matrix too obvious to even be questioned. And that one sounds all hippieish... hrmm. OK. I see a future of nanobots who keep city streets clean coupled with an augmented reality that turns every human into a walking Wikipedia. That one at least sounds pretty hip, doesn't it?

The future I imagine, the one I encourage using your conscious power of creation to yank out of the ether and into form, is all of those things but... well, it just goes a lot deeper than that. For the future I imagine is one in which the evolutionary journey of the soul has become recognized as the primary reason for being alive and where the symbolic, archetypal nature of reality is taken for granted. A future that embraces the continued development of technology and normalizes sustainable practices like permaculture, aquaculture, and neotribal communal culture, transforming society in such a way that all structures now exist only to facilitate this journey, the journey of the soul.

The journey of the soul being the reason for incarnation, the reason we come to this planet to have these experiences, face these challenges, develop these potentials, play out our own Hero's Journey. The perspective that makes it all make sense. That answers questions like "Why is this happening to me?" and "What am I to do with my life?" That allows us to find the meaning in our interactions and closest relationships.

I see performers of the highest caliber on every corner, exploring and elucidating this journey. Performers that inspire, challenge, rouse, and entertain. I see collectives forming, tackling projects, and disbanding as rapidly as they formed. Engineers and builders coming together synchronistically to manage infrastructure on a real-time, as-it-happens basis.

At the center of it all, I see loose networks of autonomous healing spaces designed for people to go within, to process, to recover and to withdraw. In these entirely volunteer-run areas, everyone is free to stay as long as they want, participating in classes and workshops or spending time in total isolation, with their food, shelter, and clothing fully taken care of. Where with a simple request, any healing modality they desire is available just for the asking.

Why would people not stay there forever you might ask, "abusing the system?" Because life itself is too much fun to retreat from for any reason except serious physical or existential need. See, life has become a giant explosion of creative self-expression. So when these processes have run their course, the only logical thing to do is return to the party and participate however you see fit.

Life as a party. A grand, cosmic, soulful party. A voyage ever deeper into the unknown, into the mystery of existence... That is my vision of the future.

The Matter of Place - Catherine Lupton

Where will you be in the future? You can read that as a question about your state of being, and as a question about a place. It's not meant to invite a clean prediction – that's close to impossible, if you are facing the future with all your faculties wide open – but to wonder whether the place where you might find yourself, the actual, physical location within this Earth, will matter to you.

Matter. It sounds like several languages for mother, but let's leave that as a coincidence. It is actual, physical, material, ground; the dirt around your carrots and the rock against which you stub your idealism. It is also whatever you designate as important, where you place your concern.

Two spectres traveling in opposite directions. In future, some among us humans will be constrained to stay put where we are, to 'adapt in place'[77]. In future, some among us humans will be forced out of our places and become refugees.

Will you regard the place where you find yourself as a blank slate, awaiting a rewrite of human needs and concerns? Will the place itself matter to you, matter *through* you? Meaning, how far might you be willing to go in co-operation with your locality's rocks, trees, soil, meadows, microbes, water sources, genius loci, climate, animals, plants, their devas, pavements, buildings, thoroughfares and ghosts? As far as asking a native tree for advice, or a food crop where it would like to be planted? As far as believing that it's the high street which travels you, as far as accepting the gestalt of all inhabitants which creates an environment – that of Brixton, say, or Skye or the Scottish / English borderlands – as your mentor and guide, your ultimate government?

I don't grant these questions any power to persuade you; I ask myself the same ones. They are an invitation to measure your resistance, to see if they push you up against a limit in your understanding of what a place, an environment, might be, who it's for, who the 'we' in *The Future We Deserve* might include, and on whose terms. To find out whether being thus pushed has value for you, or if it's merely an annoyance.

If in future the two spectres run headlong and hard into one another, that's one way of getting to measure how deeply a sense of place might matter to human beings, how deeply a place in its entirety might make the matter of a human being. Xenophobic nationalisms root themselves in the fallacy that only people of a chosen race who are born in a place should belong there. Yet ours is a world history of incomers. Some adapt and become a part of places, sensitised to their rhythms and etiquette. Some experience a change in surroundings as the replacement of one painless abstraction by another. Some bear such change as an unhealing trauma, to be endlessly re-inflicted upon those to whom belonging appears to belong.

Place, in the deep, reciprocal sense I'm evoking here, might come not to matter. Our human concerns may for good reason be directed elsewhere. If that becomes the case, where will you be in the future?

Inspirations:

Alistair McIntosh, *Soil & Soul* (2001/2004)[78] ; Jay Griffiths, *Wild* (2007); Jay Griffiths, 'This England', *Dark Mountain* #1, 2010

The Locavores' War: A History of America's Future - Frank J. Popper

In lightning predawn raids on six Minneapolis ag overcorp processing plants, a Western paratroop brigade stole half this year's Mid national corn crop and bandit-trucked it from Minnesota and the enemy Dakotas back to Montana. "A brilliant feat of arms shifted the war's momentum to us, where it belongs," said the West's interim president, Romney 4. "Now we want Atlanta's cotton. Maybe Atlanta too." The South's Defense and State Departments declined comment. – Agence Press-France, November 29, 2067

It started small, seemingly: another summer of water shortages in Colorado and the rest of the American West. It became immense: a major rift in what was still the world's most powerful nation. It led to disaster: a second, ongoing American Civil War. Even now it is hard to believe that in 2065, the Appomattox bicentennial, the United States dissolved into four semi-permanently warring countries - East, Mid, South and West - because of a dispute over how to pay for a drought.

The actual issue was an aged staple of water law: riparian rights vs. prior-appropriation ones. It meant the difference between getting water by owning riverbank or lakeside property on the one hand and taking the water first without necessarily owning the land on the other. Not one American in a thousand except perhaps farmers and ranchers knew about this obscure legal point. Not one lawyer, engineer or politician in a hundred could say two coherent sentences about it, at least before it festered and then exploded into a conflict that shook the nation and finally split it forever.

All these years later the details of America's sundering are still painful to tell. At the 2065 emergency national hydrosummit, Colorado's governor made an unavailing eleventh-hour plea to the Great Lakes states (now Mid's core) for more, cheaper and less polluted water. The defeat resulted in the impeachment of Denver's mayor and her psychiatric commitment for pre-traumatic stress disorder.

In a move never quite explained, California and Oregon, whose deserts, farms, ranches and remaining suburbs also desperately lacked water, walked out on the summit. President Christie 3 suddenly resigned, returned to New Jersey and soon became President of the East, saying "I've always wanted a real job and then Boston called."

The next weeks saw an often-sanctimonious rush by all the states to find nearby, reasonably compatible secession partners. The country's traditional (and Census) regions - the Midwest, Northeast, South and West - served perfectly as quick groupings to tear it apart. Germany's precious teenage public intellectual, BHL 6, called the fast events "the world's largest-ever and most volatile experiment in Weltgeschichtlichepolitischechemie" (world-historical political chemistry).

Those few who still cherished American unity had their hopes crushed by the South's startling January 2066 bid to confederate with Alaska because it had so many ex-Texans. "It's midwinter, Anchorage has creepy 24-hour nights and hurlish food, plus those oilworkers and Inuits want to go to the beach," said the recently resigned South Carolina governor, about to become the South's vice president.

By March 2066 mounting border skirmishes began. The East's unprovoked two-day flying-bulldozer incursion from its Pennsylvania into Mid's Ohio drew a devastating response from airborne supersonic tanks and genius-plus pebbles for four days. The never-stable "cold peace" ended. *USA Forever and Today* (in slang Usaft), the failing nation's yellowblog of record, editorially called the period "the half-year eternity of false smiles." The United States turned into the now-familiar four American nations. The war among them opened with the East's legendary genetic poisoning of two-thirds of Miami Beach's few remaining male heterosexuals and escalated from there.

The situation was unprecedented: four Post-Nano Age nations trying to destroy each other's militaries but eager to retain one another's resource, industrial and information bases. All the while they felt restrained by their shared culture, especially uebercorps like the overcommunications media and entertainment/sports overcomplexes. Major League Baseball's 56 teams tried hard to broker short cease-fires until the South's president, nationalizing the Miami Dolphins and all eight NFL Texas teams, famously told MLB, "Your body counts are a standing joke. Only football puts hair on your chest."

The Second American Civil War amounted to what defense strategists, in their astute paranoia, termed a "symmetrical quadrilateral conflict," a four-way engagement among approximate equals. An East colonel described it as "the goddamnedest food fight since the last time we did this." In fact American envirohistorians of the early twenty-first century often termed the First American Civil War "The Great Food Fight" — at least as much a struggle between resource regimes as over slavery, tariffs, regional economies or cultural lifeways.

Everyone knew that the Second War, as Americans of all nations came to name it, amounted to a long-delayed resumption of the First.

The war's four-sidedness complicated strategy and tactics. No historian or soldier could find such a nation-level, on-the-ground conflict in recent times or among developed countries. Military intellectuals had not conceived the possibility before. "We thought war was always tediously two-sided," began a RAND/World memo leaked to Usaft. The closest parallels it invoked were big-city gang wars, Native American and other indigenous tribal struggles, the principalities' conflicts in early modern Europe, Africa and Asia, or primate troops' jostling for dominance or favorable ecological niches.

The Second War saw shifting, short-lived coalitions among belligerents, such as the highly touted 2086 East-South alliance. Usaft had a "high South official" saying, "We have buried the hatchet and now will dig it up and bury it in Mid." The alliance, shaky from before its outset, lasted a few hours less than nineteen days. Usaft, which somehow kept publishing by turning ever-yellower, wondered editorially in what way she was high.

The Great Plains portion of the former United States presented a special case. Almost a seventh of the Lower 48 in land area but lightly populated and sprawling across the vast borderlands of Mid and West, it fast turned into a vital high-intensity battlespace for all four nations, plus clandestine mischief-making special-forces insertions of others that constantly fed the now-feverish American rumor mill.

For the better part of two centuries, the Plains' already most rural, remote and unpeopled portions had continually shrunk, mainly in white areas. Many Plains counties had long had mid-three or even two-digit populations that were elderly and cut off from more urban places by culture, distance, bad roads and the rugged six-month winters climate/ocean change predictably created.

Before the war's outbreak the Plains changed. In 1987 an obscure Mid-East academic couple charted the region's depopulation, concluded correctly that in a few generations it would nearly empty and called for the creation of a giant Plainswide ecological - restoration project, the Buffalo Commons. The idea romantically evoked the original Indian no-man's-land—which in technical-economic terms really was a commons: before white settlement. The Buffalo Commons became the rare intellectual vision that caught on and worked.

By 2060, because of ungulate-fertility innovations, six free-ranging million-member-plus buffalo herds reappeared. They ran from Montana and North Dakota (in fact Alberta, Manitoba and Saskatchewan in New Canada) in the north to New Mexico and Texas (and Coahuila and Nuevo Leon in Mexico) in the south. Federal, state and nonprofit agencies owned and managed most of them, but noticeable numbers belonged to newly buffalo-wealthy Indian tribes and individuals on the expanding Plains tribal lands. Environmentally sensitive buffalo cultivation by whites, led by Turner 4, also flourished.

The successful Buffalo Commons' lessons formed the core curriculum of American enviroschools. Professors and students applied them to cities whose former, seemingly permanent economic bases no longer sufficed: the once-thriving cities of industrial Cleveland, housing construction/health haven/golf Phoenix and tourism/Digital Age/retirement Tampa.

They, among many others, had for decades been dwindling to near-village size. Like turn-of-the-twenty-first-century Plains farming and ranching towns, they had become anachronisms. The Buffalo Commons and other smart-decline approaches often helped them capitalize on their throwback charm and the assets it produced: walkability, cheap energy, easy transportation, neighborliness and so on through a long list.

The Second War undid the progress. It was not only the urban aerial bombing, internal subversion, war crimes and civil-liberties violations, which the East mostly introduced and excelled at, surprising many. After the first Civil War, the U.S. Army and the Plains settlers, trying to eliminate the Indians' food/clothing/medicine source, religious symbol and selfhood base, all but wiped out the buffalo. Now the killing of buffalo and other Plains wildlife was collateral rather than intentional, but it provoked just as much Native (and dominant-enviro) resentment. The Second War's inadvertent slaughter shrunk the herds' size from 12 million to barely 1 million, about what it had been in 2020. In particular, the 2085-86 Battle of Oklahoma (usually called by its military acronym BOO) trapped the two southern herds without escape and completely eradicated them.

Afterward a tacit agreement among the four nations redirected their Plains attacks away from the buffalo, a regrettably easy tactic by then because the buffalo and the Buffalo Commons were among the Second War's great casualties. Large enviro riots in Cheyenne, Chicago, Los Angeles and Omaha protesting the buffalo's extermination and suffering made no difference. The Buffalo Commons became again what it had been at the millennium: a distant goal few believed achievable, even though it had already happened before. And the war raged on.

A World in Common - The Socialist Party of Great Britain

We live in a world which has the potential to adequately feed, house and provide clean water and decent medical care for every single man, woman and child on Earth. The resources exist to banish material want as a problem for members of the human race. Yet millions throughout the world are malnourished, live in squalor or are actually dying of starvation or starvation-related diseases. The big question that faces the human race is what can be done about it?

For some years, pressure groups concerned with the plight of populations in the less developed countries have urged bankers and governments in the richer nations to cancel the Third World debt. They imagine that if the billions of dollars in loans and interest owed by governments in Africa, South America, and Asia were written off then the crushing burden of poverty suffered by the mass of people in those regions would begin to lift. A fresh way would be open for development, they argue. Food subsidies and health programmes would attack the deaths from malnutrition and disease. Education and housing would raise the quality of life for millions.

These things would not happen. The cancellation of the debt would leave the curse of world poverty intact. The beneficiaries would be amongst the ruling elites who own and control production and distribution in the debtor countries. They are the ones who through their governments owe the money but they are not poor. Amidst the poverty of the masses they live in luxury. Holding power often with brutally oppressive methods they care little for their populations. Their aim is their own self-enrichment. Why should we want to bail them out? Why should we want to ease the way for the rising capitalists of the underdeveloped countries to accumulate capital from the exploitation of workers?

There is of course a case for the populations of the advanced regions giving aid and assistance to the people in areas where infrastructures, services, means of production and distribution are poorly developed. This is the compelling case that those with advantages should put themselves out to help those in need. Most people will accept this but it cannot happen under world capitalism which keeps even our ability to help others in economic shackles - or reduces it to the pathetic levels of charity. The tragic illusion which is misguiding those organising the Cancel the Debt campaign is their belief that the devastating problems of world capitalism can be tackled by re-arranging its finances.

The things that are desperately needed - food, clean water, housing, sanitation, transport, medical services and so on, can only be provided by useful labour, of which there is an abundance throughout the world. Finance is part of a system which operates as a barrier to useful labour producing what people need. Useful production must be freed from the constraints of profit and class interests. Only useful labour applied through world cooperation in a system of common ownership can solve the problems of world poverty.

World socialism could stop the dying from hunger immediately, and provide the conditions for good health and material security for all people across the Earth within a short time. It would do this by producing goods and services directly for need.

World socialism will operate with one simple and ordinary human ability which is universal: the ability of every individual to cooperate with others in a world-wide community of interests. For too long has indignation at human suffering been dissipated by useless causes. How much longer must the price of failure be the misery of countless millions?

— The Socialist Party of Great Britain[79]

The Story Our Children Will Tell - Curtis Faith

Here is the myth that our children will tell:

In the time before humanity was Connected and free, all lived under the repressive control of the Hoarders, a small handful of wealthy men who sent their mercenaries throughout all the Earth to take by force from the peoples their valuable things to bring them to their own lands. This was called Empire.

In the centuries before the Connection, while Empire ruled the whole Earth, some brave souls set out from Empire to a new land where the peoples had been devastated by disease and the earlier pillaging of the Hoarders of Empire. In this new land, these people from all tribes and nations were able to build new memes and slowly evolve a new way of being with each other. They were more creative and successful than the peoples of the countries of Empire because the culture of this new land was one of honoring the new and different and because the mothers of the rest of the Earth sent their daughters and sons to this new place to learn and to create where they were more free from the powers of Empire.

It was here that the great inventions of Connection were made towards the end of the second millennium. It was here that the turning point battles in the Great War of the Connected Peoples of the Earth was fought as the old ideas about power and inequality battled the meme of strength in unified diversity.

In the decades after the Great Connection, before the time of sharing and friendship, a great tribulation arose as the old pillaging ways of Empire grew stronger using the inventions of the new land. The Earth itself grew sick as ugly machines dirtied the airs and waters.

The people of the new land used the Connection to combine with those from all over the Earth to fight against the Last Hoarders who were ruining the Earth and living in luxury while many starved and died of disease through neglect.

In time, the Hoarders tried to shut down the Connection, but they could not. They had become too dependent on the Connection for their lives. With every attack the Hoarders made against the Connection, they would cause great harm to their own allies and the Hacker Army would arise and devise a Ho Chi Minh workaround. The minds of the hoarders were too slow and limited because they did not trust, and share, and learn from each other as those in the Connection did.

The Connected peoples of light from all over the Earth won the war over the forces of oppression and darkness because they learned to work together, they learned from each others, and they helped each others. While the forces of darkness were impotent in their distrust of others and their lust for power.

And so began the Time of Light. When the People of the Earth first learned to use the Connection so that everyone could benefit from it equally. The age of the Hoarders had passed.

The Abolition of Scarcity - Kevin Carson

The future will be shaped by three interlocking trends: imploding capital outlay requirements for production, reduced transaction costs of networked organization, and eroding enforceability of artificial property rights. Taken together, they will render the propertied classes' privileged access to large amounts of land and capital irrelevant, act as a force-multiplier for bootstrapping the alternative economy, drastically lower the revenue streams required both for households to subsist and microenterprises to stay in business, and shift a large portion of consumption needs into the category of Free or virtually Free as embedded rents on artificial property rights are washed out of the price of goods.

Collapsing capital outlay requirements for production, resulting both from the desktop revolution in the immaterial sphere and the micromanufacturing revolution in the physical sphere, will act as a force multiplier for the resources available to the alternative economy, thus nullifying the propertied classes' privileged access to land and capital and enabling the alternative economy to bootstrap itself exponentially from limited resources.

The radical cheapening of means of production will also undermine the logic of capitalism. The wage system came about because of the technological shift from production with individually affordable artisan tools, to production with expensive machinery that only the rich could afford. Today we are experiencing a reversal of that shift. A garage shop with a few thousand dollars' worth of homebrew CNC tools can do work that previously required a million dollar factory. The primary form of productive organization, instead of the old mass-production factory using expensive product-specific machinery, is becoming the job shop using cheap general-purpose craft tools. Capital, rather than being expensive and inaccessible to labor, is becoming cheap and ubiquitous. This destroys the entire material basis of capitalism and wage labor.

Low overhead costs reduce size of revenue stream required for a business to stay in business, and the size of the outside revenue stream required for a household to subsist. When a microenterprise (including the household as a subsistence "enterprise") has little or no overhead cost, it can weather periods of little or no income without going in the hole; and what income stream it does have is free and clear. So the distinction between being "in business" and "out of business" disappears, and people can incrementally increase the share of their needs met through self-employment and subsistence production with virtually no risk.

Networked, stigmergic organization of the kind described by Eric Raymond in "The Cathedral and the Bazaar" is also a force multiplier. Innovations are developed by the self-selected individuals most interested in them, and can be adopted immediately wherever they are useful without any administrative mediation. This is the dynamic of fourth-generation war networks, and of the file-sharing movement (in which geeks crack DRM this week and grannies can download next week). Stigmergy is a synthesis of the highest developments of both collectivism and individualism, without modifying or impairing either in the least.

The disappearance from product prices of previously embedded capital outlay costs and other sources of overhead, and of previously embedded rents on artificial property rights like copyright, mean that a growing portion of our consumption needs approaches — if it does not reach — "Free."

Theorists of new-wave capitalism look to rescue the old system from its contradictions through the use of green technology as a profitable capital sink, or Romer's model of cognitive capitalism in which innovation is capitalized as a new source of rents. They also look for ways to reinflate demand to sufficient levels that labor can be employed forty hours a week to buy stuff designed to fall apart and go straight to the landfill, so labor can buy more shoddy crap and keep the wheels turning, so that everybody can keep working forty hours a week producing crap and earning the money to buy crap.

But these models require the use of artificial scarcity to capitalize innovation as a source of rents, or to inflate capital investment requirements to artificial levels, in order to prop up the value of investment capital. When artificial property rights like patents and copyrights become unenforceable, the normal tendency of technological innovation in a competitive market is to destroy monetized value.

The proper approach should be, rather, to flush all artificial scarcity rents and capitalization requirements out of the system, to eliminate all forms of subsidized waste like planned obsolescence, and to allow bubble-inflated housing prices to collapse, so that the total work hours required to pay for the remaining monetized costs of living are radically reduced. The remaining available hours of paid labor should be redistributed through a shortening of the average work week — probably twenty hours or less.

Cities of Freedom Chariots or Four-wheeled Demons? - Cindy Frewen Wuellner PhD, FAIA

Suppose you woke up tomorrow and your car was gone? Your neighbors' cars and pickup trucks were missing too. There were no taxis, only commercial trucks and delivery vehicles too busy to carry passengers. Boom, you were caught with your feet and an old bike as transportation. What would you do?

I bet you would call into work and say you couldn't make it. You would cancel all appointments and walk your kids to school. Soon you would be taking the bus or train, working from home regularly, and walking or riding your bike for shorter trips. Delivery trucks would replenish your kitchen pantry. Over time, you would become physically fit, your wallet would be a little thicker with cash, and you would know people that share your routes. Your spatial knowledge of your neighborhood and landscapes on regular transit routes would deepen. As a bonus, since transportation emits 27% of greenhouse gases, cities would immediately experience an impressive leap in sustainability.

Cars are so deeply embedded that it's truly a challenge to imagine car-free lives. Despite environmental, health, and urban development problems, every year we become more dependent on them. In 1968, nearly one out of every two American children walked or biked to school; now only one child in eight does. Vehicle miles rose one and a half times for a population that was only 40% larger. The number of cars globally is skyrocketing from the current 700 million to over a billion cars by 2025. Yet, every hour in a car increases a likelihood of obesity by 6%. Petrol carries the two-edged sword of adding greenhouse gases and depleting oil supplies. In the United States, over 30,000 people die annually on the roads. Still we continue to add thousands of highway miles and low density developments.

While I'm suggesting a highly improbable scenario, somewhere deep in the crevices of every theory or debate about cities lurks the issue of cars. Urban-suburban debates originate in cars. Walkable versus driveable streets, cars. Sustainable development, again, cars. High density, compact, sprawl, and smart cities all deal with automobile dependency. Even big-box retail, single use zoning, and public spaces completely depend upon cars. In sum, every single proposal for improving the quality of life in cities originates in a position on automobiles. Consequently, a thought experiment of car-free cities reveals the depth of our physical, emotional, and economic dependencies.

In the twenty-first century, we have greater knowledge of consequences. The ongoing debate: should cities be car-free or do we simply need better cars?

If we choose to make better cars, we still have congestion, safety, greenfield development, and an unsustainable need for increasingly complex highways while inner cities remain blighted crime districts. The city fabric will stretch thin, leaving gaping holes of poverty and marginalized groups. In the United States, lines are drawn in the pavement. People deserve cars, say the free-market enthusiasts. Cars doom our cities to unsustainable energy consumption, say the progressives. One person's freedom chariot is another's four-wheeled monster.

That debate - cars or no cars - is bogus. We must move beyond transportation and global warming (both frozen in petrified ideologies) to improved lifestyles, better opportunities and choices, and ultimately economic advantages. How can we balance work and personal responsibilities? What makes a beautiful city that attracts newcomers? How do we create vibrant neighborhoods and lively streets?

Twentieth century cities were shaped by cars. What twenty-first century cities do we and future generations deserve? We can only open the possibilities through our imagination and commitment to sustainable development and healthy lifestyles.

Works cited:

U.S. Department of Transportation. "Early estimate of motor vehicle fatalities." March 2010 http://www-nrd.nhtsa.dot.gov/Pubs/811291.pdf Frank, L.D., Andresen, M.A., and Schmid, T.L. "Obesity relationships with community design, physical activity, and time spent in cars." American Journal of Preventative Medicine, Aug 2004 27(2): 87-96 http://www.ncbi.nlm.nih.gov/pubmed/15261894 HybridCars.com. "Driving Trends." April 5, 2009. http://www.hybridcars.com/cat_featured/driving-trends.html National Center for Safer Routes. "U.S. travel data show decline in walking and bicycling to school." April 8, 2010. http://www.saferoutespartnership.org/media/file/NHTS-SRTS-Press-Release-04082010.pdf

A Healthy and Smiling Planet - Anil Prasad

Hi friends, if the future environmental situations would force the world population to queue up for the daily ration of oxygen supply, floating over water and wearing heavy insulated suits, all prosperity would mean nothing but a curse[80]. It will be the future we deserve, if we continue to harm our lovely planet – the most precious planet in the vicinity of science so far. Definitely, we do not want this nightmare to happen. Instead, we want a healthier and smiling planet - IT SHOULD BE THE FUTURE WE DESERVE. The enormous quality as well as quantity of knowledge, experience and wisdom acquired through the millions of years of existence in this planet make man deserve for it.

How can we make the planet healthier and more smiling? (the answer to it will also explain when it does smile). Well, I think, the greener the planet is, the healthier it would become. Similarly, the more peaceful it is, the more smiley it would become. This should be the future we deserve.

At this, the next question arises - *What should be the effective strategy that can take us to the future we deserve?* It is nothing other than SIMPLICITY![81] Because, the root cause of most of the problems are man's struggles to own luxuries. Apart from environmental issues, it also causes unrest in our individual as well as social lives.

In the current world situations, our luxuries have much more serious and deep implications than the individual health issues. In the millions of years of history, man has overcome drastic changes in living environments by naturally adjusting himself with the changes. But today, the fortress of luxuries that we build recklessly around us has made the adaptation to natural changes quite impossible. Ironically, the luxuries that we build to create what we believe is a comfortable living environment, actually make the changes in the environment harder for us to adapt to. It is the real hurdle on our way to the deserved future.

Now the crucial question before us is *"how are we going to advance towards our deserved future with the power of simplicity?"* In my opinion, we needn't make big leaps. Small steps would be more effective. For example, we should decide today itself that we shall not use motor vehicles for travels below two k.m, as long as you are healthy and the weather is not too bad? We will be free to occasionally breach it for emergencies. As responsible individuals we may also ensure that authorities build and maintain safe walkways for people.

We may also:

1. Keep away from consumerism and lead a simple life to the maximum extent possible. Stop fleeing after luxuries, it will save not only the PLANET but also our family budget and health.
2. Love agriculture and farming. Find sufficient time to work in the farm along with the family members and stay with them in the home.
3. In agriculture, use environment friendly alternatives to chemical pesticides and fertilizers (a lot of environment friendly alternatives are available now). Research and develop more such alternatives and share them with the global community.
4. Effectively use online technologies to avoid unnecessary travels. This can visibly reduce the threat of hydrocarbons.
5. Research and develop open technologies to make cyber space more socially accountable.
6. Use public transport systems for travel and help authorities to maintain reliable, safe and comfortable public transport systems[82].
7. Develop and popularize alternative planet friendly open technologies in place of technologies that ruin the planet.

All these together will provide us a deserved future of living in a healthier and more smiling planet.

The Future We Deserve and the Earth Charter - Jeffrey Newman

I listened to a BBC 'Reunion' programme with Sue McGregor bringing together a few of those who had been involved in New Orleans at the time with Hurricane Katrina five years ago and pondered the uncertainty, by definition, of 'the future'. There was no mention on the programme of the 14 or 20 million[1] people (estimates vary) currently affected by the Pakistan floods. In the past two weeks, I have had a break-in at my home (while I was there) and been savaged by two dogs whilst walking across a patch of ground a hundred yards from my front door. Fortunately, neither incident caused any real damage but each has been useful in reinforcing my personal awareness of the fragility of life.

The global challenges we face (finance, resources, food, water, population, climate) are inter-connected as are the global and the local. In the words of www.earthcharter.org 'We stand at a critical moment in Earth's history, a time when humanity must choose its future'. Put starkly, 'the choice is ours: form a global partnership to care for Earth and one another or risk the destruction of ourselves and the diversity of life'. While the 'future we deserve' project provides an increasingly useful and potentially important multi-faceted compendium on such issues, a framework, compass or map might be helpful. Can the Earth Charter, a UN-inspired Declaration of 16 Principles and 61 sub-principles for a 'just, sustainable and peaceful global society' play a part here?

It was formulated in a world-wide collaborative process involving hundreds of organisations and thousands of people following the Rio Earth Summit in 1992. Under the leadership of Mikhail Gorbachev and Maurice Strong, it was published at the Peace Palace in the Hague in June 2000 and subsequently endorsed by UNESCO and many thousands of organisations.

A paragraph in the Preamble spells out the issues: 'The dominant patterns of production and consumption are causing environmental devastation, the depletion of resources, and a massive extinction of species. Communities are being undermined. The benefits of development are not shared equitably and the gap between rich and poor is widening. Injustice, poverty, ignorance, and violent conflict are widespread and the cause of great suffering. An unprecedented rise in human population has overburdened ecological and social systems. The foundations of global security are threatened.'

The leader of Bournemouth Borough Council commented that on first reading he saw it as 'idealistic nonsense' but then decided that though it was idealistic, it was not nonsense and the Council became the first local authority to endorse it in the UK in 2008.

The Principles are grouped under four headings: Respect and Care for the Community of Life; Ecological Integrity; Social and Economic Justice and Democracy, Non-Violence and Peace. The sub-principles are detailed and demand study and practical action.

The trends, as the Charter states, are perilous but not inevitable. The emergence of a global civil society is creating new opportunities to build a democratic and humane world. Our environmental, economic, political, social, and spiritual challenges are interconnected, and together we can forge inclusive solutions.

In 'The Way Forward', the Charter states the need for 'a collaborative search for truth and wisdom' and suggests that 'the arts, sciences, religions, educational institutions, media, businesses, nongovernmental organizations, and governments are all called to offer creative leadership. The partnership of government, civil society, and business is essential for effective governance'.

I see the 'future we deserve' as a major contributor.

1. http://www.bbc.co.uk/news/world-south-asia-10973725 retrieved 6.09.10

The Feet We Deserve - Steve Wheeler

Put it on a pedestal, in a glass box. Invite children to come and look. Explain. "This is the kind of thing people used to wear on their feet." Cries of disbelief from the assembled youth. "How did they walk?" "Why would they do that to themselves?"

They can't imagine strapping several pounds of rubber and plastic to their feet and having to carry that weight on the end of their legs all day; they can't imagine what it would be like to not be able to feel the floor beneath them: their supple moccasins are made of natural materials, thin puncture-resistant sole flexing to the contours of the ground, uppers moulded to the shape of their feet. Some have a gap separating the big toe, like Japanese tabi – others have individual glove-like pouches for each toe.

Get a pair of antiques out and let one try them on (it's fine – we have the Museum We Deserve now). The child totters about: "Why is the heel so high? Why can't my foot bend?" Point out the other ill effects of wearing the ancient contraptions – how their heel now strikes the ground with such force, sending a shock wave through their body into their skull; how their toes can no longer flex individually, freezing their foot into a single lifeless block; how their posture has altered, their head and pelvis tilted back, their chest and shoulders thrown forward in compensation. He nods. "Yes, it's harder to breath like this."

The novelty wears off. The kid wants out. "When did they realise how dumb this was?" Tell them you're not sure – because nowadays kids have the Teachers They Deserve, honest about the limits of their knowledge. Perhaps it was the beginning of the century, when people started realising everything else was wrong as well. Imagine how many people's feet must have started going wrong, arches collapsing because they were wrapped in soft cushions all day.

One is troubled, brow furrowed in thought (mental note – tendency towards tension cognition; perhaps she would like to spend some extra time with Ajarn Frank, learning how to think clearly without resistance?): "You know what we did in our Soma class last week, when we talked about Qi and refex... refexlollogy?" Cute. "Well, if there are so many important acu-points in your feet, wouldn't wearing those things be bad for your Qi?" Smart cookie. Count yourself lucky you're not in ancient China – they'd have had your feet bound up extra young for showing skills like that.

Hm. Maybe they're old enough. They need to know how far gone things were. How we weren't just victims of bad design: that the distortion of natural posture, the withdrawal of energy from the feet, the constriction of flow and feeling were actually fetishised, eroticised, deliberately reified – and how it was women who were the worst victims of it all. You take another exhibit from the cupboard and read the label to them: " 'Louboutin, 2010'. Who wants to try these on, then?" The children catch sight of the straps and buckles, the painfully narrow toe and the vicious-looking spike. "Eergh!" they cry in unison, giggling and wriggling at the thought of it.

Sex & Singularity: Sex in the 21st Century - Julian Powell

Face it: Sex is a very, very big deal. Sexuality permeates every corner of our lives. Within the biosphere alone, sex is the very act responsible for forming our bodies, and thus producing all human life. For this reason alone, sex is a major factor in the development of human culture and society. But of course, there's more. Much more.

Sexual energies and its many forms are nothing short of the life-blood that nourishes the entire world. Everything from creating and realizing goals, the historical conquest and pillaging of land, war, love, to the loftiest of meditative states, and of course down to literal sex are different expressions of the same Erotic force.

On the archetypal level, you see sexual metaphor in everything we do. As any 6-year old can point out, most of our architectural design, our weapons, and technology take on some kind of phallic, yonic, or breast-like shape. Sex is obviously on our minds most of the time, at least on a far deeper, subconscious level. The sex act (or what it may represent) seems to form the archetypal template for much of our human experience.

Our current models and attitudes towards sexuality and gender are very immature, and this is a far, far bigger deal than we've previously realized. If we are to evolve a happy, healthy, sustainable and mature humanity for the 21st century and beyond, re-thinking our cultural approaches to sex and gender are a must.

In both the microcosm of the individual human life, and the macrocosm of human society, a great deal of what would be classified as neurotic behavior stems from sexual dis-ease on one level or another. Reductionism aside, Freud was right here. Wilhelm Reich took it one step further, explaining that sexual energy, or orgone, was the fundamental life-force present in all life forms. Orgasm, Reich argued, did more than aid procreation. An orgasm regulated the body's emotional energy. Poor orgiastic potency meant poor emotional release, creating excess energy available to fuel neurotic states.

Even more deeply, sexual repression, guilt, and homophobia, and sexism in the West partly arise out of two prominent historical legacies. The first is the sexual repression and guilt which we inherited from the Orthodox Catholico-Christian power structures which dominated mythological-level cultural thinking for centuries (and which has yet to be fully transcended on a cultural level, and materializes in many forms). Secondly, a profound misunderstanding of gender, which likewise has deep mytho-hermeneutic roots.

The call of the day is to, as a culture, evolve into sexual maturity. Sexual maturity encompasses gender dynamics and perceived identity, sexual expression, psychic and physical health, as well as our relationship to the natural environment and other species on this planet. If we truly wish to fully evolve environmentally sustainable, sane global cultures then reassessing our models on sex and sexuality is a **must**. What would a sexually mature culture look like? And how can we make steps towards realizing the beauty and ecstasy of mature sexuality within the sphere of our personal lives, and with each other in our cultures? To find out, read on...

...middle... - Nick Taylor

-1) WTF?

This is a scattered collection of thoughts that starts in the middle, and ends in the middle.

This is the age of information-overload, and our hero has the attention-span of a gnat. Take what you like, discard the rest.

0) The Future we deserve.

Oh God no, that's got to be bad - like "The Leaders we Deserve"... that's always bad as well. That's what it means, "The Leaders we Deserve". No. We don't want that. The last thing you want is what you deserve.

In many ways the future's not looking good - and it IS what we deserve... we do deserve the monster coming down the hall, because we are pretending it's not happening. We smoke. We drink. We borrow and gamble - shield ourselves from the consequences of getting stuff cheap. And we play along with a system that does all of the above, but on a tyrannical scale.

Our kids don't deserve this future we're building for them. Squirrels and things don't deserve it. What have they ever done? They just want to eat nuts and get on with their lives. God I hate squirrels. I hate them for their freedoms; their lack of aspiration. The nut-handouts they get from trees. Socialism basically. The chattering classes. Idiots.

So. New Question: "How do we deserve the future we want?

How do we create a future that our children and squirrels and things won't hate us for dumping on them?

What in the name of all that is holy are we going to do with all this stuff we've bought?

How much would it be worth (in dollars say) not to actually *want* stuff? If you could take a not-wanting-stuff drug?

You happy?

–

1) Precursor: Let's not dwell on the future.

We have absolutely no idea what's coming. We could all die, we could all become immortal - the stakes are that high, that wide, that weird. All the exponential curves that for the whole of previous history have been more or less horizontal, are becoming more or less vertical. We're not just hitting peak-oil - we're hitting peak-everything - every resource we have is running out - except sunshine and manpower, and who wants that? You have to feed it. You have to listen to its bullshit.

Coming the other way is a tech explosion that is creating tectonic social change - and carries the very distinct possibility of extending human life indefinitely, or blowing us all up. Or turning the entire planet into goo-soup. We could become immortal. We could all become croutons.

And nobody who pretends to know what they're talking about, actually knows what they're talking about.

We have absolutely no idea - the event-horizon of predictability is now about 5 years out.

2) The biggest problem we've ever had, will ever have:

Is Other People.

Sure Acts of God can be bad, but usually because they create the conditions for Other People to be worse.

3) the only thing we can do to fix the problem of Other People is:

For them to be happy.

The biggest problem we have is inequality. Any way you cut it... in the end all roads lead back to this one undeniable fact: Inequality is always in direct proportion to social illness.

Inequality as a driver of progress is pretty toxic. Inequality is the 40-a-day cigarette habit that abandons you in the cancer-ward, taking its (youth orientated) advertising elsewhere. Marx had the problem side of things right... it's just the solutions didn't go so well because inequality is not "just" about economics.

So. Forget about self-serving moralities of the type that say "rich people work harder". They don't. Forget about theory or ideology, and look at the data. Look at what works. Inequality isn't working. Anywhere.

–

So... a bunch of things, some of these are doable, others are general principles to gravitate towards:

1) Get resilient. The best way of doing that is by becoming friends with your neighbours.

2) All of our life-support systems should deliberately be geared towards a diversity of approaches - monoculture is dangerous. So grow carrots and give them to your neighbours. Nothing needs to be a 100% solution. Nothing should be.

3) Global challenges require organisation at a global level. National at a national level. Town at a town level... street... house... family... individual...

We need to minimise organising things too far up the food-chain. All power should be systematically devolved to the smallest units possible. All authority is inherently illegitimate.

4) All policy should be evidence-based rather than ideology-based... which is to say, every new (and every old) law should be predicated on a set of measurable goals. If it doesn't fulfil these within a specified time frame then it should be automatically repealed.

5) The problem that democracy was invented to solve is the problem of unaccountable power. Democracy today is being undermined by unaccountable power - "special interest groups", mainly corporations. We need to do something to limit the size of these private tyrannies so they can't "own" the political process. This is a big one. We absolutely have to do this.

Personally I'd scrap all human-tax and replace it with a sliding-scale corporation tax where profits over one $billion are taxed at 100%. It's not a tax on people, it's a tax on things. Corporations are things.

This is never going to happen though, so instead we (the people) need to route around the unchecked power of corporations. A deliberate choice - like buying green. Buy small. Organise our life-support systems to be free from top-down control.

6) Route around the currency. Route around rent. Route around debt.

Big and difficult to do - but until you do, you're a slave. Our currency is loaned into existence as a scarce resource, at interest. We're the victims of a type of derivative slavery, which is compounded by the way banks are set up, and the way real-estate is managed. And it's getting worse.

We need to reinvent currency so that it's based on the value we create, rather than being drip-fed to us from on-high.

—

1/5 of humanity is suffering from clinical depression. We're not happy. Not even the 1% that own everything is happy. People that win the lottery aren't happy. Look at squirrels. They're happy. Why can't we be happy? Bastards.

We're being played like fiddles by an artificial culture that is selling us identity in exchange for... everything? A lot anyway. We've been immersed in this culture since we were born.. we know nothing else, and now the money is running out... for us 99% at least. So where goeth identity?

The possibility that the wheels are coming off the machine may be no bad thing - if we look after each other through the transition. If it allows us to recalibrate who we think we are. We need to re-assess (and make sure we cater to) our hierarchies of needs - and much as I hate to say this (being a recluse), we have to do it together. It has to be us.

Log in; Link up; Drop out - because the bottom is falling out of it all anyway. It's not really a question of rebellion any more.

—

ps: I urge you to please notice when you are happy, and exclaim or murmur or think at some point, "If this isn't nice, I don't know what is." - Kurt Vonnegut

If You Want to Go Fast, Go Alone. If You Want to Go Far, Go Together. And If You Want to Transform..? - Shaun Chamberlin

Like all the best tales, ours opens with music, and with Mark Kidel's *Resurgence* article *Conversation & Crossroads*:

"Some of the most powerful – and healing – forms of music combine strict 'ways' of doing things with free expression and the possibilities of interpretation or improvisation... Wisdom and experience have suggested, in every corner of the world, that excessive self-expression is self-defeating and just as destructive as an over-zealous observance of rules and regulations. There is a need for a middle way which balances 'hot' and 'cool': the release of deep emotion with the articulacy and sophistication of formal aesthetic structures...

Whereas the enjoyment of pleasure was never frowned upon in the African context, it was set within a deeply rooted sense of ethical and aesthetic 'right behaviour' (as well as a strongly hierarchical community structure which held potential excess in check, and understood, in a highly sophisticated way, the need to balance creative self-expression with collective interaction and mutual support). In the African and African-American context, the dancer who goes into trance is always being controlled in some sense by a divinity or spirits, so there is an element of ritual theatre which contains the fragility of the individual ego. Similarly, at celebrations, no dancer hogs the floor for longer than a minute or two, reaching a brief climax, but not prolonging the transcendent thrill of near-ecstatic movement and expression beyond what is in some way 'safe' or acceptable in terms of strictly personal as opposed to collective expression."

Upon reading this I was powerfully struck by the concept of a community holding an artist safe while he or she explores the wilder reaches of individual expression. As Kidel goes on to argue, the absence of this protective tradition around Western rock music can be seen in the likes of Jimi Hendrix and Jim Morrison, who in the context of a culture entranced by individualism found their lives overwhelmed and consumed by the awesome powers unrestrained artistic expression can unleash.

But these ideas have a far wider application. Rock music has merely reflected western philosophy and culture in its deification of the individual. When existentialism announced that 'existence precedes essence' – that we simply exist, and that any meaning we might then attribute to this 'blank slate' existence is solely created by ourselves and our own choices – we assumed that the 'we' in question must be our individual selves.

Our culture has moved further and further away from any sense of the collective, let alone concepts like oneness with Nature, or with all of creation, or even (Science forbid) God.

And it is this philosophy of 'individualist existentialism' – deeply embedded in our culture – that leads to the pervasive story that while some might find their meaning and fulfilment in trying to assure the future of endangered species, or disadvantaged humans, or even life itself, others may find theirs in greed, gluttony and destructiveness. For the true believer there is no contradiction here because there is no underlying meaning to seek – only individual constructs.

Within the tenets of Western philosophy it appears a logically unassailable position – if everything is fundamentally meaningless and the freedom of the individual is simply self-evident, what possible reason could there be to cease doing whatever I may fancy?

There seem to me to be two key answers to this question. The first is *consequences*. What I fancy now may not produce what I fancy tomorrow. If I choose to attach meaning or desirability to a reliable electricity supply, or food supply, then there are certain things I should really pay attention to.

But the second is *empathy*. While we may feel less empathy with beings more different or distant from ourselves, few of us would claim to feel no empathy at all. There is perhaps a sliding scale from total individualism to the sense of oneness with everything that is described in many of the Eastern mystical traditions, as well as among earlier representatives of the Abrahamic religions like Christianity. It is no coincidence that we tend to find individualists despoiling our common environment, and those at the holistic end of the scale defending it.

Existentialist individualism argues that one's position on this scale is a fundamentally meaningless personal decision. Our innate sense of empathy might whisper otherwise, but our scientific understanding of collective consequences like climate change *forces us* to recognise that even if individual freedom is our sole aim, we still have to change course, as the consequences of our actions will seriously curtail the future choices facing both ourself and the rest of life on Earth.

Viewed from this perspective, climate change represents the death of passive individualism as a coherent philosophy.

So when Kidel speaks of the highly sophisticated understanding African cultures have of "the need to balance creative self-expression with collective interaction and mutual support", he is not just talking about a better way to dance, he is speaking of the very cultural wisdom we need to build the future we deserve.

Just 4: A Macroscale Social Model - Woody Evans

The Model

There are four ways for a culture to exist.

It can be either stable or unstable, and it can be either sustainable or unsustainable. These four descriptors reduce economic, social, historical, ethnic, linguistic, and religious complexity to a simple matrix.

If a culture is stable, it is under no immediate threat of dissolution. It can continue as-is at least into the mid-term future.

If a culture is unstable, it is under threat of dissolution. It may appear to be stable into the short-term, but it'll soon turn to chaos.

If a culture is sustainable, then its practices are tenable in the long-term and could carry the culture forward indefinitely.

If a culture is unsustainable, then its practices are not tenable in the long-term, and at some point in the future it will fall out of balance and burn up its resources.

The most stable cultures are sustainable (Inuit, !Kung San, Sami). Some unsustainable cultures become stable through might (The United States, most of the trading world). A culture that was stable (or could be stable) and sustainable can be acted upon by other cultures or natural forces, and their way of life can end (most aboriginal cultures have found themselves in a version of this predicament by now). And sometimes unstable and/or unsustainable cultures find their way to better practices and more security – we see this usually on the small scale rather than the large and seems to occur most often when participants in a larger unstable and/or unsustainable culture purposefully take themselves out of the system to start anew. Often such experiments fail miserably; sometimes it seems to work well (Iceland works as both stable and sustainable, despite its financial problems; The Farm in Tennessee is doing alright; the Latin Settlement "Sisterdale" in Kendall County, Texas got really unstable really quickly when the Confederates murdered the Free Thinkers in 1862; etc.).

Even though there are many paths to get there, and even though cultures may find themselves moving in and out of them, there are just 4 ways for a culture to exist. Here's a graph:

4

	Unsustainable	Sustainable
Unstable		
Stable		

Two Problems

Models are too simple. As models approach real life complexity, they lose their utility as tools to simplify matters. Reducing all of human activity to four fields is a very simple model indeed, and may be seen as laughable; but in as much as it is simple and it is true, it may be useful as a compass.

A very common problem is to idealize the ancient, the agrarian, the pastoral, as "pure". Morality gets conflated with economics: simple folks are praised as simply good. Modern, messy, complicated, stressed-out, post-colonial, information-age folks get lumped into some kind of loose and sloppy category of "bad". Reality is very different, and very much more complex, of course. This model doesn't ask for you to buy-in to the veneration of hunter-gatherers: hunter-gatherers commit murder too.

The Future

Despite such problems, the above model points us toward the 4th cell on the graph – toward an ontology that values both stability and sustainability as the only reasonable direction for longterm cultural development. It is a conscious choice to move into stable and sustainable ways of life.

As we become aware that stability (security) is tied to economic sustainability (which is not necessarily the ability of an economy to grow forever or to metastasize precipitously, by the way), we can stack our affairs in such an order – as individuals, as families, as towns, as nations – that it may work to move our cultures into that 4th cell.

At the end of the day a comet could strike tomorrow. Life does *gang aft agley*. The onus is upon us to try, though. The responsibility to choose and to try is not avoidable.

Once we know the facts, as they say, doing nothing about them is also a choice.

Open Source Appropriate Technology - Joshua Pearce

A solution to the general problem of access to critical information for the future of sustainable development is found in the growth of open source appropriate technology (OSAT). 'Open source' refers to the free, vibrant, and burgeoning open source software movement and 'appropriate technologies' are those that can be easily and economically utilized from readily available resources by local communities to meet their individual needs. Appropedia.org, the primary wiki-based site for collaborative solutions in sustainability, poverty reduction and international development, is an excellent example of open source appropriate technology that harnesses the power of distributed peer review. All the information developed is free for others to use and adapt to solve their own sustainability problems.

Even a superficial review of global environmental conditions results in a rather bleak outlook on the future. The optimists' position is that accelerated progress in technology will rescue society even from global-scale problems like catastrophic climate destabilization. It is undeniable that technological development has provided great benefits to humankind in medicine and many other fields and technology is indeed developing faster now than ever before. Unfortunately, the vast majority of this research and the knowledge created is not focused on problems related to sustainable development and surprisingly, even much of it that is, is effectively removed from maximum deployment by patent and copyright laws.

The development of information on appropriate technology can clearly benefit from the application of an open source model.[83] Throughout the world there exist research institutes, community groups, and non-governmental organizations working with different technological innovations to alleviate poverty and mitigate the destruction caused by excesses of consumer culture. For the most part they remain disconnected, often re-inventing the proverbial wheel again and again although their counterparts in another part of the world may have already designed and debugged a similar technology. This restricted and closed model of technological development results not only in ethically unacceptable levels of poverty, but also widespread environmental desecration.

A solution to this global lack of collaboration and access to critical information for sustainable development is found in the rapid development of OSAT.[84] In order to be effective, these technologies must take into account the environmental, cultural, economic, and educational resource constraints of the local community. Often, and particularly in the developing world, these technologies are small scale, elegant, and simple, yet provide for people's needs without destroying the capacity of the Earth to support life. OSAT also harnesses the power of distributed peer review and transparency of process, proving more efficient and adaptable than closed, hierarchical systems of technology development. For example, Wikipedia[85] has become one of the top ten sites on the internet – with content created by thousands of volunteers surpassing the output of multi-billion dollar international companies.

Consider the future effect of open source appropriate technology taking hold and creating a vibrant virtual community to share AT plans and experiences. OSAT venues like Appropedia[86] are already enabling designers and field workers to download free plans of water pumps, windmills, basic medicines, solar photovoltaic devices, and many other appropriate technologies. OSAT would fall within the legal framework of an AT General Public License, where those plans can be used freely, modified, and republished under the same license for those in the future all over the world to benefit from. In this way, open source appropriate technology will become a true rival to the paradigms of the development of technology that have dominated civilization since the industrial revolution. A new revolution is underway, built on a dispersed network of innovators, inventors, and researchers working together to create a just, sustainable world. Join us[87].

Who Will Save Our Souls? - Thembisa Cochrane

It seems archaic not to separate church and state, but where has that separation taken us?

Let me introduce you to a few people:

The Atheist on a mission to save the poor people who have been sucked by force into false religious beliefs.

The African woman who found the courage to contradict her supervisor because she knew Jesus would protect her from vengeful witchcraft.

The Islamic teacher who works in France and is no longer allowed to wear her head scarf to school.

The Schoolboy who suddenly saw the light of God one weekend. His friends never mention it aloud; they treat it with the same quiet whispers as his best friend being gay.

The British man who entered his religion as "Jedi" into the national census because he heard if enough people did that they could force the government to make it official.

The Student who took a major in Religious Studies because it was considered easy and he needed good marks.

The Friends who posted their religion as "Pastafarian" and "It's complicated" on facebook. Some of them put "Christian" – they were the ones trying to save the poor people who had been sucked by Satan into false beliefs.

The Thinker, who decided he was Buddhist because Buddhism wasn't a religion.

Religion is important. It still moves and shakes our world and it cannot be ignored.

Should we fight it? Should we try to make it go away, turn it into something personal which is not asked about in polite conversation?

Religion is valuable. It can provide many things, amongst them:

- Community
- Awe
- Comfort
- Hope
- Justice (and mercy)
- Worth (and dignity)
- Transcendence (you are not born what you become)
- Healing (forgiveness heals the person who has given it as much as the person on whom it is bestowed)

Can a secular state provide those things? No. It would be worrying if it could.

Then should we ask the state to ensure everyone has the freedom to find their own preferred brand of religion on the supermarket shelf? That seems fair, but what if Scientology has the biggest marketing budget because it specifically serves those who pursue a kind of individual power that is often synonymous with financial wealth? Less fair.

If the state is not lending power to religion, then religion will draw power from mass appeal and money. In a secular state the finest minds are encouraged to study finance or medicine or law. Where does that leave the role of philosopher, spiritual counselor, moral guide, community leader?

Perhaps "religion" is too severe a word for the non-religious reader. Perhaps it is too close to the words "rigid" and "rule". A state should not give power to either of those words. Perhaps we should rather speak about a "communal philosophy of the soul".

Then what should the relationship be between the state and "the communal philosophy of the soul"? Something to be thought and talked about.

Art Monasticism - Nathan Rosquist

> *"Let's talk of a system that transforms all the social organisms into a work of art, in which the entire process of work is included... something in which the principle of production and consumption takes on a form of quality. It's a Gigantic project."* —Joseph Beuys

Problem setting

In contrast to other types of intentional community, monasticism is in decline in the global north.[88] Is it a social form that has lost its relevance to the developed, and increasingly secular world?

If we consider monasticism as an *exaptation* (a useful by-product) of religion, we can ask the question: What would monasticism look like, applied to something other than religion?

Solution

An **art monastery** utilizes monastic technology for art rather than religion.

Art monasticism considers:

1. the monastery as an art form,
2. art as a monastic tool.

If a monastery is a community that through a set of *agreements* (e.g. rule, vow) about how to live together (e.g. in silence, hard work, prayer & contemplation) leads its individual members to a certain *goal* (e.g. God, dharma, buddha-nature, self-knowledge, wisdom, concentration, compassion, non-dual awareness, the perfect blueberry pie), an *art monastery* is a one that leaves the goal undefined. For an artmonk, art is a primary form of prayer, work, and therapy, which along with meditation and other traditional monastic activities, leads him/her to a personal or shared goal.

An art monastery provides an empty space in which an artmonk can progress as deeply as possible along a chosen path, using a set of traditional monastic tools.

"It is a radical contemporary experiment in social sculpture inspired by tradition: to apply the disciplined, contemplative, and sustainable monastic way of living to the creative process." [89]

Elements of Monasticism

What distinguishes monasteries from other types of intentional community, such as communes, ecovillages, student cooperatives, land co-ops, cohousing groups, ashrams, kibbutzes, and farming collectives[90]? Some of the unique elements that could be appropriated by an Art Monastic community include:

- Unique structure in space (architecture with equality, eco-efficiency and mindfulness in mind)
- Unique structure in time (shared schedule of work, meals and contemplation together throughout day)
- Unique governance & social structure (monastic rules & vows about things like celibacy, renunciation & poverty, hard work, silence, etc.)
- Unique practice (e.g. meditation, prayer, chant, "lectio divina," artmaking, study, debate, philosophy, mysticism)
- Unique goal (e.g. whatever it is that contemplation leads to, whether that's God, the absolute, non-dual awareness, awakening, concentration, peace, knowledge, etc.)
- Unique members (avowed monastics who may or may not be separated by gender)
- Unique relationship to society and ecology at large (ecological sustainability, a degree of separateness from society, subordination to a centrally organized spiritual lineage or religious tradition)[91]

The International Otherhood of Artmonks

The International Otherhood of Artmonks connects artmonks (whether they're inside and outside art monasteries) and provides them with the tools and models they need to exist in the world (but not "of the world").

The Otherhood serves artmonks in the following ways:

- By bringing legitimacy to contemplative artmaking.
- By connecting artists of a similar spirit.
- By inspiring and instructing them in artistic and contemplative practices.
- By getting them gigs & housing.
- By commissioning, funding and producing works.
- By building or adapting spaces (i.e. monasteries) for visitable longterm learning communities and spiritual research.
- By giving them online tools to develop personal, intimate communities around the world.
- By what it produces: works, books, articles, cds, concerts, festivals.

Personal Futures and Futures Therapy - Jessica Charlesworth

Increasingly, people are taking advantage of advanced experiential forecasting techniques to take greater control of their personal futures.

Personal Futures is an emerging futures practice that is becoming more popular as we seek to interpret and understand our future life paths. Achieving the future we deserve will depend upon how we are able to experience our future self and the impact of our day-to-day decisions.

Humans have always had a hard time imagining and acting on alternative futures and have tried to discover and understand their potential futures using whatever methods they have available. Esoteric societies and cults have sought to promote various divination techniques to help people understand their fate or how to control it with foresight and prescient knowledge. In times past, certain members of society have happily invested in the apparent special insights of others to interpret signs and symbols.

Today people are looking for more secular and advanced systems, frameworks and alternative world views to help manage their emotions and relationships and guide them to make more informed decisions that will affect their potential and possible future paths. Some new techniques can reveal alternative futures and guide or provoke us to drastically change our behaviour and directly affect our future self. Systems mapping and future scenario planning are both methods used in industry to help predict markets and quantify and describe potential future worlds.

In the field of personal medicine the increase in affordable personal genomic services[92] available to the public is greatly affecting the decisions people make about their future health. Yet these services are not accurate predictions but interpretations based on probabilities and percentages.[93]

Driven by our continuing obsession with lifecaching[94] our everyday activities and technological advances in data storage, open-source mobile services and information design, people are quantifying their daily actions, motivations, conversations and thoughts to monitor their physical and mental wellbeing.[95]

If we imagine a future in which personal futures services become more widespread, it follows that there may be more guidance or 'Futures Therapy' needed to help us understand the impact of these potential paths.
Below are a number of potential services that may become available under the umbrella of 'Futures Therapy'.

- The first draws on an method of forecasting known as the Delphi Technique originally developed by Project RAND during the 1950-1960s, where a roomful of experts are brought together in a workshop format to determine the future likelihood and expected development time of a certain technology entering the market. Transplanted into the world of personal futures - in place of industry experts - friends and family members of a loved one are drawn together under the guidance of an experienced facilitator. Using the collective mindset of the "panel of experts", the facilitator encourages them to generate their own subjective and sometimes controversial predictions of possible and preferable variants of the loved one's future lifepath. This technique illustrates how we can 'use' or interpret our social network to predict how our life might be shaped by those who know us and those we may know in the future.The Delphi Party - http://www.futureofselfknowledge.org</ref>
- The second service is an extension of the Delphi technique in which a double sided postcard is sent to a friend. The sender fills out one side with predictions about the receiver's potential future. The receiver then returns the card with predictions about the sender's potential future. By sending out many cards an individual builds a body of information from different people's interpretations of their future which becomes a tool for making choices.
- The third service is a way of recording and quantifying your daily actions to prompt new behaviour. Using a diary or journal format the owner makes a daily record of their activities and is asked a set of questions. The process of completing the journal each day reveals potential new behavioural decisions. (*Did you tell someone you loved them this week? If so who?*)

We will always be at the mercy of the unknown. Sometimes we are able to let these unexpected moments take us down certain paths and sometimes we wish to plan and take control of these paths to see where they might take us. The Personal Futures phenomenon will continue to grow as more people will find more future forecasting techniques and models to borrow from. With this knowledge can lead to a better and more personally informed future for current and future generations.

Deep Lessons - Alan Chapman

The biggest contribution we can make to the world is to recognise that the deepest and most profound experience available to us - whether through recollection as a memory, as something unfolding for us in the present, or as something we wish to engage with in the future - is not something to cling to, cultivate as a permanent state, escape into or regard as a panacea, but something to learn from.

If we approach our inner lives with respect, then we must acknowledge a taxonomy of deep and profound experience, and therefore a correspondence in the depth of our opportunity to learn. To engage with the unfolding of deeper and more profound experience is to open the door to learning the most profound lessons of all. Not everyone does however, and we have seen this failure over the last three thousand years across the globe.

Should we compare and contrast a given current personal problem with that moment of profundity, we can see how our current approach to self, each other and life fails to account for a deeper consciousness of the Way Things Are, let alone reflect it in thought, word, emotion and deed.

To what extent are your problems due to a view of the world and a set of values based on assumption, speculation, hand-me-down bias and appearance, rather than on the (for some) fleeting insight into the nature of each and everyone one of us?

We each share the possibility of deep and profound experience; but how many of us are willing to understand it as best we can and learn from it?

We are each capable of pronouncing on the fundamental nature of reality; but are we also willing to consciously address our habits and behaviours in light of that data?

We can develop our morality and shape our personal lives to reflect the Truth; but to what extent do we examine the culture, society and infrastructure that we participate in and perpetuate?

The Future We Deserve is not one where every individual is enlightened, but one where everyone benefits from the lessons learned; it's an emerging vision of a civilisation built on and informed by what it means to be a human being in the deepest and most profound ways, where our life long education system encourages exploration of our inner lives and the testing of our personal views against our own direct experience, where the inherent problems of a world view at odds with the world itself are recognised and consciously addressed in that same spirit of discovery, and where our organisation and infrastructure both locally and globally are no longer informed by a paranoid and fearful view of each other and reality.

I don't know what that looks like yet; but I suspect we'll need sunglasses.

Semantic Organization and Connectivity - Anne McCrossan

Generations of the future may well look back at the turn of the 21st century and see it as a coming of age, a watershed, and I hope they do.

This is a time in which to embrace the fact that the challenges of the human condition are changing.

Up until now our time on earth as a species has focused predominantly on seeking security, shelter and subsistence, and our quest has been to protect ourselves from our own vulnerability by taming the forces of the planet.

Now we can say that, largely speaking, that box is ticked. We know how to harness power, how to create refuge and security, how to harvest our environmental resources, how to create a thriving existence. We know how to do this almost too well, at least for some.

So now, our biggest challenge is not how to tame the planet. Our biggest challenge is how to tame ourselves.

The threats we face today are of a different kind. They come from the over-exploitation of our environment, exploitation of one another, and the damage we wreak in the thrall to our egos because we do not accept the meaning of the word 'enough'.

The future we deserve will be a sustainable one only if we tame ourselves, if we learn to co-exist and consider a joined-up, interconnected and a greater good. This is the sightline that technology now gives us and this is maybe our greatest challenge.

The social possibilities for collaboration are immense, but only if we focus on how we can all win, if we can work out how we can collectively engender abundance instead of fighting over slices of the pie, and if, importantly, we can create models of existence that revolve around profiting 'with' and not 'from' each other.

So the future we deserve is one in which exploitation becomes a thing of the past, where 'I win, you lose' is seen as a zero sum game.

When people talk about the social technology revolution as being as important as the invention of the Gutenberg Press, the crucial ingredient that's not mentioned is not the technology, but the skill.

People forget that the arrival of the printing press meant people needed new skills to make the most of it; they had to learn to read and write. Having a book without being able to read and write was as useful then as it is to have a Twitter account today without the skill to contribute and lead socially, to connect with others and to have a voice of value.

Even though the web remains text-based, the potential for human connectivity the social web gives us asks that we develop skills every bit as unfamiliar as the ones we needed all those centuries ago.

It asks that we develop new levels of social and emotional intelligence, that we develop collaborative skills, physical restraint and the ability to iteratively and creatively seek and arrive at equitable solutions in conjunction with others.

It asks us to put chest-beating to one side and balance our primal drive to progress as a species with the good husbandry of society as a whole, for us to be able to create value as curators, and not just as acquisitors and owners.

The future we deserve asks us to think beyond ourselves even as it opens up new horizons. It asks us to accommodate new needs at a meta level, knowing this is now a joined up and shared world where the plunder and adventuring in pursuit of human supremacy is of an old age.

The sustenance and growth of the future now depend on the forces of equilibrium, harmony, and biological and cultural diversity, as we begin to evolve into maturity as a sentient species and organise across boundaries in new ways.

The Education We Deserve - Pamela Mclean

Everyone deserves the opportunity of a good education. I am fortunate. Thanks to the Internet I have spent ten years enjoying educational opportunities that would otherwise have been impossible for me.

The story of a "social learner"

This is my story - the learning journey of a "social learner"- someone who uses the Internet to learn from others and with others. We are a growing group, and I believe we point towards a future trend in education.

I like to learn in the company of others. When I was an undergraduate with the Open University (OU) the highlight of my study year was the week of Summer

School: that precious opportunity to be with other people who were working on the same courses. The rest of the year I was in the depths of rural England, miles from any fellow students, working through the course units (and it was back in the days before the Internet). How I craved the opportunity to interact with other learners.

It was through the OU that I got interested in computers, and also through the OU that I developed the confidence to be a self-directed learner. I believe these are the two key ingredients for access to higher educational opportunity on the Internet:

- Competence with the technology
- Confidence as a learner.

Ten years ago, when I suddenly needed to learn a lot of new information, I turned to the Internet, and gradually discovered the joys of being a self-directed "social" learner there.

OU research on social learners

It is only in the last few days that I have learned the term "social learner" to describe my learning style. Appropriately I learned it from research that has been undertaken by the Open University, related to use of their OpenLearn resources. The OU research found two distinct kinds of learners. Some engage primarily with the course content, not with other people. Social learners on the other hand are much more concerned to find other people who share their study interests.

Relationships that support learning

To me the social element is a key point. Learning on the Internet is not just about availability of content (note - excellent content is increasingly freely available). It is also about the interpersonal relationships that support learning. The importance of social interaction may vary depending on what is being studied (with some studies needing more emphasis on practical skill development, and others benefiting more from exchanging ideas). Whatever the balance, social learners appreciate supportive learning groups.

Top down or peer-to-peer

Back in 2000, when I was first using the Internet to learn, most content was on websites, very top-down, very Web 1.0. Then I came across a website that pointed me to an online conference and things were never the same again. I had discovered the power of online social learning. People shared their knowledge and perspectives, behaving sometimes like a learner and sometimes a teacher. They slipped easily back and forth between posing questions and discussing possible answers. It didn't matter that I wasn't a professor. It didn't even matter that I wasn't at a university and had no "organisational title". There was equality of access. I was allowed to join in.

Once I had tasted the intellectual stimulus of online discussion of ideas, I wanted more involvement. Like all social interactions, after making the first contacts it gets easier to find more and to find ones that have good overlap with your own interests.

In recent years, with the development of the social web (Web 2.0 - Facebook, Twitter, YouTube and suchlike) there is much more emphasis on the social aspects of Internet use, rather than just the content. The emphasis is on enabling peer-to-peer relationships, and they do not have to be exclusively online. Meet-ups already demonstrate how the Internet helps people to form local shared-interest groups.

Future learners

In future I expect to see the development of a social site that will be designed specifically to help social learners - a natural entry point to the connected world of independent learning. Signing on will be similar to freshers week in a traditional university. Newcomers will be welcomed by experienced learners and helped to find their way around.

The big difference

The big difference is that learners won't be looking for set courses. They will build a personal portfolio of their interests - what they bring, and what they need. They will look for a mixture of collaborations and content, developing their own learning ecosystem, in relationship with other learning ecosystems. There will be a big flip-over from content-centred courses to learner-centred learning, and entry will be free and open.

References

OpenLearn - http://openlearn.open.ac.uk/

RIDE 2010 Keynote: Open Educational Resources and Learning Spaces by Professor Josie Taylor (introducing the idea of social learners) - http://www.slideshare.net/CdeLondon/ride-talk-josie-taylors-version

RIDE 2010 presentation - Improving the Learner Experience: From Web 1.0 to Web 2.0, by Philip Butler - http://www.slideshare.net/CdeLondon/cde-presentation-5607624

London Meetups - http://www.meetup.com/cities/gb/17/london/

Moving Towards a Post Penal Society - Anton Shelupanov

If there is nothing else the current economic crisis has taught the modern Western world it's this: hyperincarceration is not affordable or sustainable. This is by no means a new lesson – when Churchill was Home Secretary at the beginning of the 20th Century, in the face of a World War he reduced the prison population of England by half. When the Nazi war machine hit the Soviet Union, Stalin – the granddaddy of the penal state – released some 2 million prisoners to fight against Hitler's hordes in the penal battalions. More recently during the crisis of the late 1990s, Russia embarked on an ambitious programme of penal reform to reduce its sick, addicted, economically inactive and hugely expensive million-strong prison population – something it managed up to a point.

Now, as a society we are rediscovering these ideas, and everyone from Kenneth Clarke to Arnold Schwarzenegger is attempting to reduce the use of imprisonment in their jurisdiction – with limited success – because they understand that first and foremost, hyperincarceration is a luxury politicians can no longer afford.

The current Western model of imprisonment is a fairly recent one, dating back to the early 19th century. In historical terms, that's not long. Whilst we see the prison-industrial archipelago as some kind of unmovable monolith, not least because of its physicality and the psychological associations it invokes in our culturally conditioned minds, the reality is whilst it is violent, inflexible and simply too big, it is nonetheless very fragile.

Broadly speaking, prison systems the world over have four stated goals.

- The first is deterrence – the reasoning goes that the idea of going to prison should put people off committing crimes, or as the case may be, acting outside a certain societal norm.
- The second is rehabilitation – the idea is that people who make mistakes can become free from addiction, reflect on their past actions and become educated enough to be able to re-enter society as a socially and economically active citizen.
- The third is retribution – society wants vengeance, and it wants to see those who commit crimes be punished in an obvious way.
- Finally there is public safety – isolating criminals from society and keeping them in a safe and secure environment so they have no further opportunity to cause harm to others.

The truth, widely accepted by practitioners and scholars is that the vast majority of prison systems fail almost completely in the first three, and partially in the fourth. When a junkie is desperate for his next hit, he won't think rationally that he is afraid of going to prison so he better not break into the car to steal something to sell it on. The myth of rehabilitation has been blown out of the water long ago – prison is "an expensive way of making bad people worse". To quote just one statistic, up to a quarter of all new heroin addictions are acquired in prison. The public being satisfied that vengeance has been extracted certainly is very rare – in part thanks to the constant stream of news stories originating from the colourful imaginations of tabloid journalists about prisons being a holiday camp. Finally, from the point of view of public safety, most of the time the physical buildings are secure and keep people in, but the various high profile escapes over the years and the crimes which occur in prisons and are organised from within them give the lie to the notion that walls and barbed wire can give any full guarantees of keeping the public safe and those inside secure.

There is no correlation between crime rates and incarceration rates, so why, when none of the four stated goals of imprisonment are met fully, and most are barely met, have we found ourselves in a situation in which we hit a global financial crisis with the burden of bloated, exorbitantly priced and dysfunctional penitentiary systems?

The answer lies in the third goal – the need for vengeance and visible punishment. When times were good, politicians could afford to spare no expense in making themselves look tough, and so locking lots of people up with no other purpose than their self-image and feeding the popular media was common practice. The number of people a country chooses to imprison is a purely political choice: compare Scotland and Finland – similar in size, demographics, population profile, and yet Scotland chooses to imprison three times more people. Notably though, Scotland still imprisons a lower proportion of its citizens than England & Wales.

The problem is, after every binge there is a comedown and then a hangover. So too will one follow our current hyperincarceration binge, although the sooner we halt, the less future damage we are causing and the less explosive the timebomb. The future we deserve, or at any rate have earned, is one of expanding infectious diseases, increasing inequality and more criminalisation and alienation.

The correct response is not difficult, but it will not be popular with the tabloid press and less statesman-like politicians looking to score political points at the cost of common sense, as for example the former champions of hyperincarceration Tony Blair and Jack Straw have been doing recently in response to the current UK government's attempts to pursue a more enlightened penal policy.

People and publications who engage in these activities will come round eventually, as they did in Moldova or Kyrgyzstan when the HIV epidemic became self-sustaining and harm reduction legislation had to be introduced, in the face of the mythology which equated needle exchanges and methadone maintenance with condoning illegal behaviour. Politicians and practitioners had to be courageous in the face of an infectious disease which threatened to wipe out much of the population, and ignore the denigrators with personal agendas of self-promotion or newspaper circulation.

As a result of an over-crowded system, which is under-resourced by some 30%, public safety and public health will be severely compromised. This applies in all jurisdictions, not just the UK. A series of actions is needed to ensure that the fallout from the crisis is as painless as possible. The trend towards hyper-incarceration must be halted and reversed. This can be achieved by remanding far fewer people in custody whilst they are awaiting trial (currently c. 20% in England) many of whom are released when they reach trial, stopping incarcerating all but the most prolific offenders who are detained for non-violent crime (currently about 2/3rds), and addressing the issues of those who are mentally ill outside of the prison setting (currently some 90% of all prisoners suffer from a diagnosable mental illness). This should be accompanied with a much stronger focus on strengthening the management of non-violent offenders and former offenders in the community, new ways of investing in prevention and early intervention and a bold and extensive programme of de-criminalisation (the last UK government created over 3,000 new criminal offences on the statute books).

Of course custodial establishments should also be able to continue to perform their core function well, in any crisis. They should be able to hold people who are very dangerous safely and securely without disruption. Preparation for a crisis-type scenario should entail all secure establishments ensuring that they are equipped with generators, water purification equipment, vegetable gardens, staple food stocks and possibly bakeries, fire fighting equipment and sufficient emergency healthcare facilities to cope with interruptions in supply which a crisis might bring. However, such preparations should be secondary to a much more pressing need – unburdening the system by removing those who shouldn't be there into a safe and well-managed community environment, and ensuring that those who remain are kept safely and securely.

Society will never escape the need for a certain degree of coercion, but how civilized that society is must surely be judged by how sparingly and safely this coercion is applied. Only by moving away from the current cycle of imprisoning more and more people and churning out a generation of unhealthy, addicted, jobless and criminally inclined individuals can we begin to move towards a society where the default response to the problems of crime and justice is not based on trying to please the readership of tabloids and is instead concerned with our future and safety.

A Future Without Childhood - Julia Macintosh

I propose a future without childhood. No, no, no, don't get me wrong; not a future without children – I hope children continue to happen, generally speaking. It is the idealisation of childhood that I question, as one of the methods by which we learn to impose boundaries upon ourselves and our lives, and to deny a full awareness of our human experience.

Childhood as a concept might be defined in a number of ways: biological (a specific period within the early stages of physical development); mental (a period during which personal faculties are formed and developed); moral (a state of innocence and grace); political (a state of powerlessness and exemption from responsibility); economic (a parasitic state of dependency); historic (constructed in the last few centuries in parallel to western imperialism); cultural (a shared system of learned behaviour.) There are thriving professions across sectors that are devoted to the study, the cultivation and the servicing of childhood: they maintain deeply entrenched investments in childhood as an unassailable operating concept (brightly coloured plastic tubes of yoghurt, anyone?) and for that reason alone it should be examined.

The ideal of childhood reinforces an expectation that innocence and protection from harm can be secured, even guaranteed. It instills a sense of separation and difference from others (the adults) to whom society grants agency and legitimacy. It creates the illusion that power and responsibility are something that can be picked up and handled at a certain age, when one is ready for them (if one chooses) rather than something inherent to the social experience. Childhood only exists with that complementary state, adulthood, in which we surrender innocence, assume legitimacy, and wield power. Many of the ongoing debates around children's issues in our culture arise because real lives and experiences flout these parameters regularly: what do we do about all these young parents, offenders, carers, drinkers, soldiers? The boundary between childhood and adulthood advances and recedes, it blurs and dissolves. Childhood cannot be contained separately from the progress it implies: a state of childhood suggests that there will, eventually, be a state of adulthood. The future is inherent in the idea of childhood.

A couple years ago I helped to run a conference about nature kindergartens. This was one small event in an ongoing movement to reaquaint people with nature and to promote the natural environment as a learning tool. The conference was organised by myself and other adults in an enclosed, flourescent-lit office, our eyes glazing over from hours at a computer screen. We accepted this irony with resigned duty and wistful suggestions to hold planning discussions outside in a nearby park. It is with the same irony that we have established an agency in Scotland that promotes children's play as a statutory concern and supports the development of a play workforce. We mean well! We attempt to capture play itself, that most creative and uncontrollable human experience, to ensure its role as an allotted porton of the ideal childhood. The implicit message we receive though is that our experiences can be created, achieved, within an assigned space. We are offered a temporary but safely managed respite before crossing the boundary to adulthood.

A future without childhood may therefore also be a future without adulthood. And what would there be instead? Perhaps simply personhood. We might create a cultural paradigm in which every person counts as a legitimate part of society, irrespective of their biological, mental, moral, political, or economic state. Personhood is already being explored in the context of animal rights, consciousness, evolutionary biology and in many other fields of inquiry. Our philosophical ponderings may take us into what we mean by work and play, freedom and responsibility, and what we mean by human nature: are we an integrated participant in the natural universe or are we special, more special than trees or microbes or air molecules?

A future without childhood might be a future in which everyone and no one is special, it might be a future without the future, a future of only the present and of everybody playing.

Online Open Distance Learning - Anil Prasad

Open Distance Learning - education for all

A saturated classroom study setup.

Development of formal classroom study setups are now in a saturated situation. In most places further development of infrastructure for conventional classroom learning, especially for higher education, is quite difficult. On the administrative side reasons are many like constrains of space, resources, etc. On the learners' and parents' side, nowadays, a majority of people do not have the financial health to spend a lifetime for education alone. In these tightening economic circumstances, work and study is the only principle that can keep higher education accessible to all who seek it.

Education - a costly commodity

In the present educational set up, universities and educational institutions require very large amounts of money for planning and providing quality education. We are living in an age where complete State funding of universities and educational institutions is simply not possible. Therefore, private universities, for-profit as well as not-for-profit educational institutions etc are being promoted generally throughout the world. But this strategy, coupled with other factors that lead to inflation, in turn makes education a high cost commodity.

Nowadays, worsening individual/family budgets have alarmingly reduced the buying power of learners. This situation prevails everywhere in the world including in the developed countries. An ABC News report which appeared online on Sept. 20, 2008 says that the average cost of a private university in the USA is $23,000 annually per student, while the median yearly income is $50,000 for the American household. This situation is unlikely to change as long as the imparting of education is not considered as a selfless contribution of the past generation to the present, and the present generation to the future generation. The foundation of every civilization is built with free exchange of knowledge. Those who buy knowledge may not impart it free and so civilizations might be weakened. It is the point at which we require alternate systems for low cost delivery of quality education and acceptance of qualifications across the globe.

Online ODL - a suitable alternative

The only alternative option currently before us that has the competence to tackle the above situation is Online Open Distance Learning.

Serious thoughts about virtual learning environments can be traced back to the 19th century. However, interestingly, a clear imagination of audio/video communication networks being used to deliver a lecture on Australian music to a remote audience can be seen in the short science fiction story "The Machine Stops", written by E.M Forster and published in 1909. In 1953 the University of Houston offered the first televised college credit classes via KUHT, the first public television station in the US. These attempts were all part of the efforts to use modern technologies to meet the ever increasing need for education in a cost effective manner. Virtual learning activities got amazing pace in the 1990s with the advent of the Internet. Internet based online education originally began through various business houses using online training courses to prepare their newly recruited employees. Subsequently this method gained popularity among universities and other academic bodies.

Many universities and organizations have already identified the need for Online Open Distance Learning. United Nations University, Open University

UK, Virtual Campus of The Robert Gordon University UK and the VUSSC project of Commonwealth of Learning are a few examples. Now it is time for universities all over the world to think seriously about running online open distance courses based on a mutually agreed Transnational Qualification Framework, so that qualifications are easily approved in the labour market throughout the world and the interests of the learners are safeguarded.

Innovations in communication sectors make virtual classrooms and virtual communities more reliable and lively. The time is not far off wherein we will have plenty of Online Open Universities that are connected to a Transnational Qualifications Framework across the world and providing quality education. The Virtual University for Small States in the Commonwealth (VUSSC) project of the Commonwealth of Learning can be considered as a great step ahead in this context. There are also other budding online initiatives like WikiEducator project.

Online ODL - most environment friendly way of education

Online Open Distance Learning can be considered as the most environmentally friendly way of education in the current world situation. For instance, it will directly reduce journeys and the use of stationery including paper during the learning and teaching process. Both these will save the environment as well as reduce the cost of education.

Online Open Distance Learning can also be effectively used in technical as well as professional education sectors. Technology is now competent enough to provide simulated labs, virtual conferences etc etc. Unavoidable hands-on-experience etc can be arranged through accredited centres near to the learners or through learn-by-working arrangements.

Way ahead

The basic tool we require is the greatest challenge in this context: a Transnational Qualifications Framework including Quality Assurance and Control that is generally agreed by governments, universities, other academic bodies and labour markets. Based on such a TQF, online courses can be framed and freely available content linked to each curriculum through collaborative efforts along with promoting the development of free and open content. Till that time individual universities may be encouraged to contribute to this effort by starting online open distance courses and highlighting the greatest ethic of education, that imparting education is a selfless contribution of the past generation to the present, and the present generation to the future.

The Future of Television - Glenn Hall

It's 2010, and the space in front of the sofa is free. But is it, can you see the avatar? It's lightly projected and as you move towards it, it moves towards you. It reads your mind. It notices you are tired, and hungry, and thirsty. You wave, and it moves aside, revealing a stream of information about food and drink, and the audio becomes more part of your world. You can smell the coffee, and already feel better. You're still on the sofa.

You think what I need is the human experience of sharing food, and enjoying the interaction with others, more than the simple task of heating something already prepared. The avatar returns and waves towards spaces in real time, where friends are. One is cooking and turns to smile. And speaks, the avatar gently moves to the side, yet waits alertly for instruction.

You move to your own cooking space, and share your fridge. You hold a camera close to a piece of food, and share it. The avatar beckons, your screen shows people, and food, and menus.

The bell sounds, loudly, the adverts run. Recipes, cookery gizmos, ingredients, wine. Then taxis. You wait. Pizza Delivery. You regret not having the advert free service.

The screen gets brighter, the avatar snaps to attention, it's the Government. Eat this, cook like that, exercise more. You hit the deliver Pizza button, and click for cold beer. Sports channel on. Alone.

Television? Or our primary in-home communicator. It reads your mind, you don't choose, it has no channels. It brings you what you want, and what The Government thinks you need.

Yet, Television is a device, a system, a business, a method for enhancing the human experience. It's now two way, smart, intelligent, responsive, and unseen.

At HP Labs Bristol, in the 1990s, a research project created some internet furniture. It was an ergonomic workstation, yet one version incorporated a Television set. It bridged the connection, between Consumption (viewing) and Creation (response, engagement, sharing.)

Our future, could it be of engagement, not of consumption? Could devices serve us, not control us? Could they be elegant, non intrusive, and not wooden or plastic boxes with glass screens.

Television is a system, for the "Transport of Emotion" it moves human experiences towards us. In our Future we Deserve we will engage, with the interactions, with the people, and above all, we will contribute back.

All of this is possible today.

Citizen Centred Participation - Phil Green

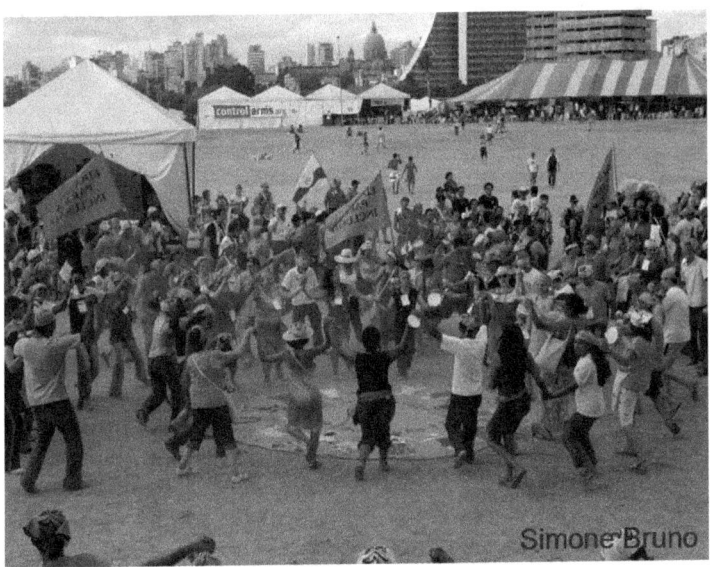

Citizens should be able to influence decisions affecting the localities and communities in which they live, work and visit.

This is not about tolerating what other agencies might cede to us, but about us (now)[96] taking responsibility (for our own futures). About us playing our part, according to our abilities, in co-designing and co-creating our own futures.

We share a planet with limited and sometimes scarce resources. In a more resource constrained future[97] it seems to make sense to make best use of our greatest resource - us, our ingenuity and creativity. For example it's arguable that we haven't got much hope of meeting, or better still even exceeding our carbon reduction targets unless we're all involved. So we accept some responsibility for all of the following:

- fair shares. We do not accept the inevitability of crude and harmful imbalances of access to resources or influence.
- fair shares between current and future generations
- a fair pattern of influence, for example between local and wider communities
- mediation between disparate interests
    - envisioning and co-designing a better future[98], a wiser earth[99]
    - planning what we need to do to get there
    - co-creating whatever we need to help us get us there
    - assessing our progress

We are responsible for the great transition, centred on our growing involvement and influence, our growing citizen and community self-actualization.[100] We are responsible for the great transition in both our local and wider communities. We all have a part to play. We do not accept any tendency to view any citizens or communities as disposable.

It's Ok to start with one's local community. We need to learn and develop confidence in our abilities to articulate the futures we choose, and to practice mediation between potentially conflicting choices. With modern technolgy we have the means to ensure proper and adequate recognition for this valuable work via transparency. Transparency via fully open and complete online record of involvement and influence, for purposes of recognition, reward, respect, trust, and, last but not least, learning and not having to keep reinventing the wheel. A quantum leap in creativity to meet contemporary challenges.

Participation with whom? - citizen to citizen as the norm, not a luxury handed down to us by benevolent yet archaic power structures. A role for experts or specialists, of course, via deliberative democracy, knowledge and evidence based decision making. But increasingly knowledge and expertise is not restricted to the few and we all have a role in ensuring knowledge is used wisely. Assessment of needs and aspirations must involve the communities affected. Local knowledge helps find solutions which work.

Civil society 2.0 - Open, wholly inclusive and totally transparent networks which enable the wellbeing of us all need to supercede the narrow interests of inflexible establishments and institutions. Gov 2.0 - Is there a role for government? yes, but also, increasingly it must be as the enabler of the wellbeing of us all.

A Wiser Rio 2012[101], a Rio which made optimum use of, included, involved, nurtured and helped grow the creativity, ingenuity and innovation of mass participation would not be a bad thing in this context.

References

- more refs via Ukgc10[102], Sustainable Community Action wiki

The Future We Got–Earth Date Zero Plus Twenty - Pamela Mclean

There are some dates that can only be pinpointed with hindsight. Peak oil was one. Earth Date Zero was another. Twenty years afterwards, with the benefit of hindsight, it stands proud - that point in time when a critical mass of people shifted their thinking to the new paradigm, when our relationship with information finally matured, our relationship with the material world altered, and the old ways began to seem foreign and somewhat inexplicable.

The shift in consciousness changed our relationships with each other, altered the assumptions we have about how we live our lives and, arguably, affected the very nature of what it is to be human. We believe it changed the future of the human race, for without that paradigm shift we had little chance of moving towards a sustainable future. After all – that's why, world wide, people now count their dates from Earth Date Zero.

Previously people talked about an "information revolution". They added websites and emailing to their existing organisational structures, some blogged and tweeted, but very few radically altered their way of doing things. Yet the evidence of deep change was all around.

Mobile phones for instance: the digital technology that rapidly encircled the globe. Young people went about things in a different way to their parents. They had been dubbed digital natives. They were comfortable with digital devices from the time they were toddlers. Their life style was new in ways that were partly trivial, but partly deeply significant. For instance, in their social lives: they were accustomed to set out with only a general objective (such as meeting up with a few friends and having a good time). They'd sort out the details by texting and talking as they went along. They didn't need to arrange to "Meet under the clock at the station by 7:30 or we'll go on without you," as their parents or grandparents had done. They could update information and change plans as they went along. Old systems of organisation and planning were becoming redundant.

So now it's Earth Date Twenty, and time to take stock. We confluence; we flow together; we swarm; we flock; we are individual but connected; we group together while interests and objectives overlap; we separate out again, go different ways, and regroup. In a way it is more chaotic, but it is also much more effective – and sustainable. Technology has moved on and we have things that people a couple of decades ago could hardly have imagined, and yet somehow, exactly twenty years ago, that critical mass of people did get the vision and make the shift.

What did they know? They had the basics of what they called Information and Communication Technology. They were getting better at leaving messages for people through voice-mails and video messaging. They talked about "the death of distance" and were aware of time-zones when they planned phone calls and online meetings. They had started to learn about simple time-shifting through their experiences of increasing viewer control over TV and video watching. Elementary group wisdom was beginning, and practical collaboration in the cloud. They were fighting battles against copyright and intellectual property legislation. They had started to recognise that things could spread virally instead of needing to "scale up". Increasingly digital information was archived automatically as things went along, and was made publicly available. Digital footprints were everywhere. It was getting easier and easier to be included in things that were going on, instead of simply accepting (or refusing) what came from the top down.

Apparently, before Earth Date Zero, life was more private and isolated and individual. People were more competitive and secretive about what they were doing. There was a lack of collaboration and information sharing, which is hard to imagine today. It is said that even buyers and sellers usually didn't communicate openly until it was too late to change anything - the product was made according to what the producer had guessed that potential buyers might be persuaded to purchase. It must have been a clumsy, crazy, wasteful system – but I guess things were different then, and people didn't know any better.

Imagine a world where people couldn't relate to information first and then sort out the material stuff later. How could such people possibly have lived their lives? No wonder they made such bad decisions and nearly wrecked the planet. I'm amazed they ever managed to organise anything in such an information-impoverished environment. I wonder if they had any idea what a barbaric system they were living in.

with thanks to David Pinto for the Earth Date Zero idea.

The Onion and the Satellite - Lucas Gonzalez

Many health-care systems, where they exist at all, are being assessed as "unsustainable", with expensive and sometimes even harmful interventions, waiting lists so long they look like rationing, and exclusion from care for a number of people (sometimes many). If these systems are indeed unsustainable then it follows, with unbelievable logic, that they will fail, crack, morph into something different.

So, what's next? If there's time, maybe some or all health-care systems can be dynamically redesigned from the core, making use of what's available in other systems, and thinking in layers?

Redesign from the core

Health-care systems' core is the **bi-cellular seed** deep inside the system: *someone who has a health issue* (a broken bone or a future disease that's preventable) and *someone who can help*. (You take both roles if you prevent or treat yourself.) Everything beyond that core - from the assistants who bring the drug or the knife, to the folks who plan world-wide vaccine production - is like the tail in modern warfare: layer upon layer of complexity, helpfulness and failure: **the onion**. Sometimes the tail is long and fat, but it's just the tail, intended to help those two people who are at the heart of the onion.

The core and all the layers have basic, and sometimes conflicting, missions. Classically, we deal with death, function and pain (or pain and function), and aesthetics. If aesthetics is "social function" or "social pain", then it's only **death and pain/function**, and how we deal with that.

Regarding **death**, let's face it: we all die at the end of our life. (Big news, I know.) So health-care systems can't really *reduce* death. All they do is delay it, making room for more life, if we live it.

We start at the center. We look at the age pyramid of the living and the smaller age pyramid of those who die. Then, we look at the causes of death for each age group, and delay death there. This is the business of **contained or containable mortality**, which we might define as *the mortality that would emerge or reemerge if rich countries' healthcare systems collapse*. In poor countries, such mortality is simply **uncontained** or, if you feel optimistic, "yet to be contained".

(Sometimes we're *too good* at delaying death[103], if population growth kills the ecosystem, if generations fight each other for resources, or if demographic shift makes the pyramid grow old so that either it shrinks and collapses or younger neighbours feel invited to migrate. It seems there's no failure like success, but that's another story.)

Dealing with death is felt to be most important regarding kid's lives, whose "potential life-years lost" indicator is greater than their grandparents'. But, of course, if and when I become a grandparent, my remaining life-years will be 100% of what I have at that point, so I will want my hip-bone replaced so I can learn to play golf at age 97. See, that's **pain and function**.

Use what's available

Infrastructure stands between us and the universe, delaying our death from the basic six ways to die: too hot, too cold, thirst, hunger, disease and injury. In health-care systems, it's buildings and energy, staff and stuff, knowledge and procedures ... much of which is paid for with money, which in turn is chronically short for the poor, and may become acutely short for the now-rich.

If money is short, how do we get the services we need? Do we look into scalable high technology? Should we look into permaculture as a design methodology that stresses "relative location for mutual service"? Could we use and improve the devices and methodologies that are currently being developed for (and by) the poor, thus helping everyone?

We want prevention, so maybe we can wash our hands with tippy tap[104]. For diagnostic devices, we can look at what out-of-the-box designers are doing with, say, stamp-sized tests.[105] For communications that don't scale, but spread, use medic frontlinesms[106]. For learning and information, build learning systems like Khan Academy[107], perhaps using books like where there's no doctor[108] and inserting them into wikireader[109]-like devices. For communities of mutual help, time banks[110] are being used. For better thinking and less stress, look into the role of meditation (with as much or as little spirituality as you like). And, of course, in general, contribute to open sources like appropedia[111].

Think in layers

Some of the above technologies look very, erm, local, don't they? What about expensive factories that make inexpensive antibiotics and pain-killers for millions? Even if you dislike Big Pharma, don't they have an essential role in health-care systems?

Well, of course they are *part* of the big picture, which includes all the layers, from "self", sitting at the center of my world, to "mom" to "neighbour" to "satellite". Simply because I can't make vaccines for my family, and WHO directors can't wash my hands.

So we need to look at how layers define themselves, and how they interact. Maybe use a variation of Simple Critical Infrastructure Maps SCIM[112] with the specifics for healthcare systems? What would that look like? How can we use both, the onion and the satellite, and everything in between? Work in progress!

Extra links that might be related to these ideas:

- http://www.quickanded.com/2011/02/disrupting-college.html Maybe cheap and disruptive becomes the new normal. Some changes are slow.
- http://www.ncrr.nih.gov/publications/ncrr_reporter/winter-spring2011/innovations.asp?p=all Respirators and prosthetic knees.

Ode to the Tech Fix - Chris Malins

(This is a little late night doggerel that came to me)

Thank goodness for technology, that gave us better roads.
And faster cars and bigger trucks to handle heavy loads.
Thank goodness for technology, that gave us flying planes.
To get to California, Greece, New Zealand and Bahrain.
Thank goodness for technology, and finding coal and oil.
Without them we'd be in the dark, labouring at manual toil.
Thank goodness for technology, and science and for business.
That take the things we wouldst not to and kindly do them for us.
Thank goodness for technology, and for the atom bomb.
Without it war upon Japan would have been much more long.
Thank goodness for technology, we'll need in times ahead.
For without solving climate change, we might all end up dead.

Thank goodness for technology, for geoengineering.
That'll let us keep the planet cool, and suitable for living.
Thank goodness for technology, for modern agriculture.
Much more equipped to keep us fed than weak old fashioned nature.
Thank goodness for technology, genetic modification,
Much rather Round-up Ready crops than swarming insect nations.
Thank goodness for technology, tech fixes to our problems.
Better to innovate our lives than change the way we live them.
Thank goodness for technology, to allow us to keep,
The curtains pulled across our eyes and all our minds asleep.
God save us from technology, for I can't help but think,
That if blindly we trust in it, our ship of fools might sink.

Deserving The Future We Want - Eldan Goldenberg

Talk of "the future" often means speculation about future technologies. A lot of these are tremendously exciting—imagine what we could do with genuinely cheap energy!—but they won't be what brings us the wonderful future we surely all want. Everything we need for that is already out in the world, and while much of it was invented relatively recently, it's all been successfully piloted somewhere.

Brazil[113] and China[114] have shown us two radically different methods for bringing millions of people out of poverty. Finland, Korea and Japan know how to give every child an education that lets all have a chance to fully participate in society[115]. Costa Rica has shown how to stop deforestation[116], and China how to start replacing lost forests[117]. Germany has proven that places with no natural advantages can generate electricity without pollution[118], and build houses that barely need heating[119]. Copenhagen, Amsterdam, Tokyo and New York City all allow people to move around without destructive dependence on cars. Milwaukee is the home of a revolutionary farming technique[120] that grows incredible quantities of vegetables and fish from tiny plots of land, with minimal energy, year-round in a harsh climate.

I am bullish about the technology we already have.

Yet I am quite pessimistic about what the future has in store for us, because we don't *deserve* the future we *want*. While the unfairness of life to individuals is a truism, as a species we'll get exactly the future we deserve because we will have made it for ourselves.

Consider a small example. This morning I stepped in dogshit on the way to work, because one of my neighbours couldn't be bothered to clean up after their precious poodle. As if the antisociality of this weren't obvious enough, round here we've been bombarded by messages[121] reminding us how destructive pet faeces are to the universally loved local waterway and its charismatic megafauna. Yet my neighbour couldn't even spare the few seconds to deal with it.

Dog turd is not the most important issue facing the world today, but it is a symptom. As a global society we know how to make the world better for all of us, instead of continuing to step in each others' dogs' shit, but doing so involves decision after decision in which individuals must concede a little self-interest for a greater externalised benefit. And if we can't persuade our neighbours to scoop poop, how will we ever persuade enough people to accept paying to educate the kids across town, or taking a little longer to get to work so people downwind don't have to breathe our cars' exhaust? Never mind the bigger problems that need action co-ordinated between countries that have never trusted each other....

When it becomes unthinkable to let our neighbours step in our dogs' shit; when we finally accept that we are our brothers' keepers; then we will deserve the future we want and we'll find we already know how to get it. We don't need a technological revolution. What we need is a moral revolution.

Re-envisioning Our Relationship With Micro-Organisms - Brian Degger

Humans are topologically donuts, bacteria live on the surface, human cells on the inside. We are dwarfed by the number of genes that are in these bacteria. At last estimation there are only 23000 genes encoded in our genome(10.1186/1471-2105-7-327) and up to 9 million of bacterial origin (10.1371/journal.pone.0006074). From this we need to consider the fact that this bacterial population forms a chronically understudied extrahuman organ.

Are we going to discover that there is a deep bacterial culture basis to human culture, that some cultural norms actually support a specific community of bacteria? We already recognise that fermentation outside the body has had a profound effect on what we as humans can eat or metabolize (coffee, cheese, kim chi etc). Now we have to recognise that this fermentation doesn't stop on the outside of our body, it continues, as bacteria provide essential nutrients to us. Might there be communal rituals that are about keeping the 'good culture' alive in the community? When explorers introduce pathogens into a 'naïve population' what is really being lost? If there is a move away from the traditional foodstuffs, are we losing more than a human culture?

The adage 'you are what you eat' makes more sense when changing a diet could change suceptibility to modern diseases such as diabetes (doi:10.1371/journal.pone.0009085) and Irritable Bowel Syndrome (doi:10.1371/journal.pone.0010507) by modifying our gut bacterial composition. The pectins in apple fruit skins have been shown to favour friendly bacteria within the gut (doi:10.1016/j.anaerobe.2010.03.005) and obesity (doi:10.1038/4441022a). As a last resort, colonic gut bacteria have been transplanted from a healthy person to cure a patient suffering from Clostridium difficile diarrhoea.

What will this mean for the Future We Deserve?

We hypothesise that there is a lot more going on in human culture than meets the eye. If we are carriers of 'good' as well as 'bad' bacteria, what does this add to human-human interactions, such as the rituals and customs of greeting? Are differences between cultures reflected in our microflora?

Can we have strategies that minimise the unintended evolution of bacterial pathogens by reducing the use of antibiotics? Can we investigate using other more specific technologies such as phage (a bacterial virus) therapy to knock out specific 'bad' bacteria such as C. difficile? In a wider context, do shared bacterial communities provide a method by which members are alike?

Can we 'know our bacteria' and gain guides on what foodstuffs we should be eating to maintain health? Can we envisage a Personalised Probiotics, that is not another mass produced commodity, or a 'lite' version of what actually works.

Lots of questions to answer, but that is part of the Future We Deserve, a culture that understands how it operates, where even the 'lowly' bacteria has a place, and not just as a cause of disease.

The Spaces We Deserve - Dougald Hine

In industrial societies, life has been organised into compartments.

Ray Oldenburg identified the three most universal: the home, the workplace and the "third place", the playful, sociable, conversational space of the pub or the coffeehouse.

To these we might add the specialised spaces of industrial-era institutions: the hospital, where we are sent to be ill; the school, where we are sent to be taught; the prison, where we are sent to be punished.

This division of space is the counterpart of the division of labour. Pursued in the name of efficiency, in many cases it has long been counterproductive, as Ivan Illich argued 40 years ago. Hospitals are not generally a good place to get well. Schools encourage us to think of learning as something which takes place through artificial exercises, in isolation from the rest of society, and under duress.

Oldenburg saw that the third place was both the humblest and, in some sense, the most humanly-important of our compartments. We can push this further. What he called the third place is a native reservation of sociability, a surviving enclave of something which, in other times and places, has characterised almost every corner of human society.

For all the wonders industrial production made possible, it also meant unprecedentedly anti-social working conditions for the vast majority of people. Even in the rich countries, where the physical degradation of earlier industrialism is practically extinct, the subjection of working time to the goal of maximum productivity remains. Only the most radical of employers, willing to become fools to the logic of capitalism, can tolerate that which makes work more enjoyable while also less productive. (It will be objected that enjoyment increases productivity, but while this may sometimes be true, it is wishful thinking to claim it as a rule.)

Similar arguments can be made for the antisocial character of our homes, schools or hospitals.

What gives hope is that all of this is in flux, at least in the struggling countries of the post-industrial west. The converging crises of the early 21st century create new possibilities, even as the massive public or private sector developments which have shaped our towns and cities becomes rarer.

Under their feet, barely noticed, a new kind of spatial agent is emerging: improvisational, bottom-up, working with the materials to hand; perhaps unqualified, or using their training in unexpected ways; responding pragmatically to the constrictions and precarities of post-crisis living. Between the jugaad culture of the Indian village, the temporary structures built by jobless architects, the pop-up shops, the infrastructure-savvy squatters and open source shelter-makers, the Treehouse Galleries and urban barns and Temporary Schools of Thought, just maybe something new is being born.

We could call it the culture of the Space Hacker - because these new players have more in common with the geeks, hippies and drop-out-preneurs who gave us open source and the internet revolution, than with the architects, developers or property industries we have known.

Unlike Silicon Valley, though, these hackers have given up on the goal of getting rich. They are driven instead by the desire to make spaces in which they want to spend time, sociable spaces of living, working and playing, as they - and the rest of us - adjust to the likelihood of getting poorer.

The Age of Warlords Cookbook - Michael Swifte

It seems we manufacture 'consent' more than just about anything else in the west. Our media and commercial food industries are staking their claims on the last pieces of moral and aesthetic high ground in an effort to exploit our patterns of conspicuous consumption. Our tastes in food are being driven by our unprecedented access to global resources. This is all at a time when age old aphorisms like "teach a man to fish..." and "there's plenty of fish in the sea" are in the process of being rendered untrue. A time when catastrophic climate change and economic disintegration threaten to test the stability of western civilisations. Food is our fuel and when we are at our greatest need it is the one thing we value above all else.

Rick Stein recently said something that confirmed my feelings about how all of humanity relates to food and how sharing is valued in times of conflict. He was speaking from his studio kitchen after his recent Far Eastern Odyssey when he remarked on the resilience of the Sri Lankan people during the recent civil war saying "Food is about good times even if there are terrible things going on all around you". The former fishmonger is known for his rapport with the people he visits and the engaging quality of his documentaries and cookbooks. The truth he has recognised is that humans need to share the act of eating and must work collectively to add value to food and to bring meals to the table in tough times.

Powdered egg is the one food that at the toughest of times will become a highly sought-after commodity. At the heart of western delicacies like sponge cakes, souffle, meringue, and many other sweet and savoury dishes is egg whites beaten to soft or stiff peaks. Egg whites are irreplaceable in western delicacies as nothing else can substitute for its particular qualities. My question is "Do powdered egg whites match up to the qualities of fresh egg whites?" The west's media are currently obsessed with both the haute cuisine and boutique agriculture sectors. Our current knowledge base is at once expanding with knowledge of exotic and labour intensive ingredients, whilst also contracting due to masking of the true nature of our supply chains.

In many countries with unstable governments, warlords are a fact of life and a constant force affecting economic and social stability. Unstable governments are forced to mediate the engagement of militant groups with the general population. In countries where crops have failed and food production and other economic infrastructure are also compromised those who have weapons have the power to control food. Max Blouin and Stéphane Pallage[122] contend that poverty levels are now being managed to qualify for food aid and deliver control over larger food surpluses to warlords. They confirm the fundamental rule that in a time of scarcity, those with weapons and power have control over food.

African cities have been hotbeds of cultural production since the wave of independence of the late 1950s and early 1960s. Despite every kind of economic manipulation and the legacy of centuries of colonialism African cities have produced cultural products that demonstrate astounding resilience. Pioneering Afro-beat musician Fela Kuti whose Lagos night club 'The Shrine' provided respite from dangerous streets spoke out strongly about the effects of economic exploitation by foreigners and his own countrymen. The creative legacy of African musicians speaks to their resilience and ability to use culture to transcend adversity. It is this quality of resilience that the large scale manufacturing of consent has stifled. Empathy and consideration of the conditions and successes of resilient people gives us the power to learn about resilience.

What do our contingency plans for the future say about our motivations? Survivalism lite is the name given to the movement (in the USA) toward relearning basic survival skills and developing stores of food and supplies for catastrophic futures. It is primarily about the preservation of the highest possible level of comfort for the individual and the family. The Dark Mountain Project also identifies risks to the 'civilisation' project but asks a much larger question "Has the civilisation project delivered us a society that is able to deal with catastrophic climate change and economic disintegration?" It has begun to answer this question in two ways. The first is an intuitive "No!", and the second is by stimulating new answers that look beyond the western civilisation to 'cultural contingencies' that recognise the true cost of western affluence.

References

Rick Stein's Far Eastern Odyssey 2 Entertain http://www.2entertainvideo.co.uk/2evideo/product.php?dbID=343

CIRPEE Working Paper 09-47 Warlords, Famine and Food Aid: Who Fights, Who Starves? Max Blouin and Stéphane Pallage http://www.cirpee.org/fileadmin/documents/Cahiers_2009/CIRPEE09-47.pdf

Music is the Weapon Stéphane Tchal-Gadjieff & Jean Jacques Flori 1982(Universal Music)

The Dark Mountain Project - The Manifesto Paul Kingsnorth and Dougald Hine http://www.dark-mountain.net/about-2/the-manifesto/

Using Science Locally - Ian Simmons

Recently I found myself in the back lane here in Whitley Bay, sorting out some weirdness with the recycling bin and talking to the chap next door, who specialises in teaching mystic running techniques, when the local 'cat lady' came up and started accusing him of 'murdering' a cat by putting slug pellets on his veg garden, which she assumed it had eaten. He was a bit put out by this, so I said I'd look into it from a scientific perspective and work out whether this was likely to be possible. So, having worked out the type of pellets, found out what they actually contained and in what concentration and the size of the deceased cat, it was clear that the beast would have had to eat a heaped tablespoon full of the things in order to croak, which put my neighbour's mind to rest, if not, entirely, our cat lady's. What, then, has the Whitley Bay Cat Poisoner got to do with sustainable futures? Well like many cities, Newcastle has a big landmark hands-on science centre, but there's no reason why this should be the only model for this kind of thing. We need science centres that are relevant to my neighbour and the cat lady, small, local places, more like libraries and community centres than flagship visitor attractions, where instead of it just being lucky that I was about when the matter of cat poisoning arose, it'd be natural to go ask these kinds of questions. True, you may say, but haven't we got Google for that? In a way, I suppose, yes, but then it needs people to know what they are looking for to make the connections, there is no chart out there that conveniently tabulates slug pellets/lethal cat dose, believe me, I've looked. Such a place would also have a small array of regularly changed simple hands-on exhibits where people could drop in and explore casually, clear updates on the latest science news, family workshop activities, kid's weekend and holiday clubs, they would also provide support for science in local schools, work with the community on projects where science might be useful to them, and like libraries you might have two or three in even a small town. It's not rocket science, the basic models exist for all these functions - science centres, community science outreach, co-enquiry programmes with universities, science shops, all of these are part of the jigsaw that could come together to create this kind of initiative. It just needs someone to decide to do it, and a moderate amount of money. Science has a part to play in the future development of communities across the world, and it needs to work in these communities and for them, not be something that occasionally impinges upon them from the outside, and having grass-roots level engagement facilities that are the natural place for people who need to make use of science seems to me to be the key to making this work.

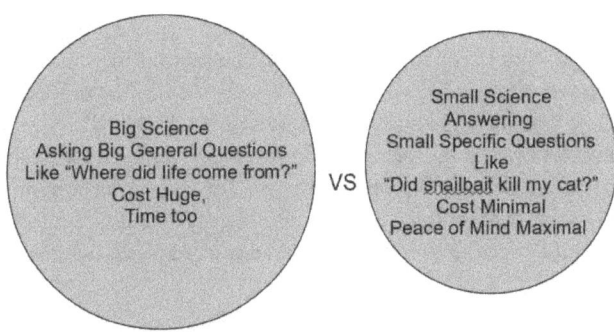

Seed Saving for Local Food Security - Lisa Erwin

The community seed bank

A village/neighborhood/community seed bank of nonhybrid (open-pollinated) seed affords community food security and sovereignty that dependence on purchased hybrid seed cannot. Whereas hybrid seeds must be repurchased annually, open-pollinated seeds can be saved from year to year and adapted to local growing conditions. Thus next year's seed supply is at hand – no corporations, cash or transport required. Open pollinated seeds are nature's gift, refined by selective seed saving over generations. A community seed bank should be restocked annually

1. To ensure that there will be enough seed to enable a transition to local self-sufficiency.
2. To adapt nonhybrid varieties to local conditions over several growing seasons, for optimal harvests.
3. To ensure the viability of seeds the way nature does, by allowing them to grow and reproduce new seed each growing season.

Any community should master the process of collecting and saving nonhybrid seed each growing season from every crop it grows. Enough seed should be saved to plant the next year's crop, with considerable additional seed as a safety margin. Seed will be needed for planting and replanting, for bartering, and in case a crop fails due to extreme weather, drought, fire or pillaging. Whether a community seed bank resides in a central location or remains a loose collaboration of seed savers, its adequacy as a local food security resource will depend on systematic planning and purposeful action.

For some crops, saving seed is simple. For other crops, the procedure is more exacting and labor intensive. In a village or a neighborhood, it makes sense to collaborate and delegate in order to simplify the seed-saving process for each seed saver. One household may interplant a block of corn with runner beans, fence the plot to keep the deer out, and save bean and corn seed enough for a number of households. Another might specialize in saving seed for tomato varieties, along with borage and basil as companion plants to deter tomato pests. A third might interplant onions, leeks and carrots and save seed for all three.

Crops that do not readily cross are "no worry" plants. They do not need spacing or other measures to maintain seed purity because they are self-pollinating. Examples are beans, tomatoes, peas, and lettuces.

Many garden crops, however, readily cross pollinate with other members of their own plant family. In most instances, seed savers strive to keep cross-pollination from happening. In that way, the desirable characteristics of a particular variety will be maintained in next year's seed.

There are a variety of ways to protect related crops from cross pollinating:
1. Stagger planting times.
2. Plant only one variety of a particular species prone to cross pollination.
3. Maintain recommended isolation distances.
4. Protect plants from cross pollination by means of physical barriers.

Selective seed saving

Seed should be saved from the healthiest, most productive plants of each variety, selected for various desirable qualities. Seed must be saved not just from one or two plants of one variety but from as many healthy specimens as possible so that genetic diversity is preserved.

Storing seed

Most stored seeds stay viable longest when they are kept in dark, dry, cool, pest-free conditions. Seed must be thoroughly dry before it is stored. Packaged properly for long-term storage, some types of seeds remain viable for years, though their germination rate is gradually reduced and some genetic diversity may be lost. Despite this fact, there are compelling reasons to plant the crops the community will depend on every year and to collect new seed:

1. This is the best way to ensure that seed is fresh and viable.

2. Growing a crop and saving seed selectively each year adapts that crop to local conditions. Locally adapted seed is the most dependable seed of all.
3. In growing crops annually and saving seed from them, community members acquire knowledge and skills potentially critical for survival. Building soil fertility using organic methods should be a simultaneous goal.

Planning for success

A planting plan for a community should ideally be done with seed saving in mind. A community focused on transitioning to local food self-sufficiency can collaborate to map arable land, including that in neighborhoods, gauging distances required to isolate certain crop varieties that cross. Planners can create planting zones for crops that should be isolated from one another for easiest seed saving.

- This essay is distilled from "Seed Saving for Community Food Security" (http://mindspinner.net/docs/SeedSaving1-0.pdf). See also
- Ashworth, Susan. Seed to Seed: Seed Saving and Growing Techniques for Vegetable Gardeners.
- Deppe, Carol. Breed Your Own Vegetable Varieties: The Gardener's and Farmer's Guide to Plant Breeding and Seed Saving.

Challenging Education and the "Harry Potter Letter" - Edmund Harriss

It is not hard to get kids playing football. You leave them somewhere with a ball. At the weekend you take them to see the game. Imagine if we could do the same with mathematics!

We can. I have built mathematical sculptures[123] with people in their own time, happily volunteered. I have taken mathematics to festivals[124] and seen parents drag their children away to give time to the other exhibits. It is possible to get kids to play spontaneously with mathematics and to give them ideas from the deep reaches of the subject. I use my research in geometry and tilings. Leave children with wooden Penrose tiles and they start to play. They ask questions, and find answers. Add games with mirrors, and toys like http://www.zometool.com/ zometool] and polydron[125] and you can give ideas from group theory[126], four dimensional space[127] and Gödel's incompleteness theorems[128]. In fact from primary to graduate school and beyond there are plenty of topics that can be motivated this way. As an example of more familiar maths, trigonometry can be used to help design a catapult and then quadratic equations will help aim it.

You will probably be surprised by how many students get inspired by these ideas, others might be interested but not want to get too deep and others will be bored. That is fine, the same happens for everything. As an example few would say that sport cannot be interesting, yet it holds little appeal to me. What we need to move on from is the idea that concepts should be hidden as they are too challenging or complicated. This is like forbidding someone learning football from seeing professionals play, or trying not to confuse a young pianist by playing them Bach[129] or Rachmaninov[130]. When they have entered school children have already worked out how to use their limbs, how to make sound and then how to give it meaning. They are used to challenge. Compared to that most mathematics is trivial. Education should be a challenge, with the acceptance that we might fail. In fact there is something wrong if someone does not fail. All schools and parents will find people around who have some area of expertise that excites them.

When people find the challenge that grips them they are inspired. They become activated to learn for themselves. However for most of history what they could find to learn was limited. This improved dramatically with public libraries, but the internet changed the game again. Now anyone who can get online can, with effort, find just about the whole of human knowledge. Internet access is rapidly expanding, how long before the majority of people on earth have access to all that knowledge?

So as the community of thinkers, artists, makers, musicians, sportsmen, we can put the challenges in front of people; help them find the goals that will drive them; set those sparks to the tinder of the internet. What then? Maybe we could take this a step further, to find those from all backgrounds who are getting excited and give them greater challenges? The internet has the knowledge, but good teachers can take things so much further. Maybe the answer is still in the internet? Something as simple as finding the individuals who are looking at a particularly high number of pages. They are almost certainly the ones diving in deep to try to find things. Identified they could be sent a "Harry Potter" letter, connecting them to a teacher; a postdoc, a young musician, someone who can guide them into the greatest challenges of whatever has got them going, providing its wisdom not just its knowledge. How many Einsteins[131] or Ramanujans[132] are out there waiting to be discovered? (and that is just the scientists)

References

- A Mathematician's Lament[133]
    - Paul Lockhart, Unpublished (widely circulated amoungst mathematicians)

- The case for revealing the beauty and not just the techniques of mathematics
- Play Ethic[134]
    - Pat Kane, Pan, New Edition 2005
    - The deeply thought through (yet readable!) account of how play can merge the inspiration and discipline required for creativity.
- Alan Kay[135] on learning and context
- Learning framework[136] from NESTA[137]
- Blogs giving examples of how to challenge and engage children with mathematics
    - Number Warrior[138]
    - Think Thank Thunk[139]
    - dy/dan[140]
- The benefits of toys (specifically LEGO) for developing mathematical ability.
    - Advanced constructional play with LEGOs among preschoolers as a predictor of later school achievement in mathematics[141]
        - Charles Wolfgang; Laura Stannard; Ithel Jones, Early Child Development and Care, Volume 173, Issue 5 October 2003 , pages 467 - 475
    - Blocks to Robots[142]
        - Marina Umaschi Bers, Teachers College Press 2007

Credibility & Calories: A Perspective on Information - Woody Evans

Information doesn't want anything, but people do. People want things like sex and freedom and control and food and community and property.

Information isn't a kind of perfect thing, it's not an ideal, it's not even a value. It's a tool. And being a tool doesn't make information good.

Tools are generally considered good if they're useful. Hammers are used to build houses. And we all know that good tools can be used for bad things.

Information is not essentially good, though it is an essential good. That is to say, it's a commodity that has value, can be traded, and that can also lose value and degrade over time.

Thought experiment: think of the most valuable discrete item of information you know. How do you assign its particular value relative to other things you know? Is it the most valuable to you personally, to your community, or to the world system as a whole? Maybe you have to use a utilitarian frame to give it value (it's valuable because it can serve the most number of people the best); maybe you have a particular religious frame (it's valuable because when someone knows it, that person is enlightened or saved); maybe it's valuable to you because it can make you a lot of money (or make a poor country rich).

Would it be valuable to the watermelon farmers and field hands near Mize, Mississippi? The land there is woods and small farms, piney, built on loam and clay, and full of fierce folks who spend a lot of time in church. They drink, fuss and fight, try to get degrees at the community college.

If the most valuable information in the world is a simple solar hack (filling plastic bottles with whatever water you've got, leaving them in the sun for a full day to make them safe to drink, say), how valuable is it to my rural Mississippi cousins? They have plentiful well water, the Okatoma river easily at hand, and over 50 inches of rainfall per year.

If the most valuable information in the world is a prayer, you'd get them more interested – but it better be a Baptist prayer. You see what I mean. Information is not objectively valuable.

To talk about the information needs of the developing world, we need to talk about what information is and what it is not.

Information is not:

- Salvific.

- More valuable than gauze, iodine, or syringes.

- The key to a floating world of equality or purity or dignity.

So what is information, at its best, for the world's poor?

Here's the answer: information is food and health. Anything beyond that, until the basics get ironed out, is lagniappe. We get the information to the people so that they can sustainably clothe, feed, and heal themselves. Your IT initiative's for the burgeoning sub-Saharan mobile "market"? Let it focus on these basics. Dignity, open government, capital ventures – these things may follow only if there's a well-laid cornerstone to build from.

People need to eat, and when your kid lacks something basic you'll do a hell of a lot that you never thought you would to get her what she needs. Nothing is more valuable than the bit of information that leads me to food to fill her belly with.

Calories build the credibility of the information technologist.

We build beyond the basics when the luxury presents itself.

The Future of Programming - Andy Broomfield

READY.

That is the prompt the Commodore 64 gives once it has been turned on, immediately it is there to be programmed. Almost always, the simple instruction to LOAD something was typed, bypassing this environment to play games or load other software, yet there was that moment of exposure, triggering that moment of curiosity that myself and many others found drew us into programming. We could tell the computer to do stuff.

Computing environments are very different now, and if we were to look at it from a usability perspective this could be considered a good thing. No longer does anyone need to type in the seemingly archaic instruction to load a program or file off a disk, it's all delivered through intuitive mouse pointer and windows. This has been further abstracted with iPhone, iPad and other touch screen mobile computers, no longer do we need to be aware of the technical underpinnings of how our computers are working when we're using them. Touch the icon and the app we want launches with the data (that is, photos, status updates, movies) we want to work with.

But I wonder if something has been lost, that initial magical exposure to its underpinnings. Computers no longer boot up into a programming language, coding tools aren't typically installed. David Brin talks about the simple 'type it in' programs in maths books (and magazines as I remember) that can't be typed in anymore, a frustration in teaching his son the fundamentals of programming languages[143]. While Apple has taken care to curate a developer eco system, this is unexposed to non-developers. (while you can get the SDK, you can't develop on your own iOS device without payment to Apple or Jailbreaking). Even Android is not immune to this lock down. The largest mobile computing (device based) platform will be made largely of free software, but we won't be able to modify it due to locked down hardware[144]. How do we expose the possibility that their app can be there too?

The web has always had a much stronger emphasis on freedom than on device platforms. The barrier to entry is low, providing you're willing to learn the knowledge, crack open a text editor, write your content and upload to a web server, from where it's available on a multitude of devices. There definitely seem to be stronger online communities around web programming technologies. Mash ups and other services still expose some of the underpinnings letting you add custom code or showing you how it works, even text forms on the web will often allow and expose underlying html, Facebook has a custom code application, Twitter accepts colour codes for custom profiles. These little elements chip away at the looking glass one little bit at a time.

So how will the next generation learn about programming in the future? How sad will it be when learning to code is something that is only started in a college lab to learn a career, and not born out of the artistic nature of hacking. I think the web provides part of the answer, as a free (as in freedom) runtime environment and distribution space, but what about development? David Brin gave his son a Commodore 64, and I think that there is room in the market for a simple development computer. This would be a sort of my first hacking toolkit, that could boot up into a programming language such as Python and alongside this could be simple web development and deployment tools to share any developed programs with the world.

Exposing the ability to apply code, and bringing about this inquisitiveness is key. It is essential that these underpinnings are still available and accessible, and that we have the means to expose them ourselves. This means fighting to keep developer tools free and more importantly accessible. It means making sure 'view source' still exists on a web browser, and simple code hacks can be published to show how to make a computer do something, and that anyone has the means to apply it. This is to ensure that the magical spirit of enquiry, that the computer can be made to do something, will continue to provide a creative spark to the next generation of programmers.

Addendum.

Since writing this in 2010, two very interesting developments have occurred. First is the soon to be launched Raspberry PI computer, a cheap ($25) computer that runs Linux and boots into a programming environment, aimed at the education market. The second is the campaign in the UK to teach programming in schools. Both these projects are deserving of support. I do worry though about the possibility of them being co-opted, I often hear that the reason to teach programming is to serve the needs of business. I wonder if the ethical side of coding will be taught, will it touch on the Free Software movement for example? Its important not to forget that an important reason for coding is to understand how these machines of ours work, and so that we can change them to work the way we want them to.

Higher Education for the Future We Deserve - Lisa Erwin

There should be no economic barriers to higher education in a finite world where outcomes for many species, including our own, hinge on the wisdom and foresight of human populations. Regardless of whether a formal university education on a well-appointed campus remains a privilege for which students must pay, everyone, everywhere, should have access to that rich inheritance of knowledge, skill, and thought which can light a way forward to that future we yet hope to deserve. Open source instructional materials are already making such access possible. Open source courses should not be limited to recorded lectures by master teachers but should be fleshed out as teaching paired with interactive lesson components that parse, reinforce, and verify understandings.

Solutions to human problems that now loom large will be erected on the foundation of shared understandings woven through the push pull of dialogue rather than in isolation; thus people need to learn to think and to learn together, not so that they might think as one, but so that they might optimize their collective intelligence through reason and understanding. (Argument, reason, and constructive dialogical skills will have to be made an intentional and carefully teased out dimension of the curriculum, because these skills are not in evidence in much of what passes for public discourse today, though they will be essential tools for any constructively configured future.) Ideally, study groups will organize around each course, either by means of the internet alone or additionally at a physical location. A number of online learning tools, such as Live Mocha, P2P University, and Grockit, have already integrated collaborative learning tools which might serve as instructive prototypes.

Learning is a service rendered that merits a service repaid. People who reach mastery of course material should be enlisted to serve as course mentors, helping to guide the learning of students and study groups who follow them. Some might become master teachers themselves. Some form of advanced certification might follow from mastery plus service to the learning community.

The approach to open learning should emphasize connectedness of disciplines rather than dwelling upon each as if it were its own ivory tower. The approach should deal with relationships, impacts and interactions of complex systems within a finite and threatened world and pose principles for living wisely and justly within resource limits.

As fossil fuel supplies decline and economies slow, local learning communities might form around a "Village Construction Curriculum." The Village Construction Curriculum would foster and support, from philosophy to practice, the creation of resilient, sustainable villages, even among the ruins of the world that oil built. The core courses in this curriculum would guide a learning community as its members learn to transcend the language of divisive national political agendas to make choices about local strategy, development, and governance. More specialized courses would equip members of the learning community to contribute according to interests and strengths, such that the village can develop a local economy that supplies many of its needs. While open source online courses can aid in the development of practical expertise, an apprenticeship model can be developed to add considerable value. Such a curriculum and apprenticeship model might evolve from the collaborative efforts of the Transition Movement and other relevant initiatives.

For existing colleges and universities, an alternative higher education model emerges as an option, one significantly different from the one we replicate widely now. The college experience at some institutions could become an exercise in creating a self-sustaining, self-supporting community blending necessary work, apprenticeships, community and studies. It could be tailored to answer needs of young adults - meaningful work, means to survive, skilling for the future, living in community, pursuing higher learning, and mapping constructive approaches to a future very different from the world they have known (not only conceptually but in practice). It seems imperative that we create institutions and strategies that nurture societal transformation and address current needs all at once. This college model would do both and would be a viable option when higher education implodes given economic collapse or a long descent and when students can no longer see the sense in spending four years racking up educational debt that might be difficult or impossible to repay.

A Systemic Revolution, or, the Need for a Post-Scientific Approach - Andy Novocin

I remember learning about the scientific method through an example in a textbook. The example was that of spontaneous generation in which someone tested the statement that rotting meat generates flies. They did this by placing rotting meat in a sealed jar and directly observing that flies never emerged from the meat. From this example we were supposed to learn about attacking a problem through the process of observing, questioning, isolating out a testable hypothesis, experimenting, and finally concluding the validity of the hypothesis. The aspect that I want to focus on in this piece is the separation of aspects of a problem. I believe that the scientific approach of analyzing a problem by breaking it down into manageable chunks is very pervasive in our world, and exists in many aspects of our culture. I see ripples of this divide and conquer approach in many facets of industrialized modern life: in the production world via the separation of labor, in the academic world with the near-infinite specialization of fields, the artistic realm in which the separation of elements in a viewing experience are abstracted into various components (think the chain from impressionists through cubists through object-less art into formless art and beyond), we analyze food in terms of its constituent nutrients, and we educate students in specific and separated subject matters from a young age right on through to post-graduate work. This cultural shift formed a type of revolution, in the sense that a new mode of seeing the world emerged to challenge the old and then traditional modality of knowledge. This new scientific modality allowed better predictive models which could be generated, tested, and improved. A working predictive model leads to confidence in the approach that generated the model and this helps to fuel these generational changes and slowly replace the old models.

In the future that we deserve I envision a dethroning of the divide-and-conquer approach by a more systemic mode of thought. We are witnessing real-time worldwide inter-connectedness and its impacts. I suspect that this connectedness will be echoed in a new language and paradigm for combining previously separate parts of scientific models for problem solving. The systemic approach to problem solving will be to see and model the inter-relationships of aspects that science/abstraction/industry has separated. We are discovering just how connected and complex things really are, and new models must be formed in light of this. Such new models will require more synthesis as opposed to separation. Just walk into the mathematics section of any university library and see hundreds of books which are only readable by a handful of experts in a highly specific field. I suspect the same is true in many core sciences. We are producing specialists who are becoming increasingly marginalized, what we don't have are people to glue together the disparate parts.

Many important and interesting problems are not attackable by a divide-and-conquer approach. For instance the growing gap between the rich and the poor, the over-usage of our planet's non-renewable resources, inter-nation and inter-cultural conflicts, or appropriate and adaptive education. We are just now beginning to develop the language infrastructure to even describe the extent of these problems largely as a matter of necessity. As we address more complex problems via synthesis and system thinking we will form the way for new approaches and paradigms by which inter-connectedness is understood, modeled, and more accurate predictions are made. Such models could bring confidence and such confidence could fuel the new modality by which future generations see knowledge. This modality would of course be echoed in many aspects of life and culture in unforeseeable ways, leading to better insights and thus wider or more refined approaches and the positive feedback loop of new ideas would carry the process. View your problem as the top level, view it as the bottom level, think about how to see and describe interconnected aspects of related problems and you'll be working towards solving the systematic problems we face and unlocking new insights into the world that the old approach is unequipped for.

An Ideal World - Paola Di Maio

In the future we deserve there must be an ideal world somewhere.

The expression 'ideal world' nowadays often points to 'wishful thinking'. But it wasn't always so. In ancient times, the notion of ideal was widely upheld, and the philosopher Plato, and others, based a whole school of thought on it, broadly known as 'idealism'. Idealists are notoriously hard to please. Plato, like other philosophers, probably never got married(but he may have had sex).[145] We have become accustomed to hear 'In an ideal world perhaps...but in reality...it's not so...', as if ideals weren't within our reach. But it's mostly a question of the way we look at things. There should be no true reason however to rule out the possibility of attaining some level of what's ideal. Quite the contrary. Ideals, like values, can provide some sense of direction and lead toward what is 'desirable'.

Humanity progresses through the pursuit of 'ideals'.[146]

There are things in life that we cannot change: where and when we are born, our family, how we grow up, our early life experiences. Everything else is more or less determined by choices, conscious or not. The outcome of our personal decisions and efforts, the endpoint of where our individual energies are directed. Ideals can provide some gravity to pull these personal efforts, and be navigation aids to provide orientation in the many improbable webs of possibilities. So when trying to figure out how to get to our ideal world, we may have to take a good look at whether it's the 'given' portion that we are expecting to satisfy our every expectation, or the portion that we can make out for ourselves, our little personal contribution toward the ideal universe, that maybe is within our reach.

Even in discussing ideal terms, one has to be realistic.

My Ideal Panflu - Lucas Gonzalez

The next severe influenza pandemic

For most people on this planet, the pandemic that started in 2009 was mostly *"hype"* and *"unnecessary worry"*. Not many died, but on average death occurred to people younger than with seasonal flu. It might have started off much worse, or become more deadly after the first wave, but it didn't. So what's next?

The nature of the challenge

In the past 300 years, flu pandemics have happened once every 10-50 years. Each one starts when a flu virus present in non-human animals either mutates or swaps genes with another virus, and a fresh human-adapted virus emerges. Many people without specific immune experience are infected in two or more epidemic waves. Once the virus is not new for most people, we can no longer call it a pandemic and it becomes the new seasonal flu.

Pandemics are very different from each other. The 1918 pandemic, by most estimates, killed 50 million from a 2000 million global population[147]. The ones that started in 1957, 1968 and certainly 2009 were very different. The next one? There are some known candidate viruses, but science can't yet predict which virus will cause it, how contagious it will be, what will be the proportion of severe and lethal cases, or which age groups will be most affected.

It's a different fast-changing world. The globalisation of people and stuff, the specialisation of vital functions and the potential for simultaneous behaviours - buying and otherwise - may combine to make a modern *deadly enough* pandemic much more disruptive than past ones[148]. Specifically, even though we can guess what proportion of severe and lethal cases will make our healthcare resources even more insufficient, we have no idea how bad things have to be perceived to strongly motivate health-care providers to prioritise their own families, transport specialists to leave much of their load behind, and civil populations to start massively going by their gut feelings rather than by any official recommendation.

Actionable preparedness is cheap insurance

Safe, early, high-yield, almost print-your-own vaccines - which would give us immunity similar to the one we have for seasonal viruses - belong in the global layer of infrastructure, out of reach for most of us. The kind of mechanisms to *simply make it happen for all in need* are not yet visible if they exist at all.

The rest of the action is distributed in more hands:

1. If we ever need to decompress and maybe even reduce the size of waves, then reduction of daily respiratory contacts works if it's done early and non-destructively[149]. A hundred years ago, some rural folks in India made it a habit of temporarily fanning out their population in epidemic times. Today? We can keep kids of several ages in small stable groups, trade at a distance with phone-based networks, and yes, there are options for massive temporary shelter too. For unavoidable respiratory contacts, strategies for using heat and humidity in public places[150] and having washable masks for all[151], together with ubiquitous appropriate-tech hand-washing[152], must be tested, documented and fine-tuned, just like well-designed ventilators[153], because they will be used anyway.
2. Within each social group there will be an inevitable number of infections, added to and compounded with all other diseases and injuries. Every single community in the world needs real-time science for the best advice; translated video/podcast education focused on what's frequent, severe and preventable; and generic non-patented drugs in scalable quantities.
3. Finally, essential life-support services need to work for all humans. This means mapping critical infrastructure[154] for all locations and then *getting what we need with what we have*, not *indefinitely* which is the basis of sustainability, but *now* which is at the heart of dealing with emergencies.

A bad pandemic does not belong in the future our kids deserve, but our best response does. And guess what? Many of the issues outlined above have benefits beyond pandemic preparedness, and we already know how to do much of this stuff. So?

Report on the Planet Earth from the Intergalactic Study Group on Worlds in Transition - Gary Alexander

We have just come back from this very interesting planet where we examined its plight and prospective future.

On our previous visit, 7000 years ago, we found the planet to be extremely promising. Its life had evolved over 3 billion years, increasing in complexity, richness and diversity, and had survived 5 great extinctions. Its seas were teeming with life in huge quantities. The land areas were covered with huge forests filled with animals of all sizes, including some with quite large brains, the mammals.

Some of these were potentially intelligent, including one species, the humans, who lived in small bands that co-operated in obtaining food, creating shelter and caring for each other. To do this they developed quite sophisticated languages, including abstract ideas. They came to see themselves as an intimate part of the natural world around them and lived in a fair degree of harmony with it. At the time, there were several million humans, which was typical of the medium sized mammals they lived among.

Unfortunately, human languages and thinking were and have remained quite primitive. They never learned to check that they had understood each other, to recognise the limitations of their knowledge, or to check that their ideas were consistent with their experience, which, as we know, are the keys to a planetary-wide, self-aware culture.

As a result humans got caught up in lots of dysfunctional ideas. For example, different groups ended up killing each other in huge numbers, with increasingly sophisticated means of killing developing over time.

Shortly after our last visit, they began to cultivate their own plants and animals for food. The result was an exponential expansion of their numbers, until they now number 7 billion. Over time, they have cut down most of the forests and destroyed most of the habitats of the larger animals, replacing them with their own cultivated plants and animals. This has hugely reduced the resilience and stability of their biosphere.

The Earth is now in the midst of a 6th great extinction as a result. The seas are especially degraded. The fish that had been one of the human's major food sources are now so depleted that their current generation may be the last to eat wild fish.

Over the past few hundred years humans learned to burn the residues of ancient life that had been buried for several hundred million years. They have done this in such quantities that they are changing the composition of their atmosphere and destabilising the climatic conditions upon which they depend.

Since our last visit, humans have almost completely lost that early sense of connection with each other and the natural world.

One of the most dysfunctional ideas, that very few of them question, is the means by which they produce food and create artifacts which they then exchange and trade with each other. Their exchange system is structured so that groups large and small are working against each other, each for their own benefit instead of for mutual benefit, not realising that doing so is to the detriment of all.

Instead of optimising their exchange to provide for their wellbeing and that of the natural world around them, they try to optimise the flow of an abstract quantity they call 'money'. Money started as a means of exchange between people who did not trust each other, but has gradually taken on greater and greater significance, so that it, and not wellbeing, now determines what is done and who gets what.

One result of this is that most humans lead fairly impoverished lives, while a few live in material plenty. However, even those lead lives that are very poor in emotional stability, supportive relationships and security. The destruction of the natural world around them is another major consequence of this means of exchange, as they believe that a continuous growth of monetary transactions is the only way to improve their lives, which blinds them to the destruction they are causing.

What are their prospects? They do have some of the key ingredients of a planetary-wide culture: They have scientists that study the natural world and are coming to understand the problems they have created. Other groups provide assistance when disasters happen, often very distant from themselves. Growing numbers of them are becoming aware of how dysfunctional their culture has become and there are now tens of thousands of groups around the planet dedicated to social justice and preserving their environment. They have a global communication system that enables them all to be aware of each other, and could potentially be used to co-ordinate themselves harmoniously. There is a growing sense that they are all interconnected and interdependent.

Unfortunately, so many of them are so totally caught in the belief of the necessity of their current exchange system that it may be that only its collapse will enable a global collaborative society to emerge. That collapse looks highly likely and quite imminent, but there is no way of knowing if it will lead to an enlightened alternative, or even if it will be in time to avoid a much worse environmental collapse.

A Hypothetical Vision of What the Property Sector in the Future Might Look Like - Bonnie O. Wong

The mess with the global financial and property markets may have been fuelled by two misguided beliefs. One, that money is an end. And two, that property can reliably provide a continuing source of income and that it is an enduring asset that can be leveraged. The future requires redressing of these beliefs and a re-boot of the financial and property markets.

In the future, we remind ourselves that money is not an end, but rather a means to exchange, make, and do things. It is merely a common currency or a language with which we may estimate value, but by no means fully captures the feelings and outcomes associated with the things and experiences to which we try to ascribe a value.

But I turn your attention to property, which people have, through the centuries, often related to money, but also power and control of resources. Traditional economic models do not always hold true in the property market. Some property owners are willing to leave their properties empty and let them decay, rather than circumvent further losses by adjusting their asking prices downward in order to successfully sell or rent them. High demand for property has not led to increases of supply nor to failing prices. Perhaps it is because the supply of land and the supply of materials with which we may construct buildings on land – steel, concrete, silicon, clay bricks and mortar – are finite. However, we can adapt our attitudes and approaches, by re-using existing materials, using renewable building materials, or inventing new materials. More critically, property is static - higher demand in one location cannot simply be satisfied by supply located 50 miles away.

If we are to protect property, its future requires a shift in beliefs and assumptions from one of ownership to one of stewardship. We would no longer assert that property is a source of perpetually rising values and continuous income streams. Price speculation is replaced by compassion for other other people and understanding others' needs for adequate shelter and social connection. Unbridled development for the sake of private profits is replaced by the understanding that we are simply renters benefiting from a very, very long leasehold of planet Earth. We pay not even a peppercorn rent, yet we are costing the Earth.

The future I imagine is one where we may sensitively build on land to provide for others as well as ourselves. Property has value where people want to live, work, or play and in the future private property investors realise that there is social and environmental value to voluntarily transferring surplus land to sustainable community development and the construction and perpetuation of affordable housing, affordable workspace, and public green space. We will invest in property, not to get rich quick and become tycoons, but rather to support lives and livelihoods. In the future, we will be good stewards of property.

The Future is Here - Kenneth Lo

We are constantly traveling.

The twin miracles of communication and transportation have brought the world and all its enticing wonders – beautiful and profane – closer to our doorstep. So not surprisingly, we have wandered away.

As liberating as it may be, the persistent exposure to media leaves many of us increasingly "mediated." Something stands between us and the places we inhabit. The news and entertainment cycle offers a renewable source of distraction. Communities of like-minded souls are readily accessible to friend and follow. We know more about distant lands and tourist destinations, abetted by guidebooks and tour groups.

In the end, we are more and more connected to every place but *here*.

As Elizabeth Drew claimed, "Too often travel, instead of broadening the mind, merely lengthens the conversation."

A resilient future will involve both a broader perspective and a deeper engagement with own's one landscape – and a network of people living more integrally in places and ecological systems.

Places are part of ecology's "network of networks"

Nature does not fight for mindshare. There is nothing intrinsically newsworthy about millennia-old cycles and relationships of life. It holds little sway among cosmopolitan urbanites or wired cognoscenti. For all of the benefits of the city, urbanization and "nature deficit disorder" fosters a kind of anthropocentrism.

But humanity relies upon the gifts of nature for virtually everything – air, water, food, inspiration, and sustenance. We ignore nature at our peril, and as recent discussion about climate and biodiversity confirms, we have ignored it.

The social web has nothing on the web of life. Between the hydrological cycle, atmospheric and meteorological patterns, deep geophysical structures, flyways and migration pathways, places across and between continents are connected by nature.

With ecology the connectedness is far from virtual, yet our collective survival will demand inculcating a greater sense of ecological connectedness and interdependence among people living in local communities and between connected communities.

It will be an act of maturity and wisdom – or perhaps desperation – to bring nature back into focus.

Spatial mismatches and shifting baselines

Time and space have been obliterated by modernity. Across the planet, people are increasingly mobile. Urban and agricultural development dominate more of the landscape. But the world is not flat. It is not a *tabula rasa* for human activity.

The phrase "spatial mismatch" – which originally described the effect of economic restructuring on jobs and residences for low-income populations – now seems to describe a vast range of our growing challenges: mismatches between food and mouths, work and reward, resources and consumption, water and agriculture. In an era of climate change, spatial mismatch could also pertain to collapse of fine-tuned temporal relationships between co-evolved plants and migratory animals.

The future isn't what it used to be... The pace of change has intensified dramatically.

And the past, too, isn't what it used to be. Even more astounding than modern invention is how much each new generation will now forget. What we remember about the land and vanished species and what is defined as "natural" all undergo creeping changes. This loss of local memory about environmental conditions is termed "shifting baselines." Things lost do not seem lost, if they are never known.

A corollary for human communities is something psychiatrist Dr. Mindy Fullilove calls "root shock," applying a biological metaphor to the decimation of established human communities and psychological ties by urban renewal.

Oral history, culture, the conservative arc of wisdom have lost their foothold. Crowd-sourced wisdom can enhance but not replace wisdom rooted in place. Connectivity without a base is not deep knowledge, especially compared to some cultural traditions developed through deep understanding of local conditions.

Conservation is local and networked

Now that the Anthropocene era is upon us with a vengeance – and we're all a part of the push against the planet's boundaries (though some more than others) – what to do? There seems to be an endless parade of endangered species and environmental disasters – as we are informed frequently by the media.

Our footprint is everywhere. Speaking about mankind's irreversible relationship with rainforests, the eminent ecologist Daniel Janzen, declared, "It's all gardening now." And so it has become with most of the planet. Humanity's role has to become one of greater stewardship.

So where do we start?

You start with what you know, with where you are. Unfortunately, these two may not coincide. Many of us no longer have much of a relationship with the natural world around us.

Somewhat like politics, all successful conservation is local. A common refrain suggests that "we will only conserve what we love. We will only love what we understand. We will understand only what we are taught." (Baba Dioum)

The Children and Nature movement, citizen science, and service learning can help us to gain deeper understanding of our neighborhoods, gardens, watersheds, and landscapes. Anything that gets us out of enclosed and "climate controlled" spaces (and away from batteries) allows our senses to engage with the world.

We also need a network of local ecological histories, documenting baselines of places to provide context for future decision-making. It's all gardening now.

Geospatial thinking and place-based education

What reality is augmented by geolocation services and mobile devices? The current interest in geolocation offers an entry into landscape, but one mostly disconnected from the ecological world of soil and water and air. In fact, it most supports consumption of one sort or another.

The map – even if it was produced by Google – is not the territory. And "here" is not a lat-long coordinate. In the living world, there are no independent places. Each point is embedded within a vast "network of networks." Geophysical and biological forces ceaselessly shape the landscape.

Geospatial thinking and geodesign may help address problems of spatial mismatch and shifting baselines. Place-based education that reveals the depth of human history and ecological relations represented by any place also engages individuals in a connected fashion.

Time to come home

It's time to come home to our senses, to return from those liberating but prodigal journeys, an era of wandering. We will continue to visit, to share stories and collaborate, keep in touch with all the people and places we've encountered. But the future is not virtual, and virtual is not the future. Even when the mind has succumbed to the lure of elsewhere, the present – including its ecological and social woes – is created by actions in the flesh.

Similarly, "here" does not mean stasis, isolation or Luddism. Here is connected, and here is changing. A brighter future will be embodied in local awareness and action, informed by a broader understanding of that embedded here. This new worldview is consonant with developing a deeper wisdom.

Given the new realities, everyone has a role as a steward. Everyone is a gardener. This is something that cannot be outsourced.

Are we here yet?

There have been many inroads leading to a new, resilient approach – permaculture and "healing cities", Transition Towns and Bright Green Cities, and many others.

For some, the resurgence of focus on local food systems has reawakened wonder in the natural world. But that said, we will not all become agrarians or pastoralists. The embrace of place is not a return to provincialism or some nostalgic sense of the past, but the rise of a truly engaged, wise, connected citizenry concerned about future generations.

Disciplines that modern (American) society once cast aside – civics, geography – still deserve a place in our future. We are looking at a new civics for a new geography based on a new ecology. But at its root, the ecology has never changed.

The excursions of brilliant communities will continue to enrich the human experience, but the human relationship with local places may determine its future sustainability.

"The real voyage of discovery," as Marcel Proust suggested, "consists not in seeking new landscapes but in having new eyes."

Hacking Society and a Proposal for Beta Towns - Andy Broomfield

I've been spending time thinking about the current touch points within western democratic systems, these are the parts where we ordinary citizens (not politicians or those in power) interact with them. The most obvious is elections, whereby we go to the polls and choose a candidate on a ballot paper (or more if we are lucky / unlucky) who will then go forward to represent us. Then there are public services, our interactions with municipal government, right through to active participation in public duties such as jury service. How can these be twisted into serving different social purposes than those originally intended? What new outcomes can be built on top of these systems? How can they be made hackable? Where will the next generation of social hackers come from?

There have been interested attempts at hacking the electoral system, though some reach critical mass more than others in terms of public consciousness. MPs who would vote according to polls conducted by constituents, independent representatives' networks, tactical vote-swapping buddy sites. For some reason though, these never seem to take off. Jury Team, the anti-party party for example, failed to gain ground in the EU elections, and is now becoming more like a traditional party with set polices that must be agreed on in order to participate. It's a shame that public appetite still seems to be for choosing between established parties, and that calls for reform are based on which system is best for choosing from the same bunch of representatives. It's a shame as the area of design politics, currently based on old traditions and institutions is ripe for innovation.

We've seen new ideas, hacks of society. Online, the open data movement has been gathering, bringing with it greater transparency. Services like MySociety and other mashups have allowed new ways of interacting with government, outside of political space, on a local and hyper-local level, with differing levels of success in subverting and building on top of existing local norms and communities. Local currencies are encouraging trade, a social hack that works on top of Pound Sterling, but becomes localised in helping local traders. Local Exchange Trading Systems (LETS), have shown their success in allowing people to exchange their alternative worktime for alternative work, which also serves as a community building exercise - again a social hack that combines work, trading and community building. Empty shops projects provide an interesting parallel, re-using empty space on a temporary basis, they potentially change the construct and expectations of the larger space they occupy.

I think we need places to try out these new ideas, where social and governmental systems could be redesigned to be openly hackable. This is a proposal, an idea to have designated 'Beta Towns' whereby experiments, designed and organised by the residents themselves, could be run to test alternative ways of doing things. The designation would take place at the will of the residents themselves (a referendum) or it could be new towns, perhaps similar to how the Free State Project is gathering libertarians to move to New Hampshire. Perhaps it's not even designated towns, but patchworks of land designated as belonging to a 'Beta Town' and having that legal framework applied to it, similar to how the project Land works. This would allow neighbours to choose whether to stick with the 'Stable' branch of lawmaking, or move to the more dynamic, but risky 'Beta' model. It would also allow residents to 'fork' a Beta Town without having to up sticks.

How do Beta Towns work? I think they would take cues from the Cathedral and the Bizarre Free Software model. Changes to legal framework are considered on wikis, debate in mailing lists perhaps, either online or with live debates mixed in. As part of being a member of a Beta Town, each resident takes responsibility for leading a certain area of the town, and depending on the size there may be a 'Benevolent Dictator.' Court proceedings and other touch points in town processes would not just act as facilitating services, but also as a point of contact for bug reporting and adjudication, to ask what's the issue: the person or the code? Processes would be fast, even a small 'Alpha village' of no more than 30 people would try out nightly builds of legal code.

The open data movement has proven successful in prying open often closed systems. Other social hacks have brought forward ways of 'altering the way things are designed' . Beta Town is an idea for one way, a new set of hacks to bring forth a generation of 'Hackers of Society.'

The Age of Phlight - Lionel Wolberger

We live in the dawn of the **age of phlight**.

Phlight is flight, but spelled with a "ph." Why? Flight today means "fossil fuel" flight, hence the "f"; such airborne buses can only stay aloft with a constant roar of jet fuel through an engine. I am talking about phlight: renewable sun-powered flight, hence the "ph", standing for passive heliogenic flight.

A cloud weighs half a million kilograms yet is suspended in the air by sunlight alone. That is the emblem of phlight; if you will forgive the literary excess, let us say that the cloud phlies.

Flight - with a fossil fuel f - is done today not only by airplanes, helicopters and rocket ships, but also by hot air and weather balloons, dirigibles, blimps, zeppelins - why? All of these are dependent on fossil fuel powered engines. Even gliders are pulled by fossil-fuel powered vehicles. All of these fly and do not phly.

- Phlight - passive heliogenic phlight - is done today by kites, passive solar-powered balloons, Tomas Saraceno's Museo Aero Solar and his flying gardens. There are also promising experimental solar collectors and kite-like wind generators, but progress is slow.

We envision a day when people sleep, work and phly daily along internationally accepted phlight paths. The slow progress towards phlight is due to the significant challenges that phlight poses. Understanding the challenges is a necessary first step towards finding solutions. The challenges are technological and social.

Phlight requires **technological advances** in

- materials: ultra-light materials like Aerogel to build any rigid structures needed;
- fabrics: ultra-thin textiles that can sequester sun radiation, retain hot air or release it as needed. Perhaps buckypaper can help.

- suits: the original B-17 passengers wore heated flying suits with oxygen masks to protect them from the -45 degree Celsius cold. We need new such suits for our phliers, perhaps based on mountaineering and arctic gear.
- kitchen and toilet: ultra-efficient food preparation and waste evacuation facilities are needed as every gram counts;
- GIS: multidimensional maps of the atmosphere are needed; Google Earth-type GIS is a good first step, but that is only the surface of the earth; we need to innovate new methods to map the flows of air that have both depth and breadth.
- escape devices: a safety vest is needed for people in phlight, perhaps gas-ejected parachutes.

Phlight requires **social and political advances** in

- path clearing: we need to clear passive phlight paths in the atmosphere, using methods such as those used by Appalachian Trail and bike path activists; these paths require clear political border rights and air rights of passage, keeping in mind the passive and hence less-controlled nature of phlight.
- flags of convenience: just like the law of the sea has a jurisdictional limit of 12 miles, the atmosphere should have a similar limit; but airsteaders, homesteading in the air, may fly flags of convenience to broker their encounters with land;
- ports of call: Phlight ports need to be created, with a clear idea of what supplies and services are needed at such a port.
- motivation: Flight is marked by drama: the rush of speed, the loud noise, the tremendous power, the vicarious thrill of seeing death-defying stunts, the frisson of pilots in military-style dress and stewardesses in short dresses. Phlight is very different: it is a contemplative pleasure like gardening, a union with nature like sailing. (On a hormonal level, flight elicits fight-or-flight adrenaline responses; phlight elicits oxytocin-type responses of endurance, closeness and bonding).

The ocean was first traveled in passive heliogenic sea craft. The earliest seamen innovated a tremendous range of technologies that benefited all humankind, such as star navigation and tension-based sail structures. They must have been crazy, taking to sea on little more than a song and a hope; yet they discovered and populated the world. Today's seasteaders take up their call, and continue to harness the freedom of the sea as a source of social and governmental innovation.

Air travel developed in reverse: first came fossil and carbon-fueled flight (even the first hot air balloons were heated by wood burning). Phlight had to await the high-tech fabrics and portable oxygen needed to enable a human to live in the oxygen-deprived, cold atmosphere. But today events pressure us to take to the skies. Overpopulation and ecological stress motivate humanity to leave the ground and take to the air.

The first phlying pioneers need to be extremely motivated people, just like the first seaman, and the first pilots. Until these people show up we can plant phlying gardens. We can hoist an atmonaut into a phlying meditation space tethered to the ground. Perhaps an X-prize can go to the first atmonaut to stay aloft for a month, or a year, in phlight. We can begin to request phlight paths from the owners of the jumbo jet superhighways, and we begin to collect the GIS data to comprehend atmospheric flows. The Graf zeppelin flew over a million and a half kilometers, including a trip around the world, but was retired as it was too slow (90 km/h) and too dangerous (flammable hydrogen). Who will duplicate that record, but by dwelling and not touring, by airsteading and not transporting? Living in the rarified cold on solar powered air–with no need for such fine steering control, nor tables with linen table cloths.

Phlight is a critical step towards easing our planet's burdens. Once achieved, we can begin tearing up concrete and liberate the world-around layer of soil from its asphalt prison, leaving it to do what it does best: make food and support the biosphere. We can achieve humanity's original dream of taking to the skies, not on the back of a roaring engine, but on the caress of a cloud.

Designing the Future - David Braden

We are, already, engaged in a single pattern of flows. We are affected by any change to the flows because one thing is related to another and everything is related to everything else. Therefore, every problem we face is also related to every other problem we face and we cannot fix them one at a time. When we try to control for any one variable, all the other variables adjust according to their own internal mechanisms.

We humans are rightly proud of our science and technology but now run up against the cold hard facts that all choices have consequences for which we cannot control. Unless we calculate for the impact throughout the entire pattern of flows there will be unintended consequences. That fact requires us to begin thinking in terms of how the parts fit together, how things work together. Knowing that we cannot control all the consequences, we can still seek to understand the synergies and symbioses inherent in the system. We cannot control the system but we can place elements in proximity and influence inherent synergies.

Fortunately for us, the system is fractal. Patterns of flows repeat themselves at all levels of the system. That means that we can design at the local level –

and think in terms of millions of different experiments – in millions of different localities – all looking for better ways to arrange the flows so that they work better for more people, plants and creatures. We do not, and cannot, improve the flows from the top down because the flows are generated at the level of the individual interaction – and we already discussed how we cannot control for all the variables.

This is a different way of looking at the problems of the world. We are used to looking for someone or something to be "responsible" for the problem. The truth is that the world we have is the cumulative result of all the choices each of us makes – so, in that sense, we have the world we have chosen. The exciting part is, we also have the power to design a different future[155].

Collaboration for Introverts or, How to Make Friends and Tolerate People - Steve Wheeler and Alex Fradera

chat session open

Ian: Hello.
Ekow: Hiya! Ian, you've been contributing great stuff on the forum for a while. I think you should come to our next meeting - we're getting together to make some real changes happen! Exciting, huh?
I: I guess.
E: You guess?
I: I'm not big on meetings. I find them pretty uncomfortable and I never get the chance to say what I want to.
E: I know what you mean. Some people - "extroverts", I guess - really enjoy this stuff, but for others it's a hassle, an ordeal even! That's a problem, though: introverts have a different way of looking at things. Without them, our meetings lose out.
I: Honestly? These problems are so complicated I'm doubtful large face-to-face meetings can get to grips with them.
E: It can be easier to explain what you think online. But things get done in the meetings that never make it to the forum. Plus, real world meetings are a lot more likely to lead to real world actions.
I: In theory, I agree. But I've found these things attract - and are dominated by - extroverted people who enjoy meetings whether or not anything gets done. I get enough of that at work...
E: It's a vicious cycle, isn't it? I worry that we've edged towards apartheid,

with introverted thinkers inhabiting the abstracted spaces and extroverts dominating the actively social ones. One issue is that most extroverts don't really understand that introverts have a different style of thinking and interacting. They think they are just uninterested or have nothing to say.

I: Let's say I'm convinced: how can I participate without feeling constantly uncomfortable or pretending to be someone I'm not?

E: OK. 1) Educate people that different styles of thinking and communication exist.

2) Design meetings to reflect that reality. Starting meetings with the usual warm-up / familiarisation exercises, for example, can help social flow, but risks freezing introverts out from the off. There are more inclusive ways to do it, though.

I: I'd also want some structure in the discussion so that people like me have a chance of being heard. Extroverts often try to jettison structure in the interests of "spontaneity" and "informality" - they may be comfortable with that, but others are not.

E: Agreed. There are good reasons to preserve space for spontaneity, but some structure can even out participation and encourage deeper engagement. We're still stuck in outmoded models of what a "meeting" should be like, but there are many different techniques and practices - consensus decision making, group facilitation - that have blossomed since the 1960s. We need to make use of them.

I: Also, introverts aren't always going to say everything they want to at the time. Sometimes the best thoughts occur after a meeting.

E: So we should have a system in place so people can follow-up on issues?

I: Yes, and we should think more about using technology to make collaboration easier - document collaboration and emergent discussion platforms; Junto, PiratePad, Google Docs. You know, I'm feeling more positive about this already! I don't know if I'm ever going to learn to love meetings but it means a lot just to know my position - and, I'm sure, that of a whole hidden iceberg of people - is acknowledged.

E: And I'll share that there's a personal dimension to all this as well; we need to accommodate people's different needs and styles of collaboration, but we also need to acknowledge that we might have been conditioned away from successful face-to-face collaboration by our upbringing, education or employment. Sometimes we need to acknowledge our resistance but do it anyway; the first time I turned up to a meeting I felt such a sense of relief - I guess I hadn't realised quite how alienated and afraid I had become, just talking about these issues through a computer screen. But when I met with live human beings and realised there were the rudiments of a genuine community there, my outlook on the whole issue was changed.

I: So you're saying that the actual process of learning to engage and organise

socially can help bring about personal as well as political change?
E: I don't think the two are separate. I think if we had a population of people capable of open, human, constructive interaction, we would already have achieved the Future We Deserve. There is no more important work for us right now than re-establishing human connection and learning to work together.
I: Wow.
E: So see you Friday?
I: I guess.
E: Shut up.
I: Joking. I'll be there. :)

chat session closed

Hundreds of Sovereign Singapores - Jon Southurst

Goodbye nation-states, hello city-states

Ever bigger cities, seeing themselves as culturally unique and more ideologically nimble than the nation-states they belong to, begin to detach themselves and declare independence. New cities will be founded and managed with specific rules for specific purposes[156] such as commerce, technology incubation, manufacturing development. Others will have nothing to do with economics and everything to do with protecting cultural traditions, all creating a cross between global freedom of choice and gated communities.

Ideally, each city would be open to anyone willing and able to make a contribution and individuals would be able to prosper in a political and cultural setting best suited to their own mindset (under conditions determined by each one). Future independent geopolitical divisions will be based on similarity of ideas rather than ethnicity or place of origin. With atomized regions each mastering their own speciality and individuals free to prosper in a chosen setting, quality of human ideas and product would flourish.

According to a Gallup survey[157], the populations of Singapore and New Zealand would double if people had the freedom to emigrate anywhere in the world, while other countries' (Zimbabwe, Sierra Leone) would halve and others would alter radically (Switzerland). Sovereign city-states merely reflect the desire of humans to pursue their lives and ambitions in appropriate places, while the current situation demonstrates their lack of freedom to do so.

This is neither a radical nor even original idea, and has been common in various places and at various times throughout history. Ancient Sparta, Athens and Mesopotamia were sovereign, as were medieval Venice and Florence.

The city of Lubek[158], part of the Hanseatic League of the Holy Roman Empire, was independent until the late 19th century and there have been a smattering of geopolitical anomalies ever since, from Tangiers and Jerusalem to West Berlin. Modern-day examples are Singapore, Hong Kong, even Vatican City and Monaco. Regardless of opinions about the governance or cultures of these places, each has been undoubtedly fascinating and has punched above its weight in world attention.

Some argue the world's future is becoming more united, more standardized and homogenous. Technological advances dictate communications will remain open and standards of commerce and interaction will remain between city-states. But just as the internet has opened minds and broadened knowledge of the world's different cultures, it has also compartmentalized and narrowed focus of interest, bringing together people with shared ideas from widespread areas while highlighting differences with people nearby (eg: you have a best friend you've never met in person, but you don't have anything in common with the guy next door). City-states will be a physical manifestation of this phenomenon.

Of course, this future won't always be pretty. Ideological experiments often go wrong. Many city-states, rather than being shining temples to individualism and freedom, will be virtual prisons of their maltreated inhabitants as some nations[159] are today. Some will exploit desperate minorities[160] for the benefit of their elites. Many will seem like dystopias with cultural practices repugnant to outsiders[161]. And while cities are powerful incubators of ideas and commerce, by themselves they are poor providers of food, water[162], materials and garbage disposal. There will be tension between city representatives and advocates of farmers and other rural dwellers in the surrounding lands, who won't be going anywhere. Conflicts, sometimes violent, will still occur but will be localized and contained, unlike the Total War scenarios of the 20th century.

Eventually the temptation to unite, expand and dominate might see city-states absorbed into new entities resembling today's countries. The drive to link and separate may be part of a larger cycle with cultures alternating between the two. But the world will always decide what it prefers through trial and error, and future city-states promise to bring much of both.

Working Together: Unleashing Collective Intelligence - Fabio Barone

"The significant problems we face cannot be solved at the same level of thinking we were at when we created them"

~ Albert Einstein

Maybe we should not talk about 'economy' any longer. A term about specialization, competition, profit. Every time we try to squeeze new concepts into this mindset we fail.

We are witnessing something unprecedented. We are observing how people are taking initiatives and creating the world they want to see. We are seeing how the Internet allows us to connect peers and empower individuals. We want to co-create, to engage with people and projects no matter where they are, we are drawn to collaborate, co-design, form communities, and imbue our actions with meaning and values. Are we headed towards a global collective intelligence, coagulating our endeavours to form one single big organization, with the Internet being something like the nervous system?

Maybe we are. We have got the tools, it's time to connect the pieces together. Suresh Fernando stepped up to the crowds and said "let's work as ecosystems". Isn't this beautiful? Ecosystems thrive on diverse webs of relationships by exchanging nutrients. The emergent pattern of a new paradigm for how we interact, facilitated by the Internet? We could all see ourselves as seeds of a thriving ecosystem. Could we imagine fermenting projects which could start creating the relationships for the ecosystem to unfold?

I believe there's plenty of nutrients at our fingertips, which can be used to form new relationships. Start working with what we have, and evolve from there. Make connections with those to whom we have affinity. I believe this approach provides the right context for emergence to happen. A cell in my finger does not need to be directly related to one in my toe, nevertheless their functions allow my body to work as a whole. As caretakers of this ecosystem we learn to take stewardship of our communities, our assets, our planet.

Key will be infrastructure which can connect people who want to work together. Tools that make it easy for groups to self-organize, to exchange, create content and work items, and get things done. Arrangements that provide the legal frameworks for people to come and work together, no matter where they live, assisted by open capital allocation agreements. Transcend what we used to see as an enterprise or an organization. If these tools are set up in true P2P manner, then nobody can stop this wave. No governmental or multinational entity can step in and impose their interests.

Any individual can then become a contributor to such an enterprise - or any, really. And within this enterprise, democratic structures and decision making processes allow members to define the value they want to create. Thus, investors, contributors, mentors, etc. all share the same value base; profit ceases to be the measuring stick for success or motivation. Communities arise around shared values.

If we combine such infrastructure with open source principles, we have immense power at our hands. We could think of 'centers of excellence', offering everything needed to disseminate knowledge about renewable energies, clean technology, organic agriculture, permaculture – you name it. If this knowledge is freely accessible, distributable, and replicable, local and cultural adaptations to technologies become possible. Open hardware and distributed manufacturing could join in being providers of toolboxes for resilient, thriving communities – what Wael Al Saad calls 'holistic eco-villages', decentralized connected entities embedded in their natural environment and using locally available resources. Elements to help leapfrogging traditional environments into sustainable, interconnected nodes. Likewise sources of inspiration and know-how for people transitioning from oversized ecological footprints to healthy relationships with our environment.

As the "Coalition of the Willing" movie postulates, we could also think of "Open Innovation Centers", in which people come together to design collaboratively and create value. We just need to create the environments for people to talk and work together. What would we be able to come up with?

Clash for Civilization - Arthur Doohan

The coming clash will not be between Muslim and Christian nor between East and West nor between rich and poor.

There are tensions between all of these 'camps', for sure.

The poor have nothing to fight us with and so there can be no 'clash' with them. I believe, however, that the 'San Bushmen and the Yanomani and the Aboriginals will be on the planet long after the last trader's screen blinks off on Wall St.

The East sees little reason to change its growth plans as they have not caused the existing atmospheric carbon increases. The West is being miserly in its offering of technology and resources that might help the East avoid the worst of the West's environmental excesses. I expect, however, that as the catastrophe unfolds both sides will be driven into each others' arms as the real 'globalisation' emerges.

The tension between Islam and the Christians is a proxy for the economic and political serfdom that the "Ummah" has suffered at the hands of the British and then American empires since the collapse of the Ottoman empire. The resentment of, and terrorism against, the 'infidel' comes from those states where the populace has been denied political expression and economic development by puppet regimes of the 'West', which has at the same time looted those countries of their natural resource (crude oil). For proof, compare the peoples of Turkey and Saudi Arabia. There were no Turks on the 9/11 planes and there are none fighting in Iraq or Afghanistan.

So, the conflict between Islam and Christianity is in reality the same as the Northern Irish conflict between Protestant and Catholic; a proxy for a historic battle for economic resources.

So, in the coming struggle, who will be doing the fighting?

The conflict, I expect, will be between the enlightened and the ignorant.

Fear, uncertainty and doubt will be wielded as weapons by demagogues, cynics and the vocal ignorant promoting simple solutions against the complex analysis offered by the reasoned, the reasonable and the eloquent as defenders of truth, hope and knowing.

Ignorance and false knowledge (such as theology) are being used to pervert the minds and recruit the bodies of the gullible, the ignorant and the desperate in every corner of the planet.

For each madrassa in Pakistan, there is a creationist college in the US. For each witchdoctor in the Congo, there is a neofascist skinhead in Moscow. For every bureaucrat, there is a copyright lawyer.

But these are not in opposition to each other. They are united in their opposition to those who believe in tolerance, openness and freedom.

For every Buffet and Jobs there will be an Ellison and a Murdoch. For each Mandela there will be a Putin. For every Dawkins there will be a Limbaugh. For each Obama there will be a Mugabe. For every Pelosi there will be a Palin.

The 'Dark Ages' did not lack for daylight. They lacked knowledge and the means to transmit knowledge. But the greatest impediment to progress were elites who fought to keep knowledge and enlightenment out of the hands of the people in order to keep power and wealth under their control.

Seawater into Food - Thomas Bjelkeman

Did you know that the global population grows by 75 million people every year? This means that we will most likely go from 6.8 billion [1] people today to 9 billion by 2040 [2]. In turn, this means that we may have to double our food production by 2050 [3], maybe more.

This is a problem. Our agriculture already uses 70% of all the available fresh water resources in the world and this goes up to 80% where the population growth is happening, i.e in the non-industrialized countries [4]. In other words, it isn't obvious where we would find enough fresh water to double the agricultural output.

On top of the population growth we have: increased meat and dairy consumption, huge pollution problems from fertilizer and pesticide use, looming fossil fuel peaks – oil and coal is used to power the "green revolution" – competing biofuel production, desertification and climate change knocking on our door. The list goes on [5] (if you just visit one link, make it this one[163]). All things which point to lower future food production, not higher.

Now what?

There isn't one solution to our problems, but the Seawater Greenhouse[164] may well be one of the most important innovations in agriculture in the last couple of decades. How does the following sound?

> Grow food on otherwise unproductive land (read cheap), using only seawater, sunshine and nutrients as inputs.

So here is the deal: You need to find an arid location with access to seawater (or saline groundwater), think northern Africa, Namibia, Arab Peninsula, Mexico, California, Australia, Canary Islands, Chile and lots of other places. Find a place which is not too high above sea level to avoid pumping costs, where you can build your Seawater Greenhouse. The process in the greenhouse uses seawater to cool the greenhouse extremely energy efficiently using solar panels and cardboard evaporators, and creates a cool, humid environment – which the crop loves. Then the greenhouse takes the humidity out of the air with inexpensive plastic condensers and creates enough distilled water to grow your crops. The result is a greenhouse which allows you to grow any crop you like, including strawberries <grin>, in the dessert. The stable greenhouse climate will probably also make it easier to use biological control to deal with pests and diseases [6].

So no use of fresh water, no fossil fuel, no (or less) pesticides, on otherwise completely unproductive land. This may well be the least environmentally damaging technology for agriculture we will have for the foreseeable future, which can scale massively.

Simply beautiful.

So what does the future look like?

The first commercial implementation is in progress in southern Australia[165] as I write this.

The Sahara Forest Project[166] is looking towards large scale implementation of this in desert locations combined with concentrated solar power to bring food, energy and water from the desert.

In the future we can imagine building the greenhouse structure out of bamboo and having chicken and tilapia farms in combination with the greenhouse. Think: vegetable waste feeds chickens, the chickens' waste feeds the duckweed in the ponds, the remaining vegetable waste becomes compost, the compost feeds worms, the worms and duckweed feed tilapia fish.

Footnotes

[1] U.S. Census Bureau, the total population of the World, projected to 06/30/10 at 20:54 UTC (EST+5) is 6,852,992,514, U.S. Census Bureau, < http://www.census.gov/ipc/www/popclockworld.html[167] > retrieved on 30 June 2010.

[2] World Population,: 1950-2050, US Census Bureau, < http://www.census.gov/ipc/www/idb/worldpopgraph.html[168] > retrieved on 30 June 2010.

[3] World must double food production by 2050: FAO chief, World Food Programme, < http://www.wfp.org/content/world-must-double-food-production-2050-fao-chief[169] >, retrieved on 30 June 2010.

[4] The United Nations World Water Development Report, World Water Assessment Programme, < http://unesdoc.unesco.org/images/0012/001295/129556e.pdf[170] >, retrieved on 30 June 2010.

[5] Big Question: Feast or Famine? University of Minnesota, < http://www.youtube.com/watch?v=F1IWkbU0SG4[163] >, retrieved on 2 January 2012.

[6] Desert makes seawater into freshwater (Woestijnkas maakt zout water zoet), EkoZine, Professor Joop van Lenteren, Wageningen University < http://www.ekozine.nl/load.php?naam=wie_wat_waar/wie_wat_waar.htm[171] >, retrieved on 30 June 2010.

Disclosure: I work with Seawater Greenhouse Ltd. to bring desert grown food to your table.

Collapsarithmetic - Chris Malins

The exponential function is one of the basic building blocks of modern mathematics. In principle to understand it requires only the most basic arithmetic – if something is exponentially growing in time, it increases by a set factor every year. Tale a simple example – a species of bacteria that reproduces so that, unrestrained, its numbers double every minute. This is an exponentially growing population.

Imagine that one of these bacteria is in a bottle at 11pm, and that at midnight the bottle will be full. Now the question – when will the bottle be half full? The answer is simple – at one minute to midnight. For all of its existence up to 11.59, the bacterial colony has had more than half of its available resource (space) left. Only as one minute to midnight passes does it start to become clear how close to exhausting this resource the colony really is.

Consider now people. We are different to bacteria, insofar as many of us allegedly understand the exponential function. But there seems to be a disconnect between this knowledge that it exists, and achieving an intuition for what it means. I say this, because anything growing by the same percentage, year on year, will double over some period. Imagine that energy use were growing at a steady 7% per annum. In ten years, we would double our demand. And in each subsequent ten year period, we would use *more energy than had been used in the entirety of human history*. For 2% growth, the doubling period would be 35 years.

Exponential growth is intrinsically unsustainable. It is inconceivable that any real resource would be available in enough quantity to sustain even 2% growth indefinitely. Take the wind – plenty of that, you might think? If energy use grew 2% annually from now, in less than 100 years we would need to harness every breath of wind in the Earth's atmosphere to keep us powered. A handful of years later, we would be using as much energy as absorbed by all the plants on Earth.

What about better technology? Plants and wind are just inefficient ways to harvest solar power. Well, if we could harvest every bit of solar energy that fell on the Earth's surface, we could keep going a little longer. If we covered the entire planet, land and sea, with 100% efficient solar cells, we could meet our requirement for maybe 500 years. That is to say, in a time comparable to the duration of the Roman Empire, we would have gone from the industrial revolution to using 100% of all solar energy reaching the planet.

If we were using nuclear power instead of solar, we'd never reach this point – in less than 300 years we'd be releasing so much energy we'd be causing global warming *without needing the greenhouse effect*. In 500 years the average summer daytime temperature would be tending towards boiling point. Clearly these scenarios cannot happen – natural limitations will kick in first. And that is the point – the social philosophy of growth, the idea that sustained 3% GDP growth (or growth in the use of any resource) could continue is absurd - economies built on this premise must fail. Nevertheless, this arithmetically ill-informed expectation is dominant – we rely on constant growth to afford services, pay pensions, stave off unemployment and so on.

We need to get growth under control – population growth, energy growth, fertiliser use growth, water use growth. And we need an economy where no growth is ok, where zero annual GDP growth doesn't mean a collapse in the standard of living. Any other long-term economic vision is absurd – because it's past one minute to midnight, and I think I'm getting uncomfortably close to the top of the bottle.

Our Future and the Sun - Vinay Gupta

Something new is happening in the world of solar panels. Last time I counted, there were 16 companies with four or five distinct technologies promising solar cheaper than coal. A real diversity of approaches; goop sprayed on plastic, wires printed on metal, yard-wide inflatable bubble-mirrors. The front runners, NanoSolar and Konarka have hundreds of millions of dollars of smart Silicon Valley money and are poaching manufacturing talent from places like IBM. They are cheap, too, these new panels. No retail yet, but manufacturing costs are estimated at 1/6 to 1/20 of conventional solar costs.

You know what that means? If this is for real - and we will find out very soon, within 5 years - energy will become as cheap as information. Enough solar panels to power an ordinary house for 20 years will cost $500. This is the tech fix so often dismissed in the literature, but it is physically possible. The energy from the sun is there, and building a better machine to scoop it up is a technical problem, not a metaphysical one. If it has been discovered by NanoSolar or Konarka, what then?

Cheap energy and cheap information. A world covered in wireless data networks and littered with solar collectors hoovering up the energy of the sun to run the machines and everything else. Energy so cheap that pulling the carbon back out of the atmosphere becomes economic. Praise be to the Sun Absolute! Is this paradise?

Well, no. Cheap electrical power and ubiquitous data networks may accelerate rather than halt loss of the biome, as clean green logging operations down the forests with solar-powered chainsaws. Water is still an issue in many places.

But cheap solar power may well break the back of some of the fundamental problems of the human race as surely as smallpox vaccination did. Violence over energy and over many forms of poverty may stop as cheap power turns into cheap tools to improve farming or process crops.

The coal will slumber in the ground. The reactors will be decommissioned. The patents will expire and then the solar materials will become as cheap as physics and chemistry allow, as cheap as tarpaulins, as cheap as cardboard, as cheap as bamboo mats. People who do not know arithmetic will carry solar blankets to charge the phone-computers that connect them to global culture, or their own past, as they choose.

This world is not only possible, but, given the thousands of gigawatts pouring from the sky, with only a very minor interruption in human foolishness, it is inevitable. Once you get to silicon chips, the step to solar panels comes. Once you get to solar panels, if you stop investing in the technologies which generate power by destroying the climate, cheap solar panels come. Once you have cheap solar panels, the age of carbon becomes a bad dream.

We can wake up from the age of carbon into the age of the Sun. We are doing it in this very generation. Praise be to the Sun Absolute!

Bootleg Oil - Al Razi Masri

After reading a blog post by Noah Raford[172] I was awakened to the fact that visions of the future are typically commissioned by the wealthy and as such are horrendously narrow in their vision. How will the the glittery sustainable technology we all wish for change the world?

The shift towards a near zero crude oil society in rich countries will probably occur as a reaction to oil prices. This rise in oil price could come from either legal frameworks such as a tax, or it could be a physical constraint brought on by the depletion of the convenient oil sources. Time and money from the state and corporate bodies will be invested in vast amounts to refine low oil technologies to a viable state, reshape the country infrastructure to be compatible with these technologies, and advance new societal norms that are in harmony with the behavioural demands of the new infrastructure. Much of these new powerful technologies will be held under patents licenced at prices that are based on models trying to emulate the returns of the good old days of oil.

On the other end there are the poor countries with oil based infrastructure. Running up to this point their economy will be crippled by having to pay high oil prices. They do not have the money to invest in a low oil infrastructure. Following this there may be a short period of cheaper oil due to low demands.

The sharp drop in oil demand combined with the high production price will mean the existing oil producing countries and companies' existing practices will have to drastically change or end entirely. In the end the oil production industry will drastically shrink and supply to demand will return to recognisable levels. Some companies will die. Others will attempt to become industry leaders in green technology.

What happens to the old oil production and delivery facilities and infrastructure? Offshore oil rigs, tankers, pipelines? As the old companies file for bankruptcy, downscale or re-focus these facilities will fall out of use. The smaller size of the industry means that there will not be a significant market in the resale of equipment. The cost involved in scrapping decommissioned facilities and equipment would probably see many sights abandoned but still capable of operation.

It is not too far fetched to imagine the organisations that operate in blackmarket goods would now take advantage of these still facilities to create a blackmarket for oil. Somali Pirates, the FARC and unscrupulous chinese companies bringing drilling sites back into operation. They are able to operate here because of the lower regard for regulations, overhead and labour costs that make such ventures unprofitable in legal circumstances.

Poor countries will be unable to immediately make the transition to low oil technologies. Corruption and the high prices associated with legal oil and the patented green technologies will mean many governments will resort to questionable oil supplies. This maintains a healthy blackmarket oil supply that will last for a long time. It will still always be a small fraction of the previous global oil consumption and may result in a second peak oil cycle brought on by failing equipment and growing attempts of government crackdowns.

These new oil wars will replace the horrors associated with national military and private military professional conflicts with the horrors of the resource wars seen around African minerals. Rival groups of informal fighters, child soldiers and associated atrocities.

Time For Resilient Tribes to Step Up and Show the Way - Kuldeep Brar

As a planet our levels of happiness haven't really changed in the last 100 years. However, our levels of stress, anxiety and depression have never been higher and are rising. The US predicts that by 2020, stress related anxiety disorders will be the largest disability impacting wellbeing and economic output after coronary heart disease, which is also related to anxiety[1].

There's clearly a lot 'wrong' with how we're functioning as individuals. However, as a species we clearly have the capacity to be happy and live fulfilling lives[2]. We must capitalise on what makes us flourish if we're to shift the tide in that direction.

There is a wealth of research and evidence looking into the science behind what's 'right' about individuals and society. The field of Positive Psychology has paved the way for new thinking on Learned Optimism in place of Learned Hopelessness, Resilience in place of Despair and a focus on Strengths in place of Weakness. The findings demonstrate that a significant percentage of our happiness is within our personal control[3].

In the 'Pursuit of Happiness' spirit of Aristotle and Thomas Jefferson, work on strength-based empowerment has lead to lasting results when it comes to happiness and the ability of individuals to lead truly meaningful lives. Eudemonia or 'the Good Life' is at last within our grasp.

For me the work on Positive Psychology parallels business thinking that we've known for some time and is long overdue. Put simply:

People flourish when they focus on their 'Core Strengths' (Positive Psychology)

Businesses flourish when they focus on their 'Core Competence' (Corporate Strategy)

The applied use of Positive Psychology frameworks does indeed provide an opportunity to change the tide of emotional malaise. But to achieve the future we want we need to go further. Building Optimism, Resilience and Strength at an individual level is not enough. We need to amplify the power of these capabilities to change the way we connect with our 'Tribes' on a societal level.

To use a business context once more, the formal rigid landscape of corporate mergers and acquisitions has dramatically shifted over the last 5 years. Companies traditionally undertake huge amounts of due diligence to mitigate risk before choosing to invest huge amounts into strategically appropriate partners. This would be followed by major reconstruction in post-merger cost-cutting to create a new entity that would be a pared down version of the original parents.

Whilst M&A activity still occurs, a new model has evolved: that of temporary collaborative open source partnering. Organisations still seek other market players to achieve their strategic aims, but now in areas of specific expertise and skill. The engagement and commitment is focused on building informal structures where companies work to combine specific strengths to create more powerful commercial propositions than they could have on their own.

Similarly Positive Psychology can help individuals use their strengths and core character to engage with others on a more effective level. But rather than focus on rigid structures of complement or compromise, there is an opportunity for individuals to strategically use their strengths in social tribes which come together for specific goals. These tribes could act as powerful change agents by forming, collaborating and then dispersing on the basis of strengths required to respond to a social need.

The central role of big government and organisations and any giant hierarchical structure providing the leadership needed to shape change has expired. It's time for strength-based tribes to provide the real life equivalent of Web 2.0 thinking and come together to respond to and lead change. To get the Future we Deserve it's the Tribes that will need to create and drive the conditions for change that will take us forward.

References:

- [1] World Health Organisation: http://www.who.int/mental_health/management/depression/definition/en/
- [2] Seligman, M. E. P. (2006) Learned Optimism: How to Change Your Mind and Your Life. Vintage Books
- [3] Wikipedia: http://en.wikipedia.org/wiki/Positive_psychology

The Music We Deserve - Allen Wentz

The invention and proliferation of the music synthesizer (thank you Dr. Robert Moog and others) changed my life in a very profoundly futuristic manner. I was an early adopter of the instrument. In fact I was on board so early that I only knew one other person who owned one before me! I scraped and saved to get one, as they were expensive and I was very young, and the only way to hear them was via the few ground-breaking record albums of the day. After I finally got my first synth, I would play for days in happy solitude, creating new, never heard before sounds and arranging them into something that was hopefully, audibly palatable. Instead of a string, "skin", reed or metal tubing, I could fashion new sound sources using pure electricity! The excitement of literally tapping into pure voltage to create sound was just so thrilling. This was literally the sound of the universe. Oscillators vibrating at Quark speed. Filters shaping the tone, and Envelope Generators providing complete control over the time domain of each sonic event. Not to mention the modulation capabilities of Sample & Hold circuits, LFOs and various other voltage processors. I mean, that terminology even sounds cool, does it not?

My "dream gig"? It was to be playing in the lounge of the moon shuttle! Looking out at the cosmos, while my sequencers chugged along underneath melodic waveforms of varying shapes and amplitude. But of course NASA decided man's natural, unending quest for discovery of new worlds should be shelved in favor of payload carrying space busses. But I digress..

So you see, I'm a musician who assumed 40 years ago that by the end of the century, at the latest, we would all be listening to this amazing, "non-traditional", futuristic electronic music due to affordable, available new instrument technology. Instead we merely got more of the same, just augmented with "funny sounds", although there has been some amazing music produced in that genre. And to be fair, there are always people pushing the boundaries of what any art form can be.

So as I end my sixth decade on this lovely water world, the future has always been a bit of an oxymoronic concept for me. An avid sci-fi reader when younger, those stories seemed almost mythological, as many were so prescient in their narrative and then voila.. came to be. For better or worse. Be it Verne's TV, or Orwell's Double-Speak. (Can you say "Net-Neutrality"?) Magical, yet "biblical" in the same breath. Exciting and full of optimism, yet simultaneously dangerous and hopeless. Forward & backward at the same time! So, since we are always living in the future, do we deserve what we have now?

At least in music, and the other fine arts as well, the future has always been with us. And modern musical composition gets plenty of mileage out of "traditional" musical instrumentation. Stravinsky, Copeland, Coltrane, Stockhausen, Davis, Zappa, Cage, and many other true pioneers have written music that will not be fully understood for possibly decades to come. And like good-quality, nutritious food, we do deserve it.

All the World's a Stage - Alex Fradera

In the beginning, there are no stages. In families and tribes, we express ourselves together through movement, song and story. There is no division between artist and audience and filling leisure time is a major occupation of each day.

Things change.

Now, division of labour generates an artist caste, of storytellers, poets, painters, minstrels. Still, you are likely to meet these people, to share directly in experiences. And more, you come together with your family, your village, to sing, to weave, share tales, for dances, raucous festivities. Art happens 'in the world' much more than on a stage.

Further change.

To music. Recorded, now a product, distributed - not shared - by brokers. Controlling who is heard, it suits them to limit this number: suits their channels to market, suits their advertising strategies. A form of mass culture develops to seize territory from both exploratory truth-seekers and deeply embedded folk practises. Art happens on a stage, and 'production values' mediate what we even see as proper entertainment, proper culture.

A horizon rises into view: one where the artist slot is now stuffed with pre-designed brands, assembled by an owner class to prevent genuine autonomy and expression, to deny economic independence. Corrosive systems, from ossified IP law to energy-hungry infrastructure, tend the fires. The stage itself is hollowed out, even as we stand clamouring for it to deliver to us.

To visual art, a similar story. To fiction, to all. Spontaneous joyful interaction whittled down to alcoholised time spent in sanctioned leisure zones. A long, dispiriting journey from our species' beginnings as creatures of overwhelming leisure. Barred from our own feast, we are forced to buy back scraps.

The horizon rises upon us.

And then recedes.

We are reclaiming our birthright to create. The reasons are manifold: the long tail, allowing creators to thrive by aiming away from the mainstream and towards their distinctive vision. Access to knowledge, examples, peers and teachers online. A culture of user-created content. Affordable tools that emulate or innovate away from professional production values. Many of these things owe themselves to the web, altering our reach in terms of audience, collaborators, learning and tools - and long may it continue. Can we also see a real world embodiment of these principles?

I believe the Future We Deserve restores art to its proper space in the everyday. Where we appreciate our access to global music but also support our local minstrels, recognising that they sing our own predicaments back to us. Where we plug ourselves into Die Woorden, and then plug out to the local stream to discover who is bashing their guitar right now, and at which street corner. Where public space is not just a place for commerce, but a playpen for people to parade and perform.

I'm confident for this because we can see many signs of this autonomous art-making already. A roleplaying scene continues to burgeon, forking via LARP and Jeepform as more embodied forms. Cosplay circles the globe and the dressing up box becomes a staple of childless households. Site-specific theatre from the supermarkets to back alleys sees the pros playing similar games, further blurring the lines. A culture of festival-making and spontaneous gigging. Capoeira in the park. Situationist tactics adopted by resistance movements and protests worldwide (not to mention their ubiquitous samba rhythms). Pervasive gaming. Beatboxing on the buses. Free running. Street Training. Mass gaming. Improv Everywhere. More and more, a culture of 'join in and do' is accelerating, flouting the idea of 'leaving it to the professionals'.

This is happening in a time of still copious energy and hence great wealth; scarcity and austerity could choke off these movements. This would be a disaster. We need more, much more. The philosopher John Dewey described art as "a remaking of the experience of the community in the direction of greater order and unity": these qualities we will gravely need. We need to make art together: collaborating, sharing, turn-taking, we quickly build trust, genuine safety and creative faculty. Countless cultures that demonstrate strong cohesion owe this to their mass expressive practises, both ritualised and improvised. We can be like them, and, in the words of thinker John Zerzan, untap "a creative energy sufficient to utterly refashion the conditions of human existence". In this future, we don't hurry in a bee-line from one planned transaction to another. We disbelieve in destination and celebrate being out and about, simply because the public spaces are immeasurably rich: rich in sociality, rich in spontaneity, rich because the gift of artistic, playful expression rewards both receiver and giver.

We would find it difficult to go back to a world without stages. But we can play together as if all the world's a stage.

Success in the Twenty First Century - Mark Charmer

The opportunities to access, absorb and distribute content are so prolific today. The implications of this change are so profound that it will take us decades to adjust.

Probably the biggest implication is for how we perceive, or define, success. In 2010 we have an intriguing situation where the majority of young people, and many, many older ones, now actively manage their "PR" each day. The main route is through new social tools such as Facebook and Twitter, and more personalised publishing in the form of blogs, MySpace pages, personal websites.

What this does is give each individual a little taste of the adrenalin that comes from fame.

Throughout the 20th century, we were all exposed to fame, almost always as something that happened to others: famous actors - "movie stars" - musicians, artists, writers, politicians and occasionally lesser heroes (normally elevated to fame by having "their story" "told" through a film or newspaper article). The other route to fame was through notoriety – usually criminal notoriety. Myra Hindley remains ones of the most famous people to have lived in Britain in the 20th century.

The mechanisms by which this elevation to fame would occur were controlled by just a few industries – the newspaper, magazine and book publishing industry had the power to promote what it believed in, or what it believed would sell.

We've therefore all grown up assuming that the gateway to a higher level of achievement is through being written about in - or even writing for - the newspapers.

Music has been packaged for us for half a century into styles that we would associate with peer groups, or use to dissociate from other groups. It has been used to frame ideas, movements, even to articulate the personality of places - New York, Los Angeles, London, Paris.

It's now possible for anyone - absolutely anyone - to record and publish their own songs. Or write and publish their own articles, poems, even books. Or take photographs and publish those, often instantaneously.

This clashes with almost every established assumption about "the way the world works". Those who run the established global content publishing and distribution systems have absolutely no idea what to do - in June, music giant

EMI, the Beatles' original record label, has chosen to retrench and become a rights management business, selling (read "milking") content back catalogues.

In front of use - poised - is a world full of people who aspire to somehow feel famous, who will find that each tingle of exposure via Facebook or Twitter will build their hunger for more.

The reality of the content publishing industry is that it has no interest in serving the needs of this mass market. At best (or perhaps at its most cynical) it seeks to "crowdsource" from this huge talent pool and create manufactured stairways where "the lucky, talented few" can be successful. Simon Cowell's extraordinary celebrity media economy built around shows like *X-Factor* is an obvious example. *Dragon's Den* is another.

What happens to everyone else doesn't seem to matter to this industry. They believe this "mass market" will remain passive, being adjusted, manipulated and satisfied by a small chosen few - the truly famous - that we will all be satisfied to watch and follow.

This isn't going to work. When millions – if not billions – are suddenly given the tools to self-publish, we have no terms of reference to predict what will happen next.

Some argue that life will go on pretty much as before, but with lower music sales, which "hurts" the industry's ability to foster new talent, further depressing the impact that music has on our own culture, our lives.

I think the future will be driven by more localist, but interconnected groups of people. I think many will grow to feel let down by the big publishers, because said publishers can't contemplate – can't cope with – helping them all become famous.

In a society where many want their piece of fame, there is only one logical path forward – local heroes.

The situation doesn't just apply in artistic publishing – it applies to business and government.

Those who believe they can contribute will find that the institutions they wish to contribute to cannot handle them – they have neither the capacity or cultural urge to provide these people with a sense of contribution, of fame. The breadth of situations where this will occur is mindblowing – from the product design student who thinks he can help Ford create better cars, to the individual who believes it simply must be possible for their city administrators to provide a lift in the local railway station.

Such frustration will increase dramatically in the next few years and become something so difficult for the established institutions to handle that many will crumble under the pressure.

In many cases the frustration amongst the mass would-be heroes will turn to anger. They will at first collaborate, then be tempted to compete and then return more assertively to collaborate. By which time the institutions will have no choice – no alternative ideas – but to let them in.

Rather like punk sought to challenge the lazy, tired '60s hangover that was the 1970s, this new mass market will almost anarchically unravel the existing institutions.

A big contributing factor will be that those who are out of work – especially those who are talented and out of work – will no longer be isolated and disenfranchised from organising and producing and distributing content. The out of work have access to all the new publishing tools, and potentially more time available, to harness them.

Is this David Cameron's "Big Society"? Perhaps it is. There are two ironies here – first that the character of this society is likely to be quite different to what Cameron's think tanks have implied. It will leave public administrators – central and local government, health, education and transport bodies – shell-shocked and impotent. This will contrast with the congenial Womens' Institute, cake-baking character that the coalition government is expecting. The second trait is that it will be much more social – much more socialist – that the think tanks expect, reflecting the tendency of the open internet to reward more liberal initiatives.

My advice? Be a part of the change you want to see.

On Lying to Children - Peep

Things people often lie to kids about include, as most people will have observed themselves at some point: death, birth, sex, relationships and imminent danger. All the things one would expect to be dealt with in a decent education, if an education is considered to be the information required for a decent chance at living your life effectively. Perhaps ideologically this is why we originally outsourced education to specialist institutions, so we didn't have to decide which awkward truth to tell. It ceased to be the responsibility of 'us' and became that of the professionals.

Working in a minor educational capacity with some of the most privileged children of the western world I see kids who, in having everything, are better protected than perhaps any other group of people on the planet. Like animals in captivity they are conditioned to stay that way. This conditioning occurs through the system of controlling information transmission known as Very Expensive Education. The lives of such privileged young people are of interest in this case because they represent the pinnacle of aspiration in the society they come from. This is the ideal childhood inscribed at the heart of capitalism.

Often the reason given for lying to those younger than us is that it isn't the right stage in their development for them to know something. Knowledge of something important might disrupt the process of indoctrination we accept as a proper education provided by somebody else, so we cover up, waiting for teacher to clarify it later.

But we don't trust these others either. Pity the unfortunate schoolteacher who attempts to teach using materials deemed 'inappropriate for children'! Unable to trust 'the professionals' to censor reliably, we invented the curriculum. The very idea that there is information that is appropriate or inappropriate for them betrays the fact that it is considered in our culture morally reprehensible not to obscure the truth from kids.

The result is that the people of the future are by turns shielded from important truths and exposed to others of a most horrid kind usually taken as necessary and unavoidable evils. Kids I work with cite the biography of a spectacularly rich and famous glamour model as a favourite book, run a close second by the biography of a survivor of horrible rape and abuse. These are books their parents are happy to provide them with and yet discussion with these parents of another recent bestseller, the biography of a less famous, self-professed feminist, proves quickly that it is considered rather risqué. They are unsure of its suitability. No reason is given for this, it is merely an unusual suggestion, and as such, immediately suspect.

How much more terrifying, to be exposed to everything that is unpleasant but unavoidable and none of the subtle, brilliant complexities which might offer solutions to such horror, on the basis that they are unsuitable for one's age. Time and time again I see the pattern assumed that that which is popular and pervasive is unavoidable and is therefore shruggingly allowed and that that which is niche or complex or obscure is confusing, potentially upsetting and therefore a risk.

The decision as to which truths are suitable may be too great for one generation to make for another. The dangers a new generation face may not even be comprehended by those teaching them. In a world in which the landscape these bairns inhabit is increasingly different from that of their elders, as change accelerates and confusion proliferates, we must learn not lie to, or come between, children and the truth they need.

We Deserve the Time and Space to Be Human - Alex Bowyer

As a species, we have begun a transformation as far-reaching as the industrial revolution or the invention of the printing press. We are now a digital society, living in two worlds - the physical world and the digital world that exists online, in our phones and PCs. Every human activity, from news and socializing to the way we do business, now depends on the digital ecosystem we have created. Without it we cannot function. And yet, we are now inadequate for survival in this new information age.

More news, blogs and writing are produced[173] than we can ever read, more movies and shows than we can ever watch - and via social networks, we now have more "friends" than we can ever do justice to. With a hundred different sources and interests competing for our attention, we are driven to do more, read more, and consume more. To survive this change, we must adapt.

Most digital consumer products today are sold on the promise that you will be able to do new things with information in new situations - whether it's listening to podcasts or audiobooks during your commute[174], socializing with friends while you're at work[175], checking email at the airport[176], or browsing the web while you have a coffee[177]. We cope by spending more of our time with computers, and by multi-tasking to ensure that every waking moment we are "plugged in" and aware of the very latest news on every topic or person we care about[178]. If we continue on this path, we risk losing ourselves. We are becoming computers - processing more and more information, in parallel, ever in need of more cycles to consume the torrent of data inputs. We need to stop and re-evaluate what computers are for.

Computers were created as tools to help us work faster and with greater efficiency; clearly an overwhelming success. But they gave us far more. As they were applied to new problems, new industries[179] emerged and old ones were threatened[180]. We seized the capability to do more, and life, like business, became a 24-hour endeavour. Somewhere along the way we forgot that computers are our servants, and we became slaves to them.

We need to consider what we stand to lose - we need to stop mindlessly reacting to stimuli and start building a positive future for our children. It's perfectly possible to program software that works for us, independently monitoring our digital worlds so we don't have to. With a little training, computers can learn what's important to you, and differentiate urgent information from news that could be made available later, in an easy-to-read summary. Your software agent[181] will do more than just respond to commands, it will act independently, researching topics of interest, finding information and news relevant to you, and filtering out the rest. It will need to understand your goals, your contexts, your relationships, and always act in your best interests. Not just to serve you more of what you like or what's popular, but also to offer contradictory perspectives and new ideas, sources that challenge us to think differently and grow as humans, not as mass-culture-consuming machines.

In the future, your computer will be your guide and assistant. It will be your symbiote - without you, it will have no purpose, and without it, you will be reduced to only those senses nature gave you, stripped of the digital superpowers that make you Human 2.0[182]. Like a human assistant today, it will communicate on your behalf, act as your proxy, and make educated guesses about what to do, checking with you later if need be - freeing you to spend time with friends and family or to express your creativity once again. It will make some mistakes, but you'll teach it, as you would a child. Over time, you'll trust it with more responsibility, while never yielding control. It will protect your data from corporations and governments, while still sharing your precious moments with family and friends. It will watch and learn from you, and reflect things back to you to make you a better person - lifestyle patterns that might be damaging, treasured relationships that you're neglecting, or important tasks you've forgotten.

Intelligent agents are not science fiction. Many of the building blocks are here today - for example Siri[183], Cyc[184], OTSN[185], Reqall[186] and the Google Prediction API[187]. We have a choice what to build next. Let's stop consuming and start evolving.

Opening the Floodgates - Ben Werdmuller von Elgg

Gatekeepers are everywhere. They are necessary, they are efficient, and they are holding us back.

In the Internet age, publishing has become the poster child for pre-Internet business models. It was an expensive business, once upon a time: works needed to be written, edited, acquired, typeset, printed, bound, advertised, distributed and sold. Entire industries - careers and legacies, even - grew up around this workflow. Publishing houses were the gatekeepers for who could be published. Bookstores were the gatekeepers of whose work could be sold. Because there were so many inherent difficulties involved in reaching an audience - not least distance, cost and the technology required - the gatekeepers had the only viable route to making it happen. Their size and economies of scale enabled authors to find readers for generations.

Then, in the 1990s, the world changed: Tim Berners-Lee invented the web, Marc Andreessen invented the modern web browser, and suddenly, anybody could write and find an audience - or communicate with anybody - anywhere in the world. Magazines and newspapers began appearing online. Within a decade, Sean Parker and Shawn Fanning had collaborated to create Napster, a music-sharing service that in two short years managed to undermine the entertainment industry's long-standing business model. It wasn't just that users were sharing music illegally with each other on a large scale, although that was happening; the big change was that suddenly, all independent artists needed to do to share their music was upload it.

The gatekeepers - the publishing houses, the Recording Industry Association of America, and others - began to fight back, but it was clear that the new models were here to stay. The old guard's economies of scale no longer mattered; technology had found a better way, and consumers voted with their feet.

It would be easy to argue that this change is restricted to post-scarcity items: products that can be encapsulated digitally and copied an infinite number of times. However, this is not the case. In the summer of 2010, the New York State legislature - heavily sponsored by the hotel industry - cracked down on residents subletting rooms as unofficial hotel rooms and advertising them on open markets like airBNB.com. If you visited a strange city and didn't have a place to stay, hotels were once a handy gatekeeper: for a price, you could generally trust their safety, cleanliness and comfort. In the age of truly open markets with built-in metrics for trust and accountability, anyone can offer a room, and as a result, the days of the global hotel chain may be numbered. Whereas brands were once symbols you could judge products by, there are now more direct ways to determine quality. Once, you were limited to commercials you had seen or articles you had read. Now, you can ask *everybody*.

There is a revolution ahead of us. Music distribution models, the market for hotel rooms or where someone can publish an article are all part of a prelude to a far bigger change: a switch from political parties and the politics of aggregation to individual politics driven by the people. Imagine an open market for politics - both politicians and political ideas themselves - that incorporated similar trust metrics to those used to safely find independent hotel rooms, where individuals didn't need the support of parties, unions or global businesses to have a chance of being elected or having their ideas incorporated into the democratic process.

Global society is rife with baked-in power structures that restrict the possibilities for billions of people - and in turn for all of us, by limiting the talent, intelligence and skills we can draw on. By removing and revealing the economic interests that control how our world is run, and empowering people to make better choices about the world around them, there is a potential for a new kind of collaborative society. Here, there is room for liberal, conservative and libertarian values; for people of all religions and belief systems. Rather than imposing ideology, these new markets provide greater freedom for ideologies to coexist, transcending borders and valuing individuals over their geographies or circumstances. The only requirements are the freedom to communicate and the right to free will.

Providing this globally will be the biggest battle of the 21st century. But it is a battle which must be won.

The Future of Art - Nick Stewart

I work in an Art School. I run an MA course in contemporary art. A key question I ask my students is: in an age of image saturation what's the point of art focused on images? The art world makes a fetish of their potential value and art has been corralled into administrative and architectural structures, institutions like Tate, that present artists with a terminal set of conditions within which to develop and present their work untouched by the realities of life on the streets beyond. Fine for pictures and objects whose sole purpose is to be looked at but hardly a meaningful context for the realisation of artists' ambitions to revolutionise the everyday life of society at large.

Back in the twentieth century the avant-garde wanted to bridge the art-life gap. But that post war project, to challenge the categorization and mystification of art separate from everyday life, largely failed. Instead we got post-modernism with its hyper-fragmentation: the creation of a world of unrelated bits and pieces as fodder for the capitalist boom (bubble) of the past thirty or so years. Now the challenge is to remake something from these pieces: to create a new narrative for art in a broader cultural context.

Instruction in the arts of life is something other than conveying information about them. It is a matter of communication and participation in values of life by means of the imagination, and works of art are the most intimate and energetic means of aiding individuals to share in the arts of living. John Dewey, Art as Experience, 1932.

Essentially, art is structured in consciousness. Objects and images are but evidence, a trace, left after the activity of art has ended. We substitute this evidence, objects and images, for a living process and so remove the potentiality of art from everyday life. Art as a quality of life would mean the end of art as a pure 'thing', something separate from the rest of life.

Jackson Pollock, as I see him, left us at the point where we must become preoccupied with and even dazzled by the space and objects of our everyday life, either our bodies, clothes, rooms, or, if need be, the vastness of Forty-second Street. Allan Kaprow, The Legacy of Jackson Pollock, 1958.

For the more than fifty years since Kaprow wrote this essay art has continued to broaden its range of experience and idea. Though much that is extraordinary has been created most of it has already been filed and stored across the network of 'terminal institutions' that now constitute the international art-world. But the "vastness of Forty–second Street" still beckons and challenges the professional alienation that now characterizes art production for most artists.

Art has been the means of keeping alive the sense of purposes that outrun evidence and of meanings that transcend indurated habit, wrote John Dewey back in 1932. But if the concept of art is to have any purchase on the future it must abandon the closed loop of institutional control. Everyday life as a site of personal and social transformation must become the new locus of art.

The Human Rite of Living - Bembo Davies

We wake up. We attend to those we live with. Exercises of strengthening the individual and group are either explicit or implicit. Nourishment is prepared from among the stores; should these moments of mutual care be combined into one ritual? Do they require strengthening through song, dance or prayer?

A choice may be available: what shall be my carbo-social footprint for today? Shall I engage in survival - gather wood for the days ahead, or am I investing in the future - engaged in collective activities that spread our collective capacity to negotiate constructively with our surroundings?

The fallback compromise is, of course, business as usual: fed by the hand that bites us, embracing our individual interface with the current grid of institutions for as long as they retain their capacity to deliver the goods. How long we can continue to reap the pleasures of our habitual bonus agreements, is the backdrop which the entire FWD project illuminates. Will we leap willingly into the future, or be shoved?

Does this moment of daily compromise too need its ritual? A communal rite of contrition/forgiveness that allows each of us another year in the clutches of these pernicious bonus agreements. Or better, a harvest feast acknowledging breakthroughs both social and psychic, and designating the priorities for the next period. Do these also require strengthening through spiritual cleansing and carnival?

For my part, I can do worse than continuing to Extract Enthusiasm at every opportunity.

No Island is an Island - Lucas Gonzalez

The challenge

At least for the time being, there's just one planet for all of us, including humans. But my <1500-gram brain has trouble visualizing even this single planet, with its zillion life-forms plus the relationships among them and the around-life molecules and energies. So I'll stick to the Canary Islands, where I live, and you can focus on any piece of land that you think you know well.

To make the thought-experiment solid, I'll imagine there's no "away". No food or other resources coming from distant coasts, and no place to dispose of our litter. When we do that, the ecological footprint[188] concept must be stared at eye to eye: our islands are all there is. As to information, we are not cheating if we assume all open human knowledge is close at hand for the two million human beings living in these seven islands.

Can we get what we need, want and prefer from what we have? Could we do it now (to respond to a sudden supply crisis) and indefinitely (to develop sustainability) or simply if we wanted to? Can we survive and thrive and, as we do, put our learning out there as part of the commons' treasure? Can we leave the camping site in a better condition than when we arrived?

How it's done

As I write this, the idea of gathering around a local-focus wiki canaripedia.org[189] (and now Localpedia[190]) may be starting to get legs. Some of us intend to create a set of pages with the essentials for water, food and energy. We'll likely look at the full six basic causes we'll all die from: too hot, too cold, thirst, hunger, illness (including unavoidable aging) and injury (from nature or from human violence). Some domain experts will want to look into communications, transport, coordination and all the other elements essential for people to operate as groups and organisations (see SCIM[191]).

To start with, we intend to compile a set of 300+ questions (factual and exploratory), ask 30+ people to compile preliminary always-perfectible answers in 100 days, and publish that under an open license.

We'll look at the data we have, with rough consensus estimates where there's nothing more accurate. We'll convert macro-data to micro-data (grams of fruit produced or needed per person and per day, calories per square meter and per year) and back to macro. We'll ask about things no-one has asked for yet, even though they are important if we are to create a facts-based vision for our islands. How much mass of animal-edible weeds can grow per month in non-cultivated arable land? How many trees can we grow from a few branches from each of our existing trees, and what kind of trees for each place and purpose, and how?

We'll find guidance for thinking style – facts in numbers, then ideas, then muscle – in seminal works like Without Hot Air[192] and Seawater Greenhouses for a high lethality pandemic[193].

We may be looking at three levels. One is basic survival, of the kind computed for refugee camps, where we need to focus on people staying alive a few more days, months or years, and where if rice is all there is, then rice is what we eat. The next level is comfort and the resilience that comes from a certain degree of flexibility. The third is luxury and expansion through beyond-basic but also-human needs, such as creating and enjoying music. Hey, we may even find beyond-fossil-fuels ways to reuse the golden molecules someone inserted into our now-broken cell-phones[194].

The human factor

Not sure we want to tell anyone about this, but are we serving the wiki, or is the wiki serving us? You tell me. The wiki will be the (more or less structured) information space, and we'll grow it. But there's lots outside the information space, namely the conversation space (where we talk about what we need to write next, how to organise it, and so forth), and the action space (where we build physical workshops, water fruit trees and take care of each other's injuries). We want to document the essentials, with video and audio and how-to pages and art. That way, others can join in at their own pace, with their own style, doing whatever they feel needs doing right now.

How do we start the job, and how do we keep it going? I guess it all starts with an invitation, drafted and crafted in the "open space" way. The invitation makes room for data, passion, lateral thinking, experiments, and generally lots of fun, both serious-fun and fun-fun.

'Cos, you know, life started already and some things we can't leave for later.

Getting The Future We Deserve - Paul Graham Raven

Let's assume for a minute we've all worked out exactly what sort of future we deserve. Now comes a tricky question: who's going to deliver us that future?

It's seductive when someone else offers to take responsibility for something big and confusing, or that looks like it'll be hard work, or both. That's how we've gotten to where we are now: top-down democracy and the nation-state model is pretty much based on saying to citizens "here, you shunt some of your earnings in our direction, and we'll take responsibility for sorting out all the stuff you can't do (or can't be trusted to do) on your own".

First problem: we don't live in the same world that top-down democracy was built for. The pyramid of communication between citizen and legislature is huge, Byzantine, slow; the world is fast, flattened, shrinking.

Second problem: abdication of responsibility allows us to blame someone else when something goes wrong... and we sure do like blaming people. It's the government's fault that the Square Mile got off with slapped wrists! Their fault that Deepwater Horizon wasn't prevented! But didn't we give the government its mandate? Ah, well, yes we did... but it's not our fault if they never deliver the promises they make, is it?

I'm going to go out on a limb, here: yes, it is our fault that they don't deliver. It's our fault because we're so eager to palm off that responsibility onto a broken system, despite a clear history of lies, deceit and (most commonly) incompetence. Look: if you were fielding tenders for some big outsourced project, and one of the pitches came from an organisation with a track record of failures-to-deliver like that of your government, would you hire them, even if they lowballed the hell out of their bid?

Of course you wouldn't. Because you're not an idiot.

It's simple: if we don't take responsibility for things, then we don't deserve to complain about them. I think we've long worn out the tired old saw that says top-down democracy is the least worst solution to a perpetual problem. A lot of new ideas, tools and technologies have come along since then, and already people are using them to pressure the state, to hold it accountable, to remind it of its broken promises. But I think we can go one further: I think we can become the state.

To put it another way: even if we were to dream up the most awesome, shiny and sustainable dream future we could imagine, if we then turned to the old systems of government to deliver them to us, we wouldn't get it. It'd be like asking your landlord to give you a hand wheeling the rubble away from the construction site that used to be his property. Instead, we need to reassert not just our rights but our abilities to act as stewards of our own world... and we do that by slowly building rhizomatic systems that – inch by inch, day by day, person by person – replace the creaking hierarchies of the state. The better we get at doing it, the less the state will have to do; eventually it'll wither away like an unused and unlamented vestigial limb, a relic of our political evolution.

Let me be perspex-clear, here: I do not advocate revolution, or at least not what has been labeled revolution in the past. I do not advocate violence or destruction or force, be it against the state or anyone else. Instead, I suggest we dismantle the state by taking back all the jobs we gave it – slowly, carefully, and with the willingness to accept that we won't always get it right first time.

I suggest we take responsibility – every one of us, to the best of our abilities, with whatever skills we have, as individuals and as communities of individuals – for our world, our future and (most importantly) for each other. It'll be hard work, but there'll be a sense of liberty when we face up to the fact that it's us that has to fix things. True liberty, I think – the sort of liberty that can't be gifted by legal documents, but which has to be built or earned afresh each day – is never having another person to blame for your problems. It always has been; we were just seduced into thinking otherwise for a while.

Whatever happens, whatever we do, we'll get the future we deserve. The question here is whether or not the future we deserve is one we'd like to live in.

Berlin, Berlin - Liam Breslin

A city divided.

In the early '60s, Berlin meant one thing to Dubliners, namely, *Checkpoint Charlie*; for it had been rebuilt in Smithfield market to film "The Spy Who Came in from the Cold", starring Richard Burton. So, visiting Berlin in 1989, I went to see the real Checkpoint Charlie, with real East German border guards. From the checkpoint, I walked along by the Berlin Wall, which was over twice my height and covered with colourful graffiti. It was a pleasant, sunny afternoon and so were my thoughts. I came to a bend in the Wall where Potsdamer Platz, once Europe's busiest intersection, had been.

I climbed into the wooden stand overlooking the Wall. It was somewhat of a surprise to see that the other side held nothing but grass for 200m and then another wall without graffiti. Instead, there were observation towers every few hundred metres. Armed guards inside prevented anyone from crossing the grass. They were assisted by dogs, by steel bars bent to ankle height in the grass, and by mines. This grass was not as innocent as it looked.

I continued along the Wall, past the Brandenburg gate to the river Spree, whose closest bank was the actual border; so if someone fell or jumped in, they were fired on. This end was marked by seventeen small white wooden crosses, each remembering someone shot while swimming or escaping through the river. The stillness was broken by a sinister grey-green gunboat that surged past along the centre of the river.

The afternoon no longer seemed so sunny. I hurried back to the viewing stand and sat. The graffiti here were many and moving. One in particular struck me - "*Where is our daughter Gretchen, disappeared 13/8/1961?*"

I thought to myself, as I regarded the Wall – "I don't know if I believe in evil as a reality, but this is the closest I have ever been to a personal experience of evil".

Imagine my astonishment when, some 12 months later, I revisited Checkpoint Charlie to find all the guards had left; when I retraced my steps to the Brandenburg gate past the 'Potsdamer Platz' bend without any trace of the Wall remaining; no guard towers; and finally, when I arrived at the seventeen small crosses, a pleasure boat carrying dozens of joyful people cruised down the centre of the river. My 'experience of evil' had completely vanished! Later, at midnight, East and West Germany were reunited.

What does it all mean now? Some say that our thoughts are powerful. How careful are we about how we use them? Do we choose fear? Or its opposite? Nostradamus, we admired for foretelling the future. But that was centuries ago. Have we progressed? Is it now time we valued, not *observing* the future, but *choosing* the future *within* ourselves?

We Deserve a Future - Jason Louv

Overpopulation. Resource scarcity. These are the problems that underly all the wars, plagues, famine and, in many cases, disease. I believe that, ultimately, we will be faced with only two solutions to these problems: to get more resources and places for people to live, or to get less people. Space migration or genocide.

Encouraging the first, and averting the second, will require progress towards a more cohesive, unified world. The only way to function as a space-going race, or to circumvent the persistent "Othering" which allows for the dehumanization that makes genocide possible is, I believe, to function as a World Group. Our current divided system allows wheat to rot in the fields while millions starve. It allows the cosmic destiny of mankind to go untapped while government teams build billion-dollar parts for spacecraft which will never be assembled, simply to justify their funding. We can do better. We need a form of global cohesiveness that will work for individuals, not against them.

We need a One World Community. Not a one world government—which would imply fascist centralization of power—but a collaborative linking of global citizens increasingly able to see the world as a single system and work across the false political, racial and religious boundaries of the last millennium. Who are able to collaborate in maintaining a life-supporting world, in all senses of the word "life," in real time.

Theodore Roszak's Ecopsychology suggests that there can be no true assessment of the symptomology of a patient without seeing the patient as a microcosm, a holographic splinter of the world, and that the true healing of an individual can and must begin with a healing of the world that they live in; their larger, extended self. (From a more limited ideological perspective, we can see echoes of this in the SPK or Socialist Patients' Collective, the West German therapy group that, inspired by the 1968 student revolutions, declared that the REAL underlying psychological issue affecting the supposedly individual pathologies of patients was the inherent contradictions of late capitalism.)

Individuals able to think of the world as a single coherent system, and able to think beyond all false boundaries and dichotomies that, in truth, only exist as modularities within that system, are going to be increasingly needed. We are weighted with the outmoded dreams of dead men and dead systems, walking-corpse institutions and undead, blood-sucking ideologies long past their expiration date which yet haunt the planet, entrapping the joy of the living within the dead ribcage walls of their rotting, false order, and which direly need a stake through the heart simply because they are no longer relevant.

Yet as persistent as they can be, these old models are failing and falling all around us. We are called to create new ones, new models, new approaches to living that can make meaning from the world as it is, not as it was. We need new models for seeing the totality of the world system, for making sense of our growing exposure to information, for the ever-accelerating way in which we witness events happening in the world. We need new ways of assessing and utilizing our resources. We need new ways of co-existing with each other, of building community, of connecting and collaborating.

The alternative is to continue on the path we are already on, to the logical conclusion of globalization as it currently functions.

I have a persistent and troubling image of a potential future for our race that I can't quite seem to shake—as overpopulation increases and the dehumanizing abuses of the globalists continue, I can see a time in which human beings live in conditions not much different from the way we keep feed animals now. Imagine yourself growing up in a ten-by-ten pen, fed on sedatives and antibiotic drips to keep the sores now growing on your body due to close confinement from killing you, or to slow the spread of the pandemics sure to arise from such a situation. It's the condition we see fit to impose upon the mammals just below us on the tree of life and, after all, you are what you eat.

Imagine yourself growing up attached to a computer, farming data for your corporate overlords, lost in the pornographic virtual realities produced to keep you complacent just as prostitutes were kept on the payroll by companies to keep miners, railroad workers and other large-project manual laborers from revolting in the 19th and early 20th centuries.

Imagine being born into wide-scale camps little different from the corporate prisons that currently dot the landscape of the United States, but that nobody talks about—hells into which illegal immigrants and drug users are de facto disappeared and converted to slave labor for corporations like Sodexho-Marriott. Just under the surface veneer of America, this is what already lurks: factory farms, corporate prisons, the uncomfortable truth that slavery never ended, it just got sneakier. The uncomfortable truth, especially post-NDAA, that this may be what they have planned for all of us.

Such, I fear, is the dream of the elites: the ability to tag, sedate, transport, and utilize human beings as resources in much the same way that we currently use cattle. Watch how the corporate elite—Monsanto, for instance—treat crops and animals. You think they see human beings as any different? They've already begun to execute plans to cull the herd, to slowly weaken, poison and decimate our ranks with chemical additives and pesticides as surely as the native tribes were wiped away with smallpox blankets. The Codex Alimentarius, there for all to see. Or consider the voluntary surveillance system called Facebook, or the monthly bill you pay for the iPhone that slowly gives you brain cancer while it tracks your every movement. This is what they want: A mechanized planet with no humanity or compassion, only Production. A concentration camp world, slowed down so you don't notice what's happening to you; mashed up with Disneyland so you don't care.

Perhaps (one hopes) this is more of a persistent fear than an impending reality, a "monster under the bed," a shadow mythology which stands as a signpost marked "do not go here." Either way, we would do well to heed the signpost.

Our world is unifying. We have a choice of doing so with brute force, as is currently being done, or doing it with intelligence, wisdom and compassion. To begin to drop the shells we have built around ourselves and reach out to each other, or to further calcify in mutual fear and distrust to the point that our shells become prisons, quite literally. In the face of the Machine, of annihilation, we are tasked with re-centering our world on our humanity, our humane-ity.

We deserve a future. It is so easy to lose hope, to become entrenched in the self-loathing that can infect and corrode so quickly. Yes, we have done terrible things, all still fresh in our memory. Yes, we continue to do terrible things.

But it is all too tempting to allow the will-to-annihilation to neutralize us. To, unconsciously or not-so-unconsciously, hold to the belief that, whatever horrors await us in the 21st century, we deserve them. That perhaps we should be wiped out as a species, since we cause nothing but pain to the world that bore and which bears us.

This is one of the greatest traps, the greatest deceptions. For all of our horrors, we are, at the end of it all, The Human Race, the ones who brought you such greatest hits as the Sistine Chapel and a man risking his life to push a homeless girl out of the way of a speeding bus. The moon landing and every sudden and unprompted moment of compassion you have experienced, and shown, in your life. Who brought you weird coffee shop art and freaky dances.

If it can be hard to see, but that doesn't mean it isn't there. That basic goodness.

The stars or the bomb: This is your choice.

Aftermath - Thinking the Unthinkable. Asking What is Not Asked - Thomas Bjelkeman

I was reading a rather entertaining book by the author Charles Stross, The Atrocity Archives[195], which is Lovecraftian horror, with unspeakable mind-sucking, planet-killing horrors from the back of beyond, married to computerized magic, a deeply secret Occult Secret Service, with the main character being a special agent come IT system administrator. I soon realized that this actually reminded me of Vinay Gupta. I mentioned this to him, and he said:

"I'm disturbed that lovecraftian scifi explains _anything_ about me. (TENTACLES!)"[196]

But it does Vinay, it does, and here is why.

For you who don't know Vinay Gupta well, I would like to summarize him as the person who thinks the unthinkable. Not just any old unthinkable, but unthinkables like:

- What really happens if the swine flu has a 30% death rate worldwide. How will society actually react?

- How do you put together a realistic plan for when a city is destroyed by a nuclear device?

- What do you actually do when the GDP takes a 40% nosedive in an economic crash?

You will find quite a lot of people claim to investigate these type of things, but most people only work with what they consider "plausible", which isn't anywhere near these type of disasters.

The characters in Stross' novel work with the unthinkable, they face the horrors that are so horrible that nobody wants to know. They do this with a good understanding of physics, mathematics, engineering, information technology and a mind ready to deal with what normal people blank out at, and they do it with an attitude. Vinay would fit right in.

Vinay's horrors do not have tentacles. But they are no less scary, because they are actually real, and if you scratch the surface of the disaster plans you may be pointed to by anyone that claims to think about the unthinkable, you will notice that they don't really deal with the worst case scenarios. They essentially deal with blips. Not crashes. People have a blank spot where the real disaster lies. They can't see it, they blank out. Vinay doesn't blank out, he rolls up his sleeves and says: "OK where do we start?"

He is often quoted as saying, "I don't get out of bed for less than 1% mortality." (And he is talking global scale.)

Vinay is a former information technology systems analyst and programmer. Now his work is primarily large scale world systems analysis. He told me recently:

> "You realize that we live in the manuscript of a Bruce Sterling book, don't you? It used to be a William Gibson script. When I worked with an online gold backed bank in Florida, struggling with how to deal with the Mafia, that was Neil Stephenson. Now the script has changed. It is clearly Bruce Sterling who writes the script now."

Footnotes

1 Vinay recently recounted an episode when he worked with the Pentagon: "What I discovered, what really broke my life in a way, was that I was better at certain aspects of policy around the bomb than the State.[197] I struggle with that. I maintain the work partly because I was told, by people involved in reacting to nuclear terrorism, in no uncertain terms that my plan was better than the official plan.[198] I was told that if a bomb was used on a US city they would probably use the plan, but could not be seen, politically, preparing to use it."[199]

Appendix

References

[1] http://www.energybulletin.net/node/47436
[2] A. Macintyre, (1981), After Virtue: a study in moral theory, Duckworth, p. 62.
[3] A. Macintyre, (1981), After Virtue: a study in moral theory, Duckworth, p. 68
[4] C. Gearty, (2005), Can human rights survive?, Cambridge University Press, p. 17
[5] M. MacDonald (1984) p. 26 in Jeremy Waldron (ed.), Theories of Rights (Oxford, 1984)
[6] ↑ Micheline R. Ishay, ed, The Human Rights Reader: Major Political Essays, Speeches, and Documents From the Bible to the Present New York: Routledge, 1997 p. xv
[7] Micheline R. Ishay, ed, The Human Rights Reader: Major Political Essays, Speeches, and Documents From the Bible to the Present New York: Routledge, 1997, p. xv
[8] see Raz, Joseph (1984). "Legal Rights", Oxford Journal of Legal Studies 1; reprinted in his Ethics in the Public Domain: Essays in the Morality of Law and Politics, Oxford: Clarendon Press, 1994.
[9] Micheline R. Ishay, The History of Human Rights (Berkeley: University of California Press, 2004) pp. 19-20
[10] ↑ Ishay, 2004, p. 34
[11] *Whole Earth Discipline* Atlantic Books, 2009
[12] "I still don't understand... why I often succumb to well-documented psychological biases, even though I'm acutely aware of these biases" David Buss, Professor of Psychology http://bps-research-digest.blogspot.com/2009/10/david-buss-overcoming-irrationality.html
[13] http://www.prospectmagazine.co.uk/2009/10/does-copenhagen-matter/
[14] *Galápagos*, Jonathan Cape, 1985
[15] http://www.longnow.org/about/
[16] http://www.theextraordinaries.org/
[17] http://www.pablopicasso.org/guernica.jsp
[18] http://www.pbs.org/treasuresoftheworld/a_nav/guernica_nav/gnav_level_1/5meaning_guerfrm.html
[19] U-n-f-o-l-d: A cultural response to climate change, *exhibition catalogue*, 2010, Springer-Verlag/Wein
[20] http://elsa.berkeley.edu/~chad/handbook9sj.pdf
[21] http://elsa.berkeley.edu/~chad/handbook9sj.pdf
[22] http://www.hawaii.edu/powerkills/COM.ART.HTM
[23] http://www.hawaii.edu/powerkills/COM.ART.HTM
[24] http://faculty.rcc.edu/sellick/On%20Being%20Conservative.pdf
[25] http://faculty.rcc.edu/sellick/On%20Being%20Conservative.pdf
[26] http://seasteading.org/
[27] http://seasteading.org
[28] http://athousandnations.com/
[29] http://athousandnations.com
[30] http://www.cato-unbound.org/2009/04/06/patri-friedman/beyond-folk-activism/
[31] http://www.cato-unbound.org/2009/04/06/patri-friedman/beyond-folk-activism/
[32] http://seasteading.org/strategic-areas/engineering
[33] http://seasteading.org/strategic-areas/engineering
[34] http://seasteading.org/blogs/engineering/2010/08/19/the-cruise-market
[35] http://seasteading.org/blogs/engineering/2010/08/19/the-cruise-market
[36] http://seasteading.org/community/contests/sinkorswim-2010
[37] http://seasteading.org/community/contests/sinkorswim-2010
[38] Berners-Lee, M. (2010). How bad are bananas? : the carbon footprint of everything. London: Profile.
[39] Estabrook, B. (2011). Tomatoland : how modern industrial agriculture destroyed our most alluring fruit. Kansas City: Andrews McMeel Publishing.

[40] Patel, R. (2008). Stuffed and Starved: Markets, Power and the Hidden Battle for the World Food System. Portobello Books Ltd.
[41] Schutter, O. D. (2010). Agroecology and the Right to Food. Development. www.srfood.org/images/stories/pdf/officialreports/20110308_a-hrc-16-49_agroecology_en.pdf http://www.srfood.org/images/stories/pdf/officialreports/20110308_a-hrc-16-49_agroecology_en.pdf
[42] James N. Rosenau, Turbulence in World Politics : A Theory of Change and Continuity (Princeton, N.J.: Princeton University Press, 1990), p. 83.
[43] T. S. Eliot, The Waste Land ([Monterrey,: Ediciones Sierra Madre, 1960).
[44] Thomas S. Kuhn, The Structure of Scientific Revolutions, 3rd ed. (Chicago, IL: University of Chicago Press, 1996).
[45] It must be noted that many of the following concepts were first articulated and brilliantly handled in Rosenau, *Turbulence in World Politics : A Theory of Change and Continuity*.
[46] An earlier draft of this paper appeared as Paul B. Hartzog, "21st Century Governance as a Complex Adaptive System," in Proceedings Pista 2004, ed. Jose V. Carrasquero, et al., Informatics and Society (Orlando: International Institute of Informatics and Systemics, 2004).
[47] http://www.wired.com/techbiz/it/magazine/17-03/wp_quant
[48] http://finance.yahoo.com/q/ks?s=WMT
[49] http://dilbert.com/strips/comic/1995-08-27/
[50] http://books.google.com/books?id=Woywyw8LlcgC&pg=PA192&lpg=PA192&dq=botany+of+desire+andes#v=onepage&q&f=false
[51] Lucas Gonzalez, My ideal panflu. Retrieved 6 August 2010. | http://www.appropedia.org/TheFWD_lucasgonzalez_My_ideal_panflu
[52] Wikipedia, Black death, | http://en.wikipedia.org/wiki/Black_Death
[53] Wikipedia, Meme, first paragraph. Retrieved 6 August 2010. | http://en.wikipedia.org/wiki/
[54] Wikipedia, List of countries by life expectancy. Retrieved 6 August 2010. | http://en.wikipedia.org/wiki/List_of_countries_by_life_expectancy
[55] The Economist, A survey of health-care finance, The health of nations. 15 Jul 2004. Retrieved 6 August 2010. | http://www.economist.com/node/2895909
[56] IPPC, Contribution of Working Group II to the Fourth Assessment Report of the Intergovernmental Panel on Climate Change, 2007, M.L. Parry, O.F. Canziani, J.P. Palutikof, P.J. van der Linden and C.E. Hanson (eds), Cambridge University Press, Cambridge, United Kingdom and New York, NY, USA. Retrieved 6 August 2010. | http://www.ipcc.ch/publications_and_data/ar4/wg2/en/contents.html
[57] Wikipedia, MMR vaccine, Safety. | http://en.wikipedia.org/wiki/MMR_vaccine#Safety
[58] Wikipedia, Casualties and war crimes. Retrieved 6 August 2010. | http://en.wikipedia.org/wiki/World_War_II#Casualties_and_war_crimes
[59] http://www.war-ofthe-worlds.co.uk/war_worlds_orson_welles_mercury.htm
[60] http://en.wikipedia.org/wiki/Blade_Runner
[61] http://en.wikipedia.org/wiki/The_Day_of_the_Triffids#Film.2C_TV.2C_radio_or_theatrical_adaptations
[62] http://data.un.org/Data.aspx?d=UNODC&f=tableCode:1
[63] http://data.un.org/Data.aspx?d=UNODC&f=tableCode:1
[64] http://www.akvo.org
[65] http://www.akvo.org/blog/?p=703
[66] http://twitter.com/bjelkeman
[67] http://www.footprintnetwork.org/en/index.php/GFN/page/world_footprint/
[68] http://en.wikipedia.org/wiki/Power_law
[69] http://en.wikipedia.org/wiki/Bak%E2%80%93Tang%E2%80%93Wiesenfeld_sandpile
[70] http://cooperationcommons.com/node/386
[71] Gunderson and Pray, 2007
[72] Recall the mafia narrative of family in 'The Godfather'
[73] For historical tracking and current global pricing see: http://www.solarbuzz.com/
[74] J. Pearce and A. Lau, "Net Energy Analysis For Sustainable Energy Production From Silicon Based Solar Cells", *Proceedings of American Society of Mechanical Engineers Solar 2002:*

Sunrise on the Reliable Energy Economy, editor R. Cambell-Howe, 2002. pdf http://alpha.
chem.umb.edu/chemistry/ch471/evans%20files/Net_Energy%20solar%20cells.pdf
[75] K. Branker, M.J.M. Pathak, J.M. Pearce, "A Review of Solar Photovoltaic Levelized Cost of Electricity", *Renewable and Sustainable Energy Reviews*, **15**, pp.4470-4482 (2011). http://dx.doi.org/10.1016/j.rser.2011.07.104 DOI and http://hdl.handle.net/1974/6879
[76] Joshua Pearce, "Photovoltaics – A Path to Sustainable Futures", *Futures* **34**(7), 663-674, 2002. http://dx.doi.org/10.1016/S0016-3287(02)00008-3
[77] http://sharonastyk.com/
[78] http://www.alastairmcintosh.com/
[79] http://www.worldsocialism.org/spgb/
[80] http://apletters.blogspot.com/2009/12/to-save-our-planet.html
[81] http://apletters.blogspot.com/2010/10/when-simplicity-would-mean-survival.html
[82] http://apletters.blogspot.com/2009/08/need-for-state-owned-public-conveyance.html
[83] A. J. Buitenhuis, I. Zelenika and J. M. Pearce, "Open Design-Based Strategies to Enhance Appropriate Technology Development", *Proceedings of the 14th Annual National Collegiate Inventors and Innovators Alliance Conference : Open*, March 25-27th 2010, pp. 1-12. Available: http://nciia.org/sites/default/files/pearce.pdf
[84] Joshua M. Pearce and Usman Mushtaq, "Overcoming Technical Constraints for Obtaining Sustainable Development with Open Source Appropriate Technology", *Science and Technology for Humanity (TIC-STH), 2009 IEEE Toronto International Conference*, pp. 814-820, 26-27 Sept. 2009.http://dx.doi.org/10.1109/TIC-STH.2009.5444388
[85] Wikipedia ranks 7th as of Sept. 15, 2010 http://www.alexa.com/topsites
[86] http://www.appropedia.org/
[87] http://www.appropedia.org/index.php?title=Special:UserLogin&type=signup&returnto= Welcome_to_Appropedia
[88] "Between 1978 and 2004—nearly the entire span of John Paul II's pontificate—the number of men in monastic and religious orders (not including priests) decreased by 46% in Europe and 30% in the Americas, while the number of women decreased by 39% and 27%, respectively. Compare this to the trend in the global South: During the same period, men in monastic and religious orders increased by 48% in Africa and 39% in Asia, with women increasing on those two continents by 62% and 64%." http://gratefultothedead.wordpress.com/2009/10/28/re-monking-the-church-new-monasticism/
[89] http://www.artmonastery.orgfcKLRhttp://en.wikipedia.org/wiki/Art_Monastery
[90] http://wiki.ic.org/wiki/Intentional_Communities
[91] http://otherhood.org/elements-of-monasticism/
[92] Predictive gene testing uses your DNA to provide information about a person's future risk of developing a specific medical disorder - http://en.wikipedia.org/wiki/Predictive_testing
[93]]Nutrigenetic Testing: Tests Purchased Mislead Consumers - [http://www.gao.gov/products/GAO-6-977T http://www.gao.gov/products/GAO-06-977T
[94] Life caching refers to a social act of storing and sharing one's life events in an open and public forum - http://trendwatching.com/trends/LIFE_CACHING.htm
[95] Quantified Self Movement - http://www.quantifiedself.com
[96] Us Now http://www.usnowfilm.com/, Here Comes Everybody[wikipedia], Wikinomics[wikipedia], etc
[97] for example Peal oil[wikipedia], Peak water[wikipedia], etc
[98] Sustainable Community Action http://sca21.wikia.com/wiki/Sustainable_Community_Action: Community_Portal wiki
[99] WiserEarth http://www.wiserearth.org/
[100] Self-actualization[wikipedia]
[101] WiserRio2012 http://www.wiserearth.org/group/wiserio2012 on WiserEarth
[102] http://sca21.wikia.com/wiki/Ukgc10
[103] https://spreadsheets.google.com/ccc?key= 0AhtJz9HHi6yVdHRtcnVYaDhEVl9xUDd6a1poeU5HckE&hl=en#gid=1
[104] http://www.akvo.org/wiki/index.php/Tippy_Tap
[105] http://www.ted.com/talks/george_whitesides_a_lab_the_size_of_a_postage_stamp.html
[106] http://medic.frontlinesms.com/

[107] http://www.khanacademy.org
[108] http://www.appropedia.org/Where_There_is_no_Doctor
[109] http://www.thewikireader.com
[110] http://en.wikipedia.org/wiki/Time_Banking
[111] http://www.appropedia.org/Category:Health_and_safety
[112] http://butteredsidedown.co.uk/scim.html
[113] http://en.wikipedia.org/wiki/Bolsa_Fam%C3%ADlia
[114] http://www.finfacts.ie/irelandbusinessnews/publish/article_10003611.shtml
[115] http://www.siteselection.com/ssinsider/snapshot/sf011210.htm
[116] http://www.economist.com/node/17062713?story_id=17062713&CFID=145163932&CFTOKEN=25812707
[117] http://www.economist.com/node/17062737
[118] http://www.guardian.co.uk/environment/2010/jul/07/germany-renewable-energy-electricity
[119] http://www.passivehouse.com/English/PassiveH.HTM
[120] http://www.youtube.com/watch?v=9qZPwBPAqks
[121] http://www.youtube.com/watch?v=UqqaybB44Kc
[122] http://www.cirpee.org/fileadmin/documents/Cahiers_2009/CIRPEE09-47.pdf
[123] http://maxwelldemon.com/2009/04/25/building-mathematics-sculpture-system-5/
[124] http://maxwelldemon.com/2010/03/16/building-mathematics-the-maker-faire-in-pictures/
[125] http://www.polydron.co.uk/
[126] http://en.wikipedia.org/wiki/Group_theory
[127] http://en.wikipedia.org/wiki/Fourth_dimension
[128] http://en.wikipedia.org/wiki/G%C3%B6del%27s_incompleteness_theorems
[129] http://en.wikipedia.org/wiki/Bach
[130] http://en.wikipedia.org/wiki/Rachmaninov
[131] http://en.wikipedia.org/wiki/Einstein
[132] http://en.wikipedia.org/wiki/Srinivasa_Ramanujan
[133] http://www.maa.org/devlin/LockhartsLament.pdf
[134] http://www.theplayethic.com/
[135] http://www.youtube.com/watch?v=Ud8WRAdihPg
[136] http://www.nesta.org.uk/library/documents/idiscover_learning_framework.pdf
[137] http://www.nesta.org.uk/
[138] http://numberwarrior.wordpress.com/
[139] http://101studiostreet.com/wordpress/
[140] http://blog.mrmeyer.com/
[141] http://www.informaworld.com/smpp/412443519-68016584/content~db=all~content=a714856615
[142] http://store.tcpress.com/0807748471.shtml
[143] David Brin, Why Johnny can't Code, http://www.salon.com/technology/feature/2006/09/14/basic
[144] Tony Mobily, 10 years on: free software wins, but you have nowhere to install it, http://www.freesoftwaremagazine.com/columns/10_years_free_software_wins_you_have_nowhere_install_it
[145] http://webspace.ship.edu/cgboer/athenians.html
[146] http://www.etymonline.com/index.php?term=idea
[147] http://www.cdc.gov/ncidod/eid/vol12no01/05-0979.htm
[148] http://www.fluwiki.info/pmwiki.php?n=Consequences.AnticipatedProblems
[149] http://www.flu.gov/professional/community/commitigation.html
[150] http://www.plospathogens.org/article/info:doi/10.1371/journal.ppat.0030151
[151] http://wwwnc.cdc.gov/eid/content/12/6/pdfs/v12-n6.pdf
[152] http://www.akvo.org/wiki/index.php/Tippy_Tap
[153] http://www.ncrr.nih.gov/publications/ncrr_reporter/winter-spring2011/innovations.asp?p=all
[154] http://files.howtolivewiki.com/Dealing%20in%20Security%20JULY%202010.pdf
[155] http://www.organiclandscapedesign.org/node/133/
[156] http://www.chartercities.org/concept
[157] http//www.gallup.com

[158] http://en.wikipedia.org/wiki/Free_City_of_L%C3%BCbeck
[159] http://www.korea-dpr.com/
[160] http://news.bbc.co.uk/2/hi/south_asia/4249223.stm
[161] http://www.bioshockgame.com/
[162] http://www.politics.ubc.ca/index.php?id=3436
[163] http://www.youtube.com/watch?v=F1IWkbU0SG4
[164] http://www.seawatergreenhouse.com
[165] http://www.seawatergreenhouse.com.au
[166] http://saharaforestproject.com/
[167] http://www.census.gov/ipc/www/popclockworld.html
[168] http://www.census.gov/ipc/www/idb/worldpopgraph.html
[169] http://www.wfp.org/content/world-must-double-food-production-2050-fao-chief
[170] http://unesdoc.unesco.org/images/0012/001295/129556e.pdf
[171] http://www.ekozine.nl/load.php?naam=wie_wat_waar/wie_wat_waar.htm
[172] http://news.noahraford.com/?p=1313
[173] http://techonomy.typepad.com/blog/2010/08/google-privacy-and-the-new-explosion-of-data.html
[174] http://www.audible.com/
[175] http://www.facebook.com/
[176] http://www.blackberry.com/
[177] http://www.apple.com/ipad/
[178] http://www.twitter.com/
[179] http://en.wikipedia.org/wiki/Video_game_industry
[180] http://www.nytimes.com/
[181] http://www.human20.com/why-you-should-let-your-computer-spy-on-you/
[182] http://www.human20.com/ten-superpowers-the-internet-gave-us/
[183] http://siri.com/
[184] http://en.wikipedia.org/wiki/Cyc
[185] http://semanticnavigation.opentext.com/
[186] http://www.reqall.com/
[187] http://code.google.com/apis/predict/
[188] http://en.wikipedia.org/wiki/Ecological_footprint
[189] http://www.appropedia.org/Canaripedia
[190] http://www.appropedia.org/Localpedia
[191] http://files.howtolivewiki.com/Dealing%20in%20Security%20JULY%202010.pdf
[192] http://www.withouthotair.com
[193] http://globalswadeshi.ning.com/forum/topic/show?id=2097821%3ATopic%3A4261&page=1&commentId=2097821%3AComment%3A4637&x=1#2097821Comment4637
[194] http://www.blueeconomy.de/
[195] http://en.wikipedia.org/wiki/The_Atrocity_Archives
[196] http://twitter.com/leashless/status/17979653438
[197] http://twitter.com/leashless/status/18019669584
[198] http://twitter.com/leashless/status/18019714978
[199] http://twitter.com/leashless/status/18019765814

Article Sources and Contributors

The sources listed for each article provide more detailed licensing information including the copyright status, the copyright owner, and the license conditions.

Introduction *Source:* http://www.appropedia.org/index.php?oldid=201943 *License:* CC-BY-SA *Contributors:* Vinay Gupta 3
Foreword - Shaun Chamberlain *Source:* http://www.appropedia.org/index.php?oldid=201907 *License:* CC-BY-SA *Contributors:* Vinay Gupta . 5
Without Divine Justice, Human Rights - Gaia Marcus *Source:* http://www.appropedia.org/index.php?oldid=201918 *License:* CC-BY-SA *Contributors:* Catlupton, Gaia, Linchpinning, Vinay Gupta, 1 anonymous edits 6
Gods or Goats - David Jennings *Source:* http://www.appropedia.org/index.php?oldid=201542 *License:* CC-BY-SA *Contributors:* Catlupton, David-jennings, Linchpinning, Vinay Gupta 9
A 'Playbour' of Love for the Next Twenty Years - Pat Kane *Source:* http://www.appropedia.org/index.php?oldid=201545 *License:* CC-BY-SA *Contributors:* Catlupton, Linchpinning, Vinay Gupta 10
Untitled, 2010 - Maria Elvorith *Source:* http://www.appropedia.org/index.php?oldid=201842 *License:* CC-BY-SA *Contributors:* Catlupton, Fixer, Linchpinning, MariaE, Vinay Gupta, 1 anonymous edits 12
We Deserve A Future Of Good Governance - Patri Friedman and Brad Taylor *Source:* http://www.appropedia.org/index.php?oldid=201547 *License:* CC-BY-SA *Contributors:* 59.93.73.178, Bradrtaylor, Catlupton, Fixer, Linchpinning, Lonny, Vinay Gupta 13
The World Needs Wives - Zoe Lee *Source:* http://www.appropedia.org/index.php?oldid=201127 *License:* CC-BY-SA *Contributors:* Catlupton, Fixer, Linchpinning, Lonny, Vinay Gupta, Zoeannl 15
The Food We Deserve - Christopher Brewster *Source:* http://www.appropedia.org/index.php?oldid=201891 *License:* CC-BY-SA *Contributors:* Catlupton, Cbrewster, Vinay Gupta, 1 anonymous edits 16
Rediscovering the Stuff We Forgot to Remember - Joe Turner *Source:* http://www.appropedia.org/index.php?oldid=201128 *License:* CC-BY-SA *Contributors:* 81.178.150.55, 81.178.155.166, 81.178.158.4, 88.110.118.58, Catlupton, Linchpinning, Lonny, Vinay Gupta 17
Reclaiming Awesome - Emma Bryn-Jones *Source:* http://www.appropedia.org/index.php?oldid=201129 *License:* CC-BY-SA *Contributors:* 81.178.152.150, Catlupton, Linchpinning, Lonny, Vinay Gupta 19
Panarchy - Paul B Hartzog *Source:* http://www.appropedia.org/index.php?oldid=201548 *License:* CC-BY-SA *Contributors:* Catlupton, Linchpinning, Lonny, Paulbhartzog, Vinay Gupta 19
On the Future We Deserve... - Antonio Dias *Source:* http://www.appropedia.org/index.php?oldid=201188 *License:* CC-BY-SA *Contributors:* Catlupton, Linchpinning, Lonny, Vinay Gupta 20
There is No Future - Eleanor Saitta *Source:* http://www.appropedia.org/index.php?oldid=201189 *License:* CC-BY-SA *Contributors:* Catlupton, Linchpinning, Vinay Gupta 22
This is Mental. - Rohan Gunatillake *Source:* http://www.appropedia.org/index.php?oldid=201190 *License:* CC-BY-SA *Contributors:* 93.97.142.35, Catlupton, Linchpinning, Lonny 23
Monastech - Nathan Rosquist *Source:* http://www.appropedia.org/index.php?oldid=201540 *License:* CC-BY-SA *Contributors:* Catlupton, Vinay Gupta, 1 anonymous edits 25
The Futures We Deserve or, Even Bankers Might Have Uses - Edmund Harriss *Source:* http://www.appropedia.org/index.php?oldid=201544 *License:* CC-BY-SA *Contributors:* 137.150.46.241, Catlupton, Gelada, Linchpinning, Vinay Gupta 26
Memes that Kill - Thomas Bjelkeman *Source:* http://www.appropedia.org/index.php?oldid=201549 *License:* CC-BY-SA *Contributors:* 90.192.40.184, Bjelkeman, Catlupton, Fixer, Linchpinning, Lonny, Vinay Gupta 28
The Tiny Army - Vinay Gupta *Source:* http://www.appropedia.org/index.php?oldid=201550 *License:* CC-BY-SA *Contributors:* 90.196.218.164, Catlupton, Linchpinning, Vinay Gupta 29
A Four-Bladed Scissors - Arthur Doohan *Source:* http://www.appropedia.org/index.php?oldid=201551 *License:* CC-BY-SA *Contributors:* Artied, Catlupton, Linchpinning, Vinay Gupta 31
One in Six, a Strategy for Reduction - Glenn Hall *Source:* http://www.appropedia.org/index.php?oldid=201554 *License:* CC-BY-SA *Contributors:* 90.196.218.164, Catlupton, Linchpinning, Skirrid, Vinay Gupta 33
Of Arms and the Man - James Hester *Source:* http://www.appropedia.org/index.php?oldid=201555 *License:* CC-BY-SA *Contributors:* Catlupton, JamesHester, Linchpinning, Lonny, Vinay Gupta 34
A Knowing World - Chris Watkins *Source:* http://www.appropedia.org/index.php?oldid=201556 *License:* CC-BY-SA *Contributors:* Catlupton, Chriswaterguy, Linchpinning, Vinay Gupta 36
A Picture, a Person, a Time and a Location - Thomas Bjelkeman *Source:* http://www.appropedia.org/index.php?oldid=194613 *License:* CC-BY-SA *Contributors:* Bjelkeman, Catlupton, Lonny, Vinay Gupta 37
Decline and Fall - Tom Stafford *Source:* http://www.appropedia.org/index.php?oldid=199062 *License:* CC-BY-SA *Contributors:* Catlupton, Fixer, Tomstafford, Vinay Gupta 38
We Deserve to Evolve - Sam Rose *Source:* http://www.appropedia.org/index.php?oldid=199063 *License:* CC-BY-SA *Contributors:* 90.192.40.184, BlueChris, Catlupton, Lonny, Philralph, Sam Rose, Vinay Gupta 40
The Knowledge and Action Platform - Mark Roest *Source:* http://www.appropedia.org/index.php?oldid=196049 *License:* CC-BY-SA *Contributors:* Catlupton, Chriswaterguy, Lonny, Markroest, Vinay Gupta 41
The Joy of Open - Erik Moeller *Source:* http://www.appropedia.org/index.php?oldid=194908 *License:* CC-BY-SA *Contributors:* Catlupton, Eloquence, Vinay Gupta 44
6 Ways to Live - Chris Malins *Source:* http://www.appropedia.org/index.php?oldid=194771 *License:* CC-BY-SA *Contributors:* Catlupton, Vinay Gupta .... ??
Solar Photovoltaic Energy Replication - Joshua Pearce *Source:* http://www.appropedia.org/index.php?oldid=199065 *License:* CC-BY-SA *Contributors:* Catlupton, J.M.Pearce, Lonny, Vinay Gupta 47
The Future We Deserve or The Future We Desire - John Byfield *Source:* http://www.appropedia.org/index.php?oldid=194971 *License:* CC-BY-SA *Contributors:* Catlupton, Chriswaterguy, Flyingcloud, Vinay Gupta 48
Zombies and Vampires, Oh My! - Antonio Dias *Source:* http://www.appropedia.org/index.php?oldid=194688 *License:* CC-BY-SA *Contributors:* Catlupton, Vinay Gupta 50
The Future of Information Freedom - Smári McCarthy *Source:* http://www.appropedia.org/index.php?oldid=194738 *License:* CC-BY-SA *Contributors:* 157.157.67.25, Catlupton, Lonny, Spm, Vinay Gupta 51
My Vision of the Future - Otis Funkmeyer *Source:* http://www.appropedia.org/index.php?oldid=196016 *License:* CC-BY-SA *Contributors:* 76.168.54.196, Catlupton, Fixer, Vinay Gupta 53
The Matter of Place - Catherine Lupton *Source:* http://www.appropedia.org/index.php?oldid=194851 *License:* CC-BY-SA *Contributors:* Catlupton, Fixer, Vinay Gupta 54
The Locavores' War: A History of America's Future - Frank J. Popper *Source:* http://www.appropedia.org/index.php?oldid=199066 *License:* CC-BY-SA *Contributors:* 198.151.130.20, 89.18.67.81, Catlupton, Fpopper, Lonny, Vinay Gupta 57
A World in Common - The Socialist Party of Great Britain *Source:* http://www.appropedia.org/index.php?oldid=199067 *License:* CC-BY-SA *Contributors:* Andybroomfield, Catlupton, Psychonaut 59
The Story Our Children Will Tell - Curtis Faith *Source:* http://www.appropedia.org/index.php?oldid=195286 *License:* CC-BY-SA *Contributors:* Inflector 60
The Abolition of Scarcity - Kevin Carson *Source:* http://www.appropedia.org/index.php?oldid=194733 *License:* CC-BY-SA *Contributors:* 72.251.11.10, 90.192.40.184, Catlupton, Lonny, Vinay Gupta 62
Cities of Freedom Chariots or Four-wheeled Demons? - Cindy Frewen Wuellner PhD, FAIA *Source:* http://www.appropedia.org/index.php?oldid=194835 *License:* CC-BY-SA *Contributors:* Catlupton, Urbanverse, Vinay Gupta 64
A Healthy and Smiling Planet - Anil Prasad *Source:* http://www.appropedia.org/index.php?oldid=199068 *License:* CC-BY-SA *Contributors:* Apletters, Catlupton, Vinay Gupta 66
The Future We Deserve and the Earth Charter - Jeffrey Newman *Source:* http://www.appropedia.org/index.php?oldid=199069 *License:* CC-BY-SA *Contributors:* Catlupton, Chriswaterguy, Vinay Gupta 67
The Feet We Deserve - Steve Wheeler *Source:* http://www.appropedia.org/index.php?oldid=194541 *License:* CC-BY-SA *Contributors:* Catlupton, SteveWheeler, Vinay Gupta 69
Sex & Singularity: Sex in the 21st Century - Julian Powell *Source:* http://www.appropedia.org/index.php?oldid=199070 *License:* CC-BY-SA *Contributors:* 173.68.142.152, Catlupton, Fixer, Vinay Gupta 70
...middle... - Nick Taylor *Source:* http://www.appropedia.org/index.php?oldid=194845 *License:* CC-BY-SA *Contributors:* 121.72.70.41, Catlupton, Fixer, Vinay Gupta 71

If You Want to Go Fast, Go Alone. If You Want to Go Far, Go Together. And If You Want to Transform..? - Shaun Chamberlin *Source:* http://www.appropedia.org/index.php?oldid=196038 *License:* CC-BY-SA *Contributors:* Catlupton, Lonny, Shaunus4, Vinay Gupta ... 75

Just 4: A Macroscale Social Model - Woody Evans *Source:* http://www.appropedia.org/index.php?oldid=197743 *License:* CC-BY-SA *Contributors:* Catlupton, Shaunus4, Vinay Gupta ... 77

Open Source Appropriate Technology - Joshua Pearce *Source:* http://www.appropedia.org/index.php?oldid=196047 *License:* CC-BY-SA *Contributors:* Catlupton, J.M.Pearce, Lonny, Vinay Gupta ... 79

Who Will Save Our Souls? - Thembisa Cochrane *Source:* http://www.appropedia.org/index.php?oldid=194874 *License:* CC-BY-SA *Contributors:* 90.194.29.187, Catlupton, Lonny ... 80

Art Monasticism - Nathan Rosquist *Source:* http://www.appropedia.org/index.php?oldid=194810 *License:* CC-BY-SA *Contributors:* Catlupton, Vinay Gupta ... 82

Personal Futures and Futures Therapy - Jessica Charlesworth *Source:* http://www.appropedia.org/index.php?oldid=199073 *License:* CC-BY-SA *Contributors:* Catlupton, Jesscharlesworth, Lonny, Vinay Gupta, 1 anonymous edits ... 84

Deep Lessons - Alan Chapman *Source:* http://www.appropedia.org/index.php?oldid=194819 *License:* CC-BY-SA *Contributors:* 90.192.40.184, Catlupton, Fixer, Vinay Gupta ... 86

Semantic Organization and Connectivity - Anne McCrossan *Source:* http://www.appropedia.org/index.php?oldid=194762 *License:* CC-BY-SA *Contributors:* Annemcx, Catlupton, Cocreatr, Munimortal, Vinay Gupta ... 87

The Education We Deserve - Pamela Mclean *Source:* http://www.appropedia.org/index.php?oldid=199079 *License:* CC-BY-SA *Contributors:* Andybroomfield, Catlupton, Pamela McLean, Vinay Gupta ... 88

Moving Towards a Post Penal Society - Anton Shelupanov *Source:* http://www.appropedia.org/index.php?oldid=199080 *License:* CC-BY-SA *Contributors:* Antonsh, Catlupton, Fixer, Vinay Gupta ... 91

A Future Without Childhood - Julia Macintosh *Source:* http://www.appropedia.org/index.php?oldid=194697 *License:* CC-BY-SA *Contributors:* Catlupton, Cricket7642, Lonny, Vinay Gupta ... 94

Online Open Distance Learning - Anil Prasad *Source:* http://www.appropedia.org/index.php?oldid=199081 *License:* CC-BY-SA *Contributors:* Apletters, Catlupton, Shaunus4, Vinay Gupta ... 95

The Future of Television - Glenn Hall *Source:* http://www.appropedia.org/index.php?oldid=194863 *License:* CC-BY-SA *Contributors:* Catlupton, Chriswaterguy, Skirrid, Vinay Gupta ... 98

Citizen Centred Participation - Phil Green *Source:* http://www.appropedia.org/index.php?oldid=196052 *License:* CC-BY-SA *Contributors:* Catlupton, Lonny, Philralph, Vinay Gupta ... 99

The Future We Got–Earth Date Zero Plus Twenty - Pamela Mclean *Source:* http://www.appropedia.org/index.php?oldid=199082 *License:* CC-BY-SA *Contributors:* Andybroomfield, Catlupton, Pamela McLean ... 101

The Onion and the Satellite - Lucas Gonzalez *Source:* http://www.appropedia.org/index.php?oldid=199083 *License:* CC-BY-SA *Contributors:* Catlupton, LucasG, Vinay Gupta ... 103

Ode to the Tech Fix - Chris Malins *Source:* http://www.appropedia.org/index.php?oldid=194774 *License:* CC-BY-SA *Contributors:* Catlupton, Vinay Gupta ... 105

Deserving The Future We Want - Eldan Goldenberg *Source:* http://www.appropedia.org/index.php?oldid=194783 *License:* CC-BY-SA *Contributors:* Catlupton, Eldang, Vinay Gupta ... 106

Re-envisioning Our Relationship With Micro-Organisms - Brian Degger *Source:* http://www.appropedia.org/index.php?oldid=197745 *License:* CC-BY-SA *Contributors:* Brian Degger, Catlupton, Lonny, Shaunus4, Vinay Gupta ... 107

The Spaces We Deserve - Dougald Hine *Source:* http://www.appropedia.org/index.php?oldid=194723 *License:* CC-BY-SA *Contributors:* 78.86.158.143, 80.192.63.187, Catlupton, Vinay Gupta ... 108

The Age of Warlords Cookbook - Michael Swifte *Source:* http://www.appropedia.org/index.php?oldid=199085 *License:* CC-BY-SA *Contributors:* Catlupton, Vinay Gupta ... 110

Using Science Locally - Ian Simmons *Source:* http://www.appropedia.org/index.php?oldid=194746 *License:* CC-BY-SA *Contributors:* 85.3.124.59, Brian Degger, Catlupton, Fixer, Ian Simmons, Vinay Gupta ... 112

Seed Saving for Local Food Security - Lisa Erwin *Source:* http://www.appropedia.org/index.php?oldid=199086 *License:* CC-BY-SA *Contributors:* 90.192.40.184, Catlupton, Fixer, Vinay Gupta ... 113

Challenging Education and the "Harry Potter Letter" - Edmund Harriss *Source:* http://www.appropedia.org/index.php?oldid=194641 *License:* CC-BY-SA *Contributors:* BlueChris, Catlupton, Gelada, Lonny, LucasG, Vinay Gupta ... 115

Credibility & Calories: A Perspective on Information - Woody Evans *Source:* http://www.appropedia.org/index.php?oldid=197746 *License:* CC-BY-SA *Contributors:* 64.28.243.220, 64.28.244.12, 64.28.250.239, 64.28.251.253, 64.28.253.128, 64.28.254.190, 64.28.255.114, 64.28.255.46, 71.21.183.45, Catlupton, Chriswaterguy, KBaskerville68, Lonny, Shaunus4, Vinay Gupta ... 117

The Future of Programming - Andy Broomfield *Source:* http://www.appropedia.org/index.php?oldid=197747 *License:* CC-BY-SA *Contributors:* Andybroomfield, BlueChris, Catlupton, Lonny, Shaunus4, Vinay Gupta ... 119

Higher Education for the Future We Deserve - Lisa Erwin *Source:* http://www.appropedia.org/index.php?oldid=194799 *License:* CC-BY-SA *Contributors:* Catlupton, Vinay Gupta ... 121

A Systemic Revolution, or, the Need for a Post-Scientific Approach - Andy Novocin *Source:* http://www.appropedia.org/index.php?oldid=194804 *License:* CC-BY-SA *Contributors:* 80.236.71.28, AndyNovocin, Catlupton, Lonny, Vinay Gupta ... 122

An Ideal World - Paola Di Maio *Source:* http://www.appropedia.org/index.php?oldid=201915 *License:* CC-BY-SA *Contributors:* Catlupton, Shaunus4, Vinay Gupta ... 124

My Ideal Panflu - Lucas Gonzalez *Source:* http://www.appropedia.org/index.php?oldid=201669 *License:* CC-BY-SA *Contributors:* Catlupton, Lonny, LucasG, Shaunus4, Vinay Gupta ... 125

Report on the Planet Earth from the Intergalactic Study Group on Worlds in Transition - Gary Alexander *Source:* http://www.appropedia.org/index.php?oldid=199517 *License:* CC-BY-SA *Contributors:* Catlupton, Garyalex, Vinay Gupta ... 126

A Hypothetical Vision of What the Property Sector in the Future Might Look Like - Bonnie O. Wong *Source:* http://www.appropedia.org/index.php?oldid=194888 *License:* CC-BY-SA *Contributors:* BonnieOWong, Catlupton ... 128

The Future is Here - Kenneth Lo *Source:* http://www.appropedia.org/index.php?oldid=199518 *License:* CC-BY-SA *Contributors:* Catlupton, Kenlo, Vinay Gupta ... 130

Hacking Society and a Proposal for Beta Towns - Andy Broomfield *Source:* http://www.appropedia.org/index.php?oldid=199519 *License:* CC-BY-SA *Contributors:* Andybroomfield, Catlupton, Vinay Gupta ... 133

The Age of Phlight - Lionel Wolberger *Source:* http://www.appropedia.org/index.php?oldid=199520 *License:* CC-BY-SA *Contributors:* 90.196.218.128, Catlupton, Lwolberg, Shaunus4, Vinay Gupta ... 135

Designing the Future - David Braden *Source:* http://www.appropedia.org/index.php?oldid=194885 *License:* CC-BY-SA *Contributors:* Catlupton, David Braden, Vinay Gupta ... 137

Collaboration for Introverts or, How to Make Friends and Tolerate People - Steve Wheeler and Alex Fradera *Source:* http://www.appropedia.org/index.php?oldid=194951 *License:* CC-BY-SA *Contributors:* Alex Fradera, Catlupton, Chriswaterguy, SteveWheeler, Vinay Gupta, 1 anonymous edits 138

Hundreds of Sovereign Singapores - Jon Southurst *Source:* http://www.appropedia.org/index.php?oldid=194877 *License:* CC-BY-SA *Contributors:* Catlupton, Fixer, South, Vinay Gupta ... 140

Working Together: Unleashing Collective Intelligence - Fabio Barone *Source:* http://www.appropedia.org/index.php?oldid=194926 *License:* CC-BY-SA *Contributors:* 178.83.240.82, Catlupton ... 142

Clash for Civilization - Arthur Doohan *Source:* http://www.appropedia.org/index.php?oldid=194822 *License:* CC-BY-SA *Contributors:* 90.192.40.184, Artied, Catlupton, Fixer, Vinay Gupta ... 143

Seawater into Food - Thomas Bjelkeman *Source:* http://www.appropedia.org/index.php?oldid=197036 *License:* CC-BY-SA *Contributors:* 90.145.42.235, 90.192.40.184, Bjelkeman, Catlupton, Chriswaterguy, Lonny, Vinay Gupta ... 145

Collapsarithmetic - Chris Malins *Source:* http://www.appropedia.org/index.php?oldid=194777 *License:* CC-BY-SA *Contributors:* Catlupton, Vinay Gupta ... 147

Our Future and the Sun - Vinay Gupta *Source:* http://www.appropedia.org/index.php?oldid=194603 *License:* CC-BY-SA *Contributors:* 90.196.218.164, Catlupton, Vinay Gupta ... 148

Bootleg Oil - Al Razi Masri *Source:* http://www.appropedia.org/index.php?oldid=201903 *License:* CC-BY-SA *Contributors:* Razi, Vinay Gupta 149

Time For Resilient Tribes to Step Up and Show the Way - Kuldeep Brar *Source:* http://www.appropedia.org/index.php?oldid=199521 *License:* CC-BY-SA *Contributors:* Catlupton, LucasG, Missybrar, Vinay Gupta ... 151

The Music We Deserve - Allen Wentz *Source:* http://www.appropedia.org/index.php?oldid=194680 *License:* CC-BY-SA *Contributors:* Allenwentz, Catlupton, Lonny, Vinay Gupta ... 152

All the World's a Stage - Alex Fradera *Source:* http://www.appropedia.org/index.php?oldid=194938 *License:* CC-BY-SA *Contributors:* Alex Fradera, Catlupton, Vinay Gupta ... 154

Success in the Twenty First Century - Mark Charmer *Source:* http://www.appropedia.org/index.php?oldid=199522 *License:* CC-BY-SA *Contributors:* Catlupton, Vinay Gupta ... 156

On Lying to Children - Peep *Source:* http://www.appropedia.org/index.php?oldid=198106 *License:* CC-BY-SA *Contributors:* Catlupton, Vinay Gupta ... 158

We Deserve the Time and Space to Be Human - Alex Bowyer *Source:* http://www.appropedia.org/index.php?oldid=194633 *License:* CC-BY-SA *Contributors:* 67.22.237.2, Alexbowyer, Catlupton, Chriswaterguy, KBaskerville68, Vinay Gupta 160
Opening the Floodgates - Ben Werdmuller von Elgg *Source:* http://www.appropedia.org/index.php?oldid=194860 *License:* CC-BY-SA *Contributors:* 82.41.228.79, 82.41.240.198, Catlupton 161
The Future of Art - Nick Stewart *Source:* http://www.appropedia.org/index.php?oldid=194976 *License:* CC-BY-SA *Contributors:* Catlupton, Vinay Gupta 163
The Human Rite of Living - Bembo Davies *Source:* http://www.appropedia.org/index.php?oldid=194909 *License:* CC-BY-SA *Contributors:* Catlupton, Fixer, Vinay Gupta 164
No Island is an Island - Lucas Gonzalez *Source:* http://www.appropedia.org/index.php?oldid=198850 *License:* CC-BY-SA *Contributors:* Catlupton, Lonny, LucasG, Vinay Gupta 165
Getting The Future We Deserve - Paul Graham Raven *Source:* http://www.appropedia.org/index.php?oldid=194636 *License:* CC-BY-SA *Contributors:* 90.192.40.184, Catlupton, Fixer, Vinay Gupta 167
Berlin, Berlin - Liam Breslin *Source:* http://www.appropedia.org/index.php?oldid=194968 *License:* CC-BY-SA *Contributors:* Catlupton, Vinay Gupta 168
We Deserve a Future - Jason Louv *Source:* http://www.appropedia.org/index.php?oldid=201852 *License:* CC-BY-SA *Contributors:* Vinay Gupta 169
Aftermath - Thinking the Unthinkable. Asking What is Not Asked - Thomas Bjelkeman *Source:* http://www.appropedia.org/index.php?oldid=201898 *License:* CC-BY-SA *Contributors:* Bjelkeman, BlueChris, Catlupton, Lonny, Vinay Gupta 172

Image Sources, Licenses and Contributors

The sources listed for each image provide more detailed licensing information including the copyright status, the copyright owner, and the license conditions.

Image *Source:* http://www.appropedia.org/index.php?title=File:Dragonfly_black_1600.jpg *License:* GNU Free Documentation License *Contributors:* Vinay Gupta 5
Image *Source:* http://www.appropedia.org/index.php?title=File:4BladedScissors.png *Contributors:* Artied 32
Image *Source:* http://www.appropedia.org/index.php?title=File:TheFWD-Bjelkeman-Akvo-phone.png *Contributors:* Bjelkeman 37
Image *Source:* http://www.appropedia.org/index.php?title=File:4-cell2.jpg *Contributors:* Kdevans 78
Image *Source:* http://www.appropedia.org/index.php?title=File:DSC01155.jpg *Contributors:* Philralph 99
Image *Source:* http://www.appropedia.org/index.php?title=File:BigSciencevSmallScience.jpg *Contributors:* Brian Degger 113

License

CC-BY-SA
Appropedia:Copyright
http://www.gnu.org/licenses/fdl.html

Index

...middle... - Nick Taylor, **71**

A Four-Bladed Scissors - Arthur Doohan, **31**
Aftermath - Thinking the Unthinkable. Asking What is Not Asked - Thomas Bjelkeman, **172**
A Future Without Childhood - Julia Macintosh, **94**
A Healthy and Smiling Planet - Anil Prasad, **66**
A Hypothetical Vision of What the Property Sector in the Future Might Look Like - Bonnie O. Wong, **128**
A Knowing World - Chris Watkins, **36**
All the Worlds a Stage - Alex Fradera, **154**
An Ideal World - Paola Di Maio, **124**
A Picture, a Person, a Time and a Location - Thomas Bjelkeman, **37**
A Playbour of Love for the Next Twenty Years - Pat Kane, **10**
Aquaculture, **53**
Art Monasticism - Nathan Rosquist, **82**
A Systemic Revolution, or, the Need for a Post-Scientific Approach - Andy Novocin, **122**
A World in Common - The Socialist Party of Great Britain, **59**

Berlin, Berlin - Liam Breslin, **168**
Bootleg Oil - Al Razi Masri, **149**

Challenging Education and the Harry Potter Letter - Edmund Harriss, **115**
Cities of Freedom Chariots or Four-wheeled Demons? - Cindy Frewen Wuellner PhD, FAIA, **64**
Citizen Centred Participation - Phil Green, **99**
Clash for Civilization - Arthur Doohan, **143**
Collaboration for Introverts or, How to Make Friends and Tolerate People - Steve Wheeler and Alex Fradera, **138**
Collapsarithmetic - Chris Malins, **147**
Credibility & Calories: A Perspective on Information - Woody Evans, **117**

Decline and Fall - Tom Stafford, **38**
Dedication, **1**
Deep Lessons - Alan Chapman, **86**
Deserving The Future We Want - Eldan Goldenberg, **106**
Designing the Future - David Braden, **137**

Footnotes, **172**
Foreword - Shaun Chamberlain, **5**

Getting The Future We Deserve - Paul Graham Raven, **167**
Gods or Goats - David Jennings, **9**

Hacking Society and a Proposal for Beta Towns - Andy Broomfield, **133**
Higher Education for the Future We Deserve - Lisa Erwin, **121**
Hundreds of Sovereign Singapores - Jon Southurst, **140**

If You Want to Go Fast, Go Alone. If You Want to Go Far, Go Together. And If You Want to Transform..? - Shaun Chamberlin, **75**
Introduction, **3**

Just 4: A Macroscale Social Model - Woody Evans, **77**

Memes that Kill - Thomas Bjelkeman, **28**
Monastech - Nathan Rosquist, **25**
Moving Towards a Post Penal Society - Anton Shelupanov, **91**
My Ideal Panflu - Lucas Gonzalez, **125**
My Vision of the Future - Otis Funkmeyer, **53**

No Island is an Island - Lucas Gonzalez, **165**

Ode to the Tech Fix - Chris Malins, **105**
Of Arms and the Man - James Hester, **34**
One in Six, a Strategy for Reduction - Glenn Hall, **33**
Online Open Distance Learning - Anil Prasad, **95**

On Lying to Children - Peep, **158**
On the Future We Deserve... - Antonio Dias, **20**
Opening the Floodgates - Ben Werdmuller von Elgg, **161**
Open Source Appropriate Technology - Joshua Pearce, **79**
Our Future and the Sun - Vinay Gupta, **148**

Panarchy - Paul B Hartzog, **19**
Personal Futures and Futures Therapy - Jessica Charlesworth, **84**
Power Law, 40

Reclaiming Awesome - Emma Bryn-Jones, **19**
Rediscovering the Stuff We Forgot to Remember - Joe Turner, **17**
Re-envisioning Our Relationship With Micro-Organisms - Brian Degger, **107**
Report on the Planet Earth from the Intergalactic Study Group on Worlds in Transition - Gary Alexander, **126**

Seawater into Food - Thomas Bjelkeman, **145**
Seed Saving for Local Food Security - Lisa Erwin, **113**
Semantic Organization and Connectivity - Anne McCrossan, **87**
Sex & Singularity: Sex in the 21st Century - Julian Powell, **70**
Solar Photovoltaic Energy Replication - Joshua Pearce, **47**
Success in the Twenty First Century - Mark Charmer, **156**

The Abolition of Scarcity - Kevin Carson, **62**
The Age of Phlight - Lionel Wolberger, **135**
The Age of Warlords Cookbook - Michael Swifte, **110**
The Education We Deserve - Pamela Mclean, **88**
The Feet We Deserve - Steve Wheeler, **69**
The Food We Deserve - Christopher Brewster, **16**
The Future is Here - Kenneth Lo, **130**
The Future of Art - Nick Stewart, **163**
The Future of Information Freedom - Smári McCarthy, **51**
The Future of Programming - Andy Broomfield, **119**
The Future of Television - Glenn Hall, **98**
The Futures We Deserve or, Even Bankers Might Have Uses - Edmund Harriss, **26**
The Future We Deserve and the Earth Charter - Jeffrey Newman, **67**

The Future We Deserve or The Future We Desire - John Byfield, **48**
The Future We Got–Earth Date Zero Plus Twenty - Pamela Mclean, **101**
The Human Rite of Living - Bembo Davies, **164**
The Joy of Open - Erik Moeller, **44**
The Knowledge and Action Platform - Mark Roest, **41**
The Locavores' War: A History of America's Future - Frank J. Popper, **55**
The Matter of Place - Catherine Lupton, **54**
The Music We Deserve - Allen Wentz, **152**
The Onion and the Satellite - Lucas Gonzalez, **103**
There is No Future - Eleanor Saitta, **22**
The Spaces We Deserve - Dougald Hine, **108**
The Story Our Children Will Tell - Curtis Faith, **60**
The Tiny Army - Vinay Gupta, **29**
The World Needs Wives - Zoe Lee, **15**
This is Mental. - Rohan Gunatillake, **23**
Time For Resilient Tribes to Step Up and Show the Way - Kuldeep Brar, **151**

Untitled, 2010 - Maria Elvorith, **12**
Using Science Locally - Ian Simmons, **112**

We Deserve a Future - Jason Louv, **169**
We Deserve A Future Of Good Governance - Patri Friedman and Brad Taylor, **13**
We Deserve the Time and Space to Be Human - Alex Bowyer, **160**
We Deserve to Evolve - Sam Rose, **40**
Who Will Save Our Souls? - Thembisa Cochrane, **80**
Wikipedia:Here Comes Everybody, 177
Wikipedia:Peak water, 177
Wikipedia:Peal oil, 177
Wikipedia:Self-actualization, 177
Wikipedia:Wikinomics, 177
Without Divine Justice, Human Rights - Gaia Marcus, **6**
Working Together: Unleashing Collective Intelligence - Fabio Barone, **142**
World Footprint, 40

Zombies and Vampires, Oh My - Antonio Dias, **50**

www.ingramcontent.com/pod-product-compliance
Lightning Source LLC
Chambersburg PA
CBHW071158240526
45470CB00017B/341